DISCOVERING ISAIAH

DISCOVERING BIBLICAL TEXTS
Content, Interpretation, Reception

Comprehensive, up-to-date and student-friendly introductions to the books of the Bible: their structure, content, theological concerns, key interpretative debates and historical reception.

PUBLISHED

Iain Provan, *Discovering Genesis*
Ralph K. Hawkins, *Discovering Exodus*
Jerome F. D. Creach, *Discovering Psalms*
Andrew T. Abernethy, *Discovering Isaiah*
Ian Boxall, *Discovering Matthew*
Joel B. Green, *Discovering Luke*
Ruth B. Edwards, *Discovering John*
Anthony C. Thiselton, *Discovering Romans*
David A. deSilva, *Discovering Revelation*

DISCOVERING ISAIAH

Content, Interpretation, Reception

Andrew T. Abernethy

WILLIAM B. EERDMANS PUBLISHING COMPANY

GRAND RAPIDS, MICHIGAN

First published 2021 in Great Britain by
Society for Promoting Christian Knowledge
36 Causton Street
London SW1P 4ST

This edition published 2021
in the United States of America by
Wm. B. Eerdmans Publishing Co.
4035 Park East Court SE, Grand Rapids, MI 49546
www.eerdmans.com

27 26 25 24 23 22 21   1 2 3 4 5 6 7

ISBN 978-0-8028-7805-2

Library of Congress Cataloging-in-Publication Data

A catalog record for this book is available from the Library of Congress.

Scripture acknowledgements can be found on p. 182.

Contents

Contents

Acknowledgements

'The [literary] work itself creates an audience' (Ricoeur 1981: 91). Authors never know who will read their book. Books will blaze their own trails, finding their way to unanticipated doorsteps and digital libraries. As I wrote, I imagined pastors and students as my audience, but, if you don't fit either category, I am glad this book reached you. One thing all of my readers may have in common is that reading *Discovering Isaiah* is a penultimate step towards far greater goals – perhaps, to better read the book of Isaiah and to better know the God of Isaiah. As you will see in this volume, the book of Isaiah has created a vast audience that you are joining. Alexandrians, apostles, apologists, artists, and activists are among its audience, and this list would be far greater if we moved past 'A' in the alphabet. If *Discovering Isaiah* accomplishes its purpose, you will be equipped to traverse Isaiah among the troop of those who have read it as Christian Scripture across two millennia.

On New Year's Eve 2019, my family and I boarded a plane in Chicago that would whisk us away from the city's wintry gloom to six months of bliss in pastoral Cambridge, UK. I would write *Discovering Isaiah* at Tyndale House and enjoy being a Visiting Fellow with the University of Cambridge Faculty of Divinity. We'd have a fairy-tale British adventure. Two months after arrival, Covid-19 had a grip on Italy. It began slowly moving towards the UK. We eventually had to shelter in place, and Tyndale House and the university closed. Thankfully, I had already written my two most research-intensive chapters amid the convenience and community of Tyndale House. By mid March, we had decided to return to the USA. Our home in Wheaton, Illinois, was being rented until the end of June, so my parents graciously made their home in Indiana available to us. In Indiana I tried to keep writing amid the chaos of Covid and limited resources. During this time, Steve Walton (Trinity College, Bristol) became a source of encouragement via regular video chats. Since my return to Wheaton College, three graduate assistants have been a great help to me in proofreading, chasing down resources, and formatting the Bibliography: Dr Mason Lancaster, Heather Zimmerman, and Katie Black. Thank you for helping to make a miracle happen – that of submitting this manuscript only one month after its due date.

I also must express my gratitude to Philip Law (SPCK) and Andrew Knapp (Eerdmans) for this opportunity and for their patience. My PhD mentor, Willem VanGemeren, is never far from my mind whenever I write on Isaiah. Financially, Wheaton College's Sabbatical and Aldeen grants have helped fund my research, and my colleague Dan Trier took the time to read one of my chapters. My wife, Katie, and our children have been invaluable companions, bringing me great joy and relief amid the labours that brought forth this volume.

As Covid-19's shadow looms across this work, the injustices in our world continue, relentlessly. This volume, especially Chapter 9, is dedicated to all who suffer injustice in this world and dare to hope in Isaiah's God for a brighter tomorrow.

> The Lord will comfort Zion;
>   he will comfort all her waste places,
> and will make her wilderness like Eden,
>   her desert like the garden of the Lord;
> joy and gladness will be found in her,
>   thanksgiving and the voice of song.
> (Isa. 51.3)

Abbreviations

1QIsaᵃ	Isaiahᵃ (Dead Sea Scrolls – 'Great Isaiah Scroll')
1QIsaᵇ	Isaiahᵇ (Dead Sea Scrolls)
4Q161	Pesher Isaiah (Dead Sea Scrolls)
4Q163	papPesher Isaiah (Dead Sea Scrolls)
AB	Anchor Bible Commentary
ABD	*Anchor Bible Dictionary*, ed. D. N. Freedman. 6 vols. New York, 1992.
BBRSup	Bulletin for Biblical Research Supplements
BETL	Bibliotheca ephemeridum theologicarum lovaniensium
BIntS	Biblical Interpretation Series
BSac	*Bibliotheca sacra*
BZAW	Beihefte zur Zeitschrift für die alttestamentliche Wissenschaft
BZNW	Beihefte zur Zeitschrift für die neutestamentliche Wissenschaft
CBQ	*Catholic Biblical Quarterly*
CBQMS	Catholic Biblical Quarterly Monograph Series
COS	*The Context of Scripture*, ed. W. W. Hallo and K. L. Younger. 3 vols. Leiden, 1997–2003.
ESV	English Standard Version
FAT	Forschungen zum Alten Testament
FOTL	Forms of the Old Testament Literature
HCOT	Historical Commentary on the Old Testament
HUCA	*Hebrew Union College Annual*
ICC	International Critical Commentary
JETS	*Journal of the Evangelical Theological Society*
JQR	*Jewish Quarterly Review*
JSOT	*Journal for the Study of the Old Testament*
JSOTSup	Journal for the Study of the Old Testament Supplement Series

JSSM	Journal of Semitic Studies Monograph
LHBOTS	Library of the Hebrew Bible/Old Testament Studies
LXX	The Septuagint
MT	Masoretic Text
NAC	New American Commentary
NICOT	New International Commentary on the Old Testament
NIGTC	New International Greek Testament Commentary
NIV	New International Version
NKJV	New King James Version
NRSV	New Revised Standard Version
NSBT	New Studies in Biblical Theology
NTSup	Supplements to Novum Testamentum
OBT	Overtures in Biblical Theology
OT	Old Testament
OTL	Old Testament Library
OTM	Oxford Theological Monographs
SBL	Society of Biblical Literature
SBLAIL	Society of Biblical Literature Ancient Israel and Its Literature
SBLDS	Society of Biblical Literature Dissertation Series
SJOT	*Scandinavian Journal of Theology*
TJ	*Trinity Journal*
VT	*Vetus Testamentum*
VTSup	Supplements to Vetus Testamentum
WBC	Word Biblical Commentary
WTJ	*Westminster Theological Journal*
WUNT	Wissenschaftliche Untersuchungen zum Neuen Testament

1

An enduring word

A voice says: 'Cry out!'

> And I said: 'What shall I cry out? All people are like grass, and all
> their faithfulness is like the flower of the field. The grass withers, and the
> flower fades because the breath of the LORD blows against it.'[1]
> (Isa. 40.6–7a)

'What shall I cry out?' As I write this book, I join the prophet and ask this same
question. The prophet sees human lives shrivelling like grass. Invasion after
invasion, siege after siege, and forced migration after forced migration have
led him to this metaphor. Human life is like grass that lacks water as the sun
blazes; it shrivels. In our own day, a once-in-a-century pandemic (Covid-19)
reminds a world proud of modern medicine that death lurks like a hungry
lion. What can the prophet proclaim amid such decay? What's the point of
writing a book when those who read it are staring death in the face? All people
are like grass.

The prophet also sees how fickle human beings are: 'all their faithfulness
[*ḥesed*][2] is like the flower of the field.' He sees an exiled nation drifting from
God, and people mistreating one another (cf. Isa. 57.1). As Covid-19 wracks
the world, revelation after revelation of our lack of *ḥesed* surfaces. Ahmaud
Arbery, Breonna Taylor, and George Floyd, among others, became symbols
of the black experience in the USA, further exposing the systemic absence of
ḥesed towards the black community. Well-known Christians are being exposed
as wicked, and some are announcing that they have left the faith. Is there
anything to proclaim when it seems like everyone is faithless, like flowers that
quickly wither? All our faithfulness is like the flower of the field.

God responds in agreement with the prophet's assessment of the people:

---

1 Translation is the author's, with the quotation marks following the interpretation by Goldingay and
Payne 2006: 1/79–85. Throughout this volume, the NRSV will be quoted unless otherwise noted.

2 The LXX translates this as 'glory'.

Surely the people are grass.
The grass withers, the flower fades . . .
(Isa. 40.7)

Yet, even amid death and faithlessness, there is one reason why the prophet can preach: 'but the word of our God endures for ever' (40.8 NIV).

Unlike grass and flowers, unlike people and their faithlessness, God's word remains and endures. It does not wither and fade. It is a word one can proclaim even in the most fragile of circumstances. It is a word worth writing a book about during the time of Covid-19 and a civil rights crisis. God's word stands for ever.

Our starting point

Discovering Isaiah is not primarily about discovering the historical prophet or prophets behind this book. *Discovering Isaiah* aims to help you discover an ancient text that claims to be the very words of Israel's God. There are countless stories about the prophets Jeremiah and Ezekiel in the books that bear their names, but the book of Isaiah is different. The prophet Isaiah only appears in character in seven of the book's 66 chapters (6; 7; 20; 36—39). When he does appear, his main purpose is to deliver the word of God. As Christopher Seitz (1988: 121–2) notes: 'In the Book of Isaiah, God does most of the talking . . . The Book of Isaiah is a book whose main character is God.' I will consider my own book a success if you are better positioned to discover and respond to the God of Isaiah's vision and to the enduring words of this God.

So, from the start, we must recognize that the fundamental posture for reading Isaiah is to read it as the enduring word of God that invites responses of obedience and trust. The very structure of the book of Isaiah underscores this. The book does not open with Isaiah's call to prophetic ministry – that comes in chapter 6 – but rather with God calling for the world and his people to 'listen':

Hear, O heavens, and listen, O earth . . .

Hear the word of the LORD . . .
Listen to the teaching of our God
(1.2, 10)[3]

---

3 On the importance of responding to God's word in the structure of the book, see Carr 1996; Conrad 1991: 83–102; Jang 2012; Liebreich 1956 (esp. 1.10; 39.5; 66.5).

In chapter 2, all nations stream to Zion to receive God's word:

> Let us go up to the mountain of the LORD . . .
> that he may teach us his ways . . .
> For out of Zion shall go forth instruction,
> and the word of the LORD from Jerusalem.
> (2.3)

Isaiah 40 and 55 frame the heart of the book around the surety of God's words. God assures the prophet that amid the uncertainties of exile 'the word of our God will stand for ever' (40.8). Even amid circumstances that point to the contrary, God declares that his word will not fail:

> For as the rain and the snow come down from heaven,
> and do not return there until they have watered the earth,
> making it bring forth and sprout,
> giving seed to the sower and bread to the eater,
> so shall my word be that goes out from my mouth;
> it shall not return to me empty,
> but it shall accomplish that which I purpose,
> and succeed in the thing for which I sent it.
> (55.10–11)

At the end of the book, 'those who tremble at my word' (see 66.2, 5) will live on God's holy mountain. As David Carr (1996: 214, italics original) puts it: 'we can read it as a drama opening with a call to repentance and closing with paired proclamations to those who answered the call and those who did not.' Thus, from beginning to end, the book of Isaiah presents itself to us as the word of God that summons obedience, invites trust, and determines destinies.

The history of the Church bears witness to the enduring word of God in Isaiah. According to St Jerome (2015: 68), 'Within [Isaiah] is contained all the Holy Scriptures, everything human language can bring forth and the understanding mortals can receive.' Jerome thought of Isaiah as the Bible in miniature, containing words that bore witness to what would happen long after the prophet Isaiah. Jerome viewed Isaiah as a fifth Gospel of sorts. He (2015: 67, 68) says:

> I shall expound Isaiah in such a way that I will show him not only as
> a prophet, but as an evangelist and apostle . . . the Scripture at hand

contains all the Lord's mysteries and proclaims Emmanuel, the one who was both born of a virgin and performed illustrious works and signs, was dead and buried, and by rising from the lower world is the Savior of all nations.

Augustine (1887: 894) follows suit when he says, '[Isaiah] should be called an evangelist rather than a prophet.' Thomas Aquinas (2017) agrees with St Jerome, stating that Isaiah's message is so clearly expressed that 'he seems not to compose a prophecy, but a Gospel'. For these church fathers, God's word in Isaiah speaks clearly and relevantly for all of time. As we will see, preachers, civil rights activists, reformers, novelists, poets, priests, artists, and musicians from many eras and from all over the world have found in Isaiah a word from God that endures far beyond the lifetime of the prophet.

Our strategy

So, what is our plan for exploring the enduring word of God presented to us in the book of Isaiah? We will draw upon historical insights, literary analysis, and reception history. Let me explain this threefold approach by way of personal narrative.

I love the book of Isaiah, but I was not planning to write another introduction on it. I had just written *The Book of Isaiah and God's Kingdom* (IVP, 2016). In that volume, I used the strategy of biblical theology to orient readers to the book of Isaiah through the lens of God's kingdom. I was happy with how my book was helping others, so I had no desire to write another introductory work. Yet, when SPCK and Eerdmans invited me to write on Isaiah for this series, I had a change of heart. What got me excited about this project was the invitation to introduce Isaiah by integrating three approaches that are often kept separate: the historical, the literary, and the reception history approaches.

Within the field of Old Testament studies, scholars traditionally divide between those who focus on 'historical backgrounds' and those who focus on the 'literary' side of interpretation. During my PhD studies, my friends who were studying Akkadian, obsessing about archaeology, and trying to piece together the ancient cultural backgrounds behind texts were on the historical side of the ledger. Although I benefit from and appreciate historical study, my expertise and primary area of academic interest are on the literary side – how should I *read* Isaiah literarily? My historically oriented friends might be most excited about reconstructing Sennacherib's siege of Lachish, but my interest would be in Sennacherib's role in the narrative plot of Isaiah 36—37. In my dissertation, published as *Eating in Isaiah* (Brill, 2014), I offer a sequential reading of Isaiah that asks how food and drink figure into the book's literary structure and message. I incorporate insights from ancient material culture within the monograph, but my primary aim is to offer a literary analysis and reading. So, the invitation to integrate the historical with the literary when introducing Isaiah seems quite natural from my vantage point in the field of Old Testament studies.

As for reception history, it took me a while to recognize its value. My training had led me to prioritize reading Isaiah in its final form to grasp the original meaning in the text, so I did not see how the Church's reception of Isaiah might be of use. From that vantage point, one needs only the text of Isaiah and ancient historical resources made available by modern scholarship. Gradually, I had a change in outlook. Georg Gadamer in particular was helpful.[4] Gadamer helped me see that we all approach Isaiah or any text through presuppositions that derive from a *history of effects*. When the book of Isaiah came into existence, it created a new horizon that led to a ripple of effects reaching up to this day. When I approach Isaiah, I am naturally influenced by the presuppositions that have moulded me due to the ripple effect across reception history. It is simply impossible to approach a historical object or ancient text without having been influenced by its effects across time. Attention to reception history at the very least helps us become aware of our presuppositions as we come to the text.

Some might complain that reception history could lead us astray in our reading of Isaiah. True, but this is where Gadamer stresses the importance of 'openness'. We come 'open' to a text like Isaiah, recognizing that our presuppositions, shaped as they are through a history of effects, may lead us to come up short when reading and trying to understand Isaiah. Isaiah is other than us, so, in humility, we can expect moments of misalignment between our current horizon and the text's horizon. It is when these horizons intersect amid moments of misalignment that growth in understanding takes place.

Over the past several decades, reception history has begun to carve out space in the field of Old Testament studies, especially for Isaiah. John Sawyer is a leading voice in this arena. His book *The Fifth Gospel* (1996) offers a masterful overview of Isaiah's reception in various eras of the Church and focuses on key topics such as the virgin birth, the 'man of sorrows', and peace.

---

4   See esp. Gadamer 1989: 267–306.

More recently, Sawyer (2018) has published a commentary, *Isaiah through the Centuries*, where he follows the flow of thought in the texts of Isaiah in conversation with interpretations throughout church history. Brevard Childs' *The Struggle to Understand Isaiah as Christian Scripture* (2004) showcases and assesses the interpretation of Isaiah by individuals from the early Church to the Middle Ages to the Reformation and up through the modern era. What I am struck by in Childs' work is how reading early Christian interpreters invites us to ask explicitly theological and ecclesiological questions when reading Isaiah. Although my interaction with the Church's reception in this volume is mainly through primary sources, the works of Sawyer and Childs are well worth consulting for those who want to go further in this area.

So, in this volume, the Church's reception of Isaiah will play an important role. While I recognize the importance of Jewish interpretation, I will need to limit my purview to Christian reception. Although there are surely more, I will alert you to three benefits from attending to the reception of Isaiah. First, reception history helps you become more conscious of which streams of tradition have most influenced you. By foregrounding your prior shaping (presuppositions), you will be better prepared to recognize the disconnections between your prior understanding and Isaiah itself.

Second, there is exegetical pay-off from reading texts in conversation with interpretative history, as earlier interpreters may see elements in the texts of Isaiah that we might be overlooking (perhaps due to our current cultural and social locations). It is a wrong assumption that interpreters prior to the modern period had no grounding in the lexical, historical, and literary dimensions of Isaiah; there is a treasure trove of exegetical and interpretative insight available from these commentators.

Third, and perhaps most significant, attending to reception history provides the opportunity to ponder how best to read Isaiah as Christian Scripture today. Most modern commentaries bracket out the faith component, so listening in on how Isaiah is being read in the light of Christ and as a word for the Church across the centuries offers an opportunity to be trained in this ecclesial craft of reading Isaiah.[5]

Obviously, the task of exhaustively integrating history, literary insight, and reception history in a short book on Isaiah is impossible. My work here is representative and introductory, though I trust it will also prove to be enriching, interesting, and provocative. *Discovering Isaiah* is an entry into

---

5   For a delightful argument for employing 'craft' rather than 'science' or 'art' as a metaphor for describing theological interpretation, see Chapman 2018.

engaging the enduring words of God in Isaiah as words that stem from a time in *history*, that are inscribed in *literary* form, and that have been *received* for several millennia as God's word to and for the Church.

The structure of our book

There are ten chapters in this book, including this one. I intentionally started with an invitation to receive the book of Isaiah as God's word because this is the starting point of Isaiah in its opening chapter.

Chapters 2 and 3 survey the history of interpretation. It will become apparent that a different set of questions animates the study of Isaiah from Qumran through to the Reformation (Chapter 2) in comparison with the questions asked after Spinoza to the present day (Chapter 3).

Chapter 4 is my attempt to sketch the historical vision that unfolds across the book of Isaiah. I trace the (hi)story Isaiah tells in four phases – from judgement by means of Assyria and Babylon, to God's plans to use Cyrus of Persia, to the role of the Suffering Servant, and finally to the final consummation of judgement and salvation.

Chapters 5–9 focus on key themes: holiness, Zion, the Davidic Messiah, the Suffering Servant, and justice. I examine each theme in the light of its historical and literary contexts in the book and the (hi)story Isaiah tells, before investigating how interpreters across the centuries understood these topics.

In Chapter 10, I conclude with how the book of Isaiah ends, by noting how the 'endgame' across Isaiah is worship of the LORD by all humanity at Zion.

So, welcome to this journey towards discovering the God of Isaiah and his enduring words. As you embark, I invite you to hear these words from God:

This is the one to whom I will look,
    to the humble and contrite in spirit,
    who trembles at my word.
(Isa. 66.2)

2

Pre-modern readings of Isaiah

When I was an undergraduate, I enrolled in a 'Biblical Interpretation' class. After two weeks of discussing the history of biblical interpretation, I dropped the course. I wanted to know how *I* should interpret the Bible, not how *others* had interpreted it. I have since repented, but my instincts tell me that you might feel the same way about this chapter and the next. As mentioned in Chapter 1, there are numerous benefits of attending to the history of interpretation.

- *It exposes our pre-understandings.* Why do you want to study Isaiah? What do you expect to find in Isaiah? How should one interpret Isaiah? Whether you know it or not, you have some opinions already. Do you expect to see lots of messianic promises? Do you expect to find insight into ancient history? Do you expect to find words of comfort? Should one read Isaiah in the light of Jesus and the Church today? Should one read it in its original historical context? You probably have instincts about reading Isaiah that have been shaped by a stream of historical and spiritual influences extending all the way back to Isaiah. By studying the history of interpretation, you will become more aware of your pre-understandings and the historical stream that has influenced you.
- *It teaches us to ask the right interpretative and hermeneutical questions.* Questions such as 'What is the literal-historical sense of Isaiah?' or 'How does this bear witness to Christ?' or 'How does this apply to today?' recur throughout history. Depending on your background, you may prioritize just one of these questions to the neglect of the others. History teaches us to ask them all.
- *It invites humility.* The history of interpretation invites us to be open to learning from others, even the ancients. Throughout all eras, interpreters are blind to certain elements of the text. What makes us in the modern era think we have the exclusive lease on proper knowledge of Isaiah? We need the history of interpretation to expose and fill in our blind spots.
- *It enables us to read commentaries with discernment.* Have you ever wondered why a commentator focuses on what she or he comments

on? A sense of the history of interpretation will sharpen your ability to understand and assess the claims made by commentators on Isaiah.

This chapter and the next offer you the opportunity to see where you fit in to this tremendous legacy of attempting to discern God's voice through the book of Isaiah.

From the Old Testament to the New Testament

Ever since Isaiah was written, the religious community has read this book, hoping to discern anew how its prophetic message continues to sound forth in contemporary times.

Isaiah in the Old Testament

Two examples will illustrate for us how Old Testament writers drew upon the book of Isaiah to address their contemporaries and look to the future. At the start of Ezra, the writer fuses a passage from Jeremiah (51.11: 'The Lord has stirred up the spirit of the kings of the Medes . . .') and verses from Isaiah 41 (vv. 2, 25; 'stir up'), 44.28 ('Cyrus'; 'Jerusalem'; 'be built'), and 45.13 ('I will stir him up . . . He will build my city'):[1]

> the LORD stirred up the spirit of King Cyrus of Persia so that he sent a herald throughout all his kingdom, and also in a written edict declared: 'Thus says King Cyrus of Persia: The LORD, the God of heaven, has given me all the kingdoms of the earth, and he has charged me to build him a house at Jerusalem in Judah.'
> (Ezra 1.1–2)

Judah's exile to Babylon culminated in the destruction of Jerusalem in 586 BC, and, now, Ezra draws upon the prophetic word of Isaiah to allude to God's faithfulness amid the opportunity to return from exile under Cyrus's decree in 539 BC.

Also, Isaiah's influence can be seen throughout Zechariah (see Stead 2009). As one illustration, Zechariah 1.14–17 fuses together numerous prophetic strands to declare God's plans to restore Zion (Stead 2009: 95–103). Most significantly, Zechariah 1.16–17 announces: 'I will return to Jerusalem with

---

1   See Williamson 1985: 8–10. Translations are the author's own.

mercy, and there my house will be rebuilt . . . the LORD will again comfort Zion and choose Jerusalem.' The promises of God's return (Isa. 52.8–9), his compassion (54.7), and God's comfort for Jerusalem and Zion (40.1; 51.3) are integral to Isaiah's message of hope. By appealing to Isaiah's prophecies, the writers of the post-exilic generation recognize that a greater era of restoration promised in Isaiah endures as a grand hope, even amid their dismay after they return to the land.

These two examples of Isaiah's use in the Old Testament demonstrate that for the post-exilic community the book of Isaiah offers a lens for discerning divine activity in the present and for envisaging what is yet to come.

Jesus ben Sira

Around 180 BC, a wise scribe in Jerusalem named Jesus ben Sira wrote a book consisting of an extended reflection on wisdom (chs 1—43) and the godly lives of the saints across the Hebrew Bible (chs 44—50). This work is referred to as either Sirach, the Wisdom of Ben Sira, or Ecclesiasticus, and is considered to be part of the 'Apocrypha' or 'Deuterocanonical' books from the intertestamental period (Skehan and Di Lella 1987: 2–20). In the latter part of the book, Jesus ben Sira turns to the life of Hezekiah, during whose time God saved Jerusalem from Assyria 'through Isaiah' (Sir. 48.20). As an explanation for why God routed the Assyrians, Ben Sira goes on to say:

> 22 For Hezekiah did what was pleasing to the Lord,
>   and he kept firmly to the ways of his ancestor David,
> as he was commanded by the prophet Isaiah,
>   who was great and trustworthy in his visions.
> 23 In Isaiah's days the sun went backwards,
>   and he prolonged the life of the king.
> 24 By his dauntless spirit he saw the future,
>   and comforted the mourners in Zion.
> 25 He revealed what was to occur to the end of time,
>   and the hidden things before they happened.
> (Sir. 48.22–25)

Four legacies of the identity of Isaiah are drawn upon here: he was (1) an intercessor to God in prayer (48.20); (2) an exhorter of kings to live righteously (48.22); (3) a miracle worker (48.23); and (4) a foreteller of comfort for Zion and of the end times (48.24–25). The first three legacies align with Isaiah 1—39, especially 36—39, and the fourth has Isaiah 40—66 in mind. Although modern scholarship will doubt whether the prophet Isaiah of the eighth century BC spoke chapters 40—66 to an audience several generations removed, 'it is obvious that Ben Sira attributed the whole Book of Isaiah to the eighth-century B.C. prophet' (Skehan and Di Lella 1987: 539). A few centuries later, Josephus shared this same outlook that Isaiah was a prophet who foretold Zion's future restoration through Cyrus many years in advance (*Antiquities* 11.5–7).

Qumran Isaiah

Around the time when Isaiah was translated into Greek (see below), there was a sectarian community in the Judean desert that cherished the book of Isaiah (200 BC to first century AD). This community had libraries of biblical and religious texts held in various caves. The remarkable preservation and discovery of these texts in AD 1948–57 captured the imaginations of the general public and scholars. Among the many Dead Sea Scrolls, it is Isaiah that drew the lion's share of attention (Brooke 2006). For our purposes, four insights are significant.

First, the book of Isaiah was extremely *important* for the Qumran community. There were 21 Isaiah texts found in the caves, with two found in Cave 1 (1QIsaᵃ; 1QIsaᵇ), 18 in Cave 4, and one in Cave 5 (for an overview, see Tov 1997; Flint 1997). In comparison, only the book of Psalms, with 36 copies, and Deuteronomy, with 26, had greater representation. What is more, there are remains of five commentaries (*Pesharim*) on passages across Isaiah (Horgan 1979). Isaiah held a central place in the religious outlook of this community.

Second, the Isaiah texts at Qumran all show a high level of *alignment with the Masoretic Text*.[2] Prior to the discovery of the 1QIsaᵃ scroll, the Leningrad Codex, dating to AD 1008, was the oldest manuscript of the books of the Hebrew Bible from the Masoretic tradition.[3] Remarkably, the discovery of the Qumran Isaiah texts shows continuity across a thousand years of textual transmission. When news of the discovery became public in 1948, Isaiah took centre stage, as William Brownlee states:

> It was pre-eminently the existence of a complete copy of Isaiah from the late second century B. C. which excited the scholarly world. Scholars,

---

2   The Masoretic Text (MT) refers to a textual tradition that was preserved by a school of scribes in Tiberias (a city on the Sea of Galilee), dating to the last three centuries of the first millennium AD. The Aleppo Codex (a partial assemblage of OT texts) and the Leningrad Codex (a complete assemblage of OT texts) date to the tenth and eleventh centuries and reflect the Masoretic tradition.

3   The Masoretic Text (MT) refers to a textual tradition that was preserved by a school of scribes in Tiberias (a city on the Sea of Galilee), dating to the last three centuries of the first millennium AD. The Aleppo Codex (a partial assemblage of OT texts) and the Leningrad Codex (a complete assemblage of OT texts) date to the tenth and eleventh centuries and reflect the Masoretic tradition.

to be sure, were interested also in other documents, but here was an astonishing discovery of which one had scarcely dared to dream: that the history of the Hebrew text of the Old Testament should in a single leap be carried back a thousand years.
(Quoted in Brooke 2006: 84)

Third, the 'Great Isaiah Scroll' (1QIsaᵃ) contained the *entire* book of Isaiah, chapters 1—66. The scroll is incredible in its size, at 24 feet (7.3 m) long and 10.25 inches (26 cm) high. Early in the modern era of Isaiah studies (see Chapter 3), many held that Isaiah 1—39 and Isaiah 40—66 were originally separate books. Some even argued that these two books were not combined together until the first century BC. With the finding of the Great Isaiah Scroll, it becomes apparent that these two parts of the book belonged together earlier than expected (copied in the second century BC). What is more, based on spacing between chapters 33 and 34, some (e.g. Brownlee 1964) suggest that the Qumran community read Isaiah in two parts: 1—33 and 34—66. This finding contributed to the new impetus to read the book of Isaiah as a unity.

Fourth, and finally, there are five 'commentaries' (*Pesharim*) on parts of Isaiah (e.g. Isa. 5; 10—11; 30.15-18; 40.11; 54.12a) that open windows into how the Qumran community interpreted the book (Wise et al. 1996: 209–14). Viewing themselves as living during the end times, the members of this community read Isaiah as speaking eschatologically about judgement coming against the Pharisees (the 'Flattery Seekers' in 4Q163; Horgan 1979: 173) and priests in Jerusalem and also about the coming Messiah (4Q161).

Greek Isaiah

By the middle of the second century BC, Isaiah became available in Greek (Dines 2004: 46). This development was monumental, for the book instantly became accessible to the Greek-speaking world. In Egypt, as part of the Greek-speaking world, Jews would gather at 'places of prayer' – precursors to the synagogue – to worship and study (Dines 2004: 44), so the Greek translation began to play a central role in these contexts. Eventually, the Greek version of Isaiah became the go-to resource for liturgy and study across the Greco-Roman world, much like English translations of the Bible are for those in the USA and UK today.

Questions naturally arise for scholars as they examine Greek Isaiah (see Porter and Pearson 1997): 'Did the translator of Greek Isaiah use a manuscript equivalent to the Hebrew Masoretic Text of Isaiah?' 'Did the translator translate for sense or word for word?' 'What social context does Greek Isaiah address?' 'Did the translator have a purpose in mind as he translated?' There are no definitive answers to these questions, although scholars have fun trying to come up with them (cf. Baer 2006; van der Kooij 2006; Wagner 2013). The most significant point for us is to recognize that a Greek translation of Isaiah was available for Jews dispersed across the Greco-Roman Empire. By the time of the New Testament, Greek Isaiah was the go-to translation for the apostles when they wrote the Gospels and their letters.

Isaiah in the New Testament

In view of Isaiah's importance at Qumran, it is no surprise that Isaiah is called to mind all over the New Testament. According to the index in the Nestle-Aland 28th edition of the Greek New Testament, the New Testament cites or alludes to all but three of Isaiah's 66 chapters, amounting to 637 allusions to and citations from Isaiah by the apostles. With this in mind, the following statement by Steve Moyise and Maarten J. J. Menken (2005: 1) is no exaggeration:

> [Isaiah's] influence is everywhere in the New Testament documents. We find quotations concerning the birth of Jesus, his ministry and mission (and John the Baptist), his opponents, his rejection, his sacrificial death, the mission of the church, particularly the inclusion of the gentiles, and a host of issues facing the early church. We also find a host of allusions, and one could even say that certain central theological concepts, such as 'gospel', derive from Isaiah.

Since later chapters in this book will consider specific examples of how the New Testament communities received Isaiah's message, I limit myself to a few comments here as to how Isaiah in general, but especially the Isaianic new exodus, seems to provide a conceptual lens for books in the New Testament.

In the Gospel of Mark, Rikki Watts (1997) argues that Mark activates in the minds of his hearers the schema of the new exodus in Isaiah to understand God's work in Christ. This new-exodus schema, with its expectation that God will deliver his people, lead them on a journey, and return them to Zion, unifies the entire Gospel.

In Luke and Acts, David Pao (2000) makes the case that the strategic placement of texts from Isaiah in Luke 3, 4, and 24 and in Acts 1, 13, and 28 establishes Isaiah's new exodus as the hermeneutical framework for interpreting the Luke-Acts duology. Pao is particularly alert to how Isaiah supports the Lukan aims of reconfiguring the identity of God's people to include Gentiles amid the Jewish hardness towards the gospel.

A final example comes from the letter to the Romans. J. Ross Wagner (2002) contends that in Romans, especially chapters 9—11, Paul draws upon Isaiah's storyline of rebellion (hardening of heart), punishment (exile), and restoration. In doing so, Isaiah offers a framework for explaining the gospel, Paul's role in Gentile mission, and the persisting hardness of the Jews. Thus, the New Testament is not informed merely by isolated verses from Isaiah, but rather by the book's grand vision.

Isaiah, then, provides a conceptual grid for comprehending the historical reality of God's saving intervention in Christ and the reconstitution of God's people.

The early Church

The interpretation of Isaiah in the early Church follows in the footsteps of the apostles, reading Isaiah in view of God's work in Christ, but there is a greater focus among the first Christians on how Isaiah addresses their contexts of suffering and how Isaiah can help the Gentile Church defend its existence in the face of Jewish and Roman questioning.

The Ascension of Isaiah

In the first half of the second century AD, an apocalyptic tale, *The Ascension of Isaiah*, about Isaiah's martyrdom, took form within a Christian community in Syria (Knight 1995). It tells of a visionary experience that Isaiah had during the twentieth year of King Hezekiah. Although bodily present before Hezekiah and the prophets, Isaiah in mind and spirit traverses the seven levels of heavenly glory where he witnesses Christ's descent from the highest heavens to take on a lowly, human form – to be born as the child of Mary, suffer, and ultimately die. This vision is both what gets Isaiah into trouble with King Manasseh, who decrees that Isaiah is to be sawn in two, and what enables Isaiah to willingly and peacefully endure the suffering of martyrdom. This account of Isaiah encourages the suffering Church with the examples of Isaiah and Christ and with the prospect of heavenly glory.

Defence of Christianity

Isaiah is also a go-to resource for defending the veracity of the Christian faith in the early Church. The first great 'apology' (defence of the faith) is Justin Martyr's *Dialogue with Trypho* (c. AD 150). Justin makes a case to a Jew named Trypho, and a few of his friends, concerning how a predominately Gentile Church believes itself to align with Israel's Scriptures. Two of the main concerns he addresses are 'Why don't Christians keep Moses' law?' and 'How can Jesus truly be the Messiah?' In both cases, Justin draws extensively on Isaiah. External conformity to Moses' laws of sacrifice and Sabbath (chs 1; 58) is insufficient, according to Isaiah, so a new covenant and expression of law is coming (55.3–5; cf. Jer. 31.31–33) that will include Gentiles (Isa. 2.2–4; 42.6–7) amid Jewish hardening (6.9–10). As for Jesus being the expected Messiah, Isaiah bears witness to a divine–human Messiah who would be born to a virgin (7.10–17) and would suffer as God's Servant to bear the curse for sin (ch. 53). Justin is an exemplar of the early apologetic use of Isaiah to prove the validity of Christianity and invite Jews to 'believe entirely as we do that Jesus is the Christ of God' (*Dialogue* 141.3; Justin Martyr 2003: 212).

Tertullian is another early apologist who drew upon Isaiah in a range of contexts to defend the Christian faith.[4] In his 'Apology' (*c.* AD 198–217) he addresses a Roman tribunal, at a time when the Romans were persecuting Christians out of ignorance, in the hope that the judges might better understand the Christian faith and even believe in Christ. The fulfilment of prophecy is a reason to believe, he argues; chief among such fulfilments are Isaiah's predictions that Jews would resist Christ's first advent (Isa. 6.9–10) and that Jesus would be God born in the flesh through a virgin (7.14). In his 'Answer to the Jews' (*c.* AD 198–208), his argument takes a similar shape to Justin's. Isaiah expects a new covenant of law-keeping that incorporates Gentiles and he also predicts a Messiah born of a virgin who will suffer. Similarly, Tertullian (*c.* AD 207) leverages Isaiah in his 'Five books against Marcion'. Marcion was a heretical teacher who drove a wedge between the allegedly evil, wrathful god of the Old Testament and the good, spiritual god of the New Testament. Since physical creation and flesh were evil, according to Marcion, he did not believe that Jesus came in the flesh. Tertullian argues that the prophets, of whom Isaiah is the chief instance, predicted two advents: one of humility and one of glory. In the advent of humility, Isaiah predicted that God would come to earth, take on flesh (ch. 7), suffer (53.2–4), die (53.12), and, as a result, have an impact on the entire world (2.2–3; 42.6–7; 55.3–5), although Jews would reject this Christ.

The final apologist we will mention is Eusebius. His *Proof of the Gospel* (*c.* AD 315) consists of ten books (see Eusebius of Caesarea 1920). Books 5–10 catalogue how prophets foretold that God would come among humanity (Isa. 35.1–7; 52.5–10) and take on flesh as a Jew (chs 7–8), and predicted specifics from Jesus' life, ministry and death. Although Justin's and Tertullian's use

---

4   The works of Tertullian can be found in Coxe 1885.

of Isaiah was directed towards their Jewish opponents, Eusebius's defence seems to be anticipating the Arian controversy.[5] Eusebius grants much more attention to the pre-existence of the Son and the expectation that the Son as Word of God would take on flesh.

Thus, as the early Christian Church took shape within an era when its validity was highly doubted, apologists, such as Justin Martyr, Tertullian, and Eusebius, appealed to the predictions of Christ in the prophets, particularly Isaiah whom Eusebius referred to as 'the greatest of the prophets' (Eusebius 1920: 1/244), to make the case for Christianity.

Commentaries on Isaiah

There was also a developing set of commentaries on the book of Isaiah in the early Church, written by the likes of Eusebius, Jerome, Cyril of Alexandria, and Theodoret. Commentaries by Eusebius and Jerome illustrate the hermeneutical approaches of this era.

The *Commentary on Isaiah* by Eusebius, translated into English (Eusebius 2013), offers a rich window into the interpretation of Isaiah at the time (*c.* AD 337–9). He opens his commentary (2013: 1) by stating:

> At times the Spirit delivered his revelation to the prophet plainly, so that there was no need of allegory to explain the message, but only an understanding of the actual words themselves. But at other times, the Spirit communicated through symbols and circumstances, placing other meanings in certain key words and even in names.

The distinction in Eusebius's preliminary remarks exposes a prioritization of the literal, plain meaning of Isaiah, unless a literal meaning is not readily apparent. Lest a modern reader be mistaken, a 'plain' or 'literal' reading for Eusebius and most ancient interpreters is not confined to understanding a passage in its eighth-century BC context. A literal reading follows the plain sense of the text across the entire sweep of redemptive history. For example, Isaiah 1.21–26 speaks of a time when the faithless, unjust city of Jerusalem will be purged through punishment to become a city of faithfulness, justice, and righteousness. Eusebius explains (2013: 8) its fulfilment as follows:

> This government was organized by the Jewish people long ago, but it has since collapsed, and now from out of the whole world it has been raised

---

5   Arius denied that Jesus was God because he believed that Jesus was created by the Father.

up again in the church of Christ and has been 'founded on the rock.' And those who preside as *judges* and *counselors from the beginning* of this beautiful city are in fact to be understood as the apostles and the disciples of our Savior. Those from the apostolic succession who were established as presiding officers of the church of God still shine through even now, for the seed of good trees bears good fruit.

A plain reading of this passage for Eusebius follows the sense of the passage – the end of a corrupt governmental structure in Jerusalem and the establishment of a just governmental structure – and identifies it in view of history, where Jerusalem's governmental structure collapsed and God's faithful governance is now across the globe in the offices of the Church.

Although Eusebius does not often resort to 'spiritual' or 'allegorical' interpretation, we find it on occasion in his commentary. For instance, in Isaiah 19.5–7 ('the waters of the Nile will be dried up . . . its canals will become foul, and the branches of Egypt's Nile will diminish and dry up'), the prophet speaks of a drought coming over Egypt that will parch its land. Eusebius argues that a plain understanding of this is not possible. Because of this he states: 'the Word forces us to adopt a figurative interpretation, so that even if we do not want to we have no other choice' (2013: 98). He goes on to interpret the waters as symbolic for Egyptian power or philosophy, which will fragment into different schools of thought (like canals) and find its wisdom destroyed before 'the evangelical word concerning the kingdom of heaven' (2013: 98).

Jerome offers us another commentary on Isaiah (*c.* AD 408–10) from this era, also translated into English (Jerome 2015). Although Eusebius and the other apologists were confined to Greek translations, Jerome was a polyglot, mastering Latin, Greek, and Hebrew. Throughout his commentary, he impressively compares the Hebrew text of Isaiah with a Jewish Greek translation (the Septuagint) and Christian Greek recensions (Aquila; Symmachus) as he offers his interpretations. His interpretative method, like that of Eusebius, attends to the literal, but he is more favourable to the 'spiritual' sense of the text than Eusebius. For, he says, 'God was speaking in the mind of the prophets' and, as a result, '[t]his is why, after the truth of history, everything should be understood spiritually' (Jerome 2015: 69). In fact:

The Scripture at hand [Isaiah] contains all the Lord's mysteries and proclaims Emmanuel, the one who was both born of a virgin and performed illustrious works and signs, was dead and buried, and by rising from the lower world is the Savior of all nations . . . Within this volume is contained all the Holy Scriptures, everything human language can bring forth and the understanding of mortals can receive. (2015: 68)

One can detect Jerome's movement from the historical to the spiritual in his interpretation of Isaiah 1.21–26. He acknowledges that the faithful Zion who becomes a faithless whore (1.21) 'can indeed be understood even of the times of Isaiah', but he goes on to suggest several lines of interpretation. This depiction of Zion becoming faithless towards God 'refers more fully to the suffering of Christ', when all turned away from him. Additionally, since Zion is the dwelling place of God, Jerome extends this image spiritually to the human soul where 'God's justice first dwelled', but later the soul falls into sin and allows demons to take up residence (2015: 87). Often, Jerome offers allegorical reflection after extended literal, historical commentary that transitions to comments about the soul, philosophy, and virtue.

Thus, as the early Church read Isaiah, several issues were paramount. In the case of the apologists, Isaiah enabled them to justify their existence because the prophet predicated a season of Jewish hardening, a lowly Messiah, and Gentile inclusion in God's kingdom. For commentators, mining the word of God in Isaiah required a balance between attending to the extended literal sense of the text and deciphering the occasions when the Spirit invited allegorical readings.

The Middle Ages

The Middle Ages was a time when the tradition of the church fathers was drawn upon and recirculated, yet there were two notable developments during this era that warrant our attention: the work of Thomas Aquinas and Jewish interpretation.

Thomas Aquinas

Thomas Aquinas, who was later proclaimed 'The Doctor of the Church' by Pope Pius V, wrote his first book around AD 1148 based on lectures delivered to undergraduate students in Cologne while he was a graduate student. This book was his commentary on Isaiah, now translated into English and available online at <https://aquinas.cc/la/en/~Isaiah>. His commentary is decisively literal and displays a number of interpretative techniques that reveal a significant development in the commentary tradition. First, he attends obsessively to the literary structure of Isaiah. As he opens his comments on Isaiah 1 (§26–7), he begins with a panoramic view of the book's two halves (chs 1—39; 40—66) before identifying three parts for the first half of the book (chs 1—6; 7—31; 32—39). Narrowing even further, the structure of the first six chapters consists of chapters 1 and 2—6. As for chapter 1, Aquinas identifies two parts, verses 2-20 and 21-31. Within 1.2-20, the following subunits organize his exposition: 1.2-6 is a reproof for fault, 1.7-9 threatens punishment, and 1.10-20 points to a remedy for punishment. This attention to structure in Aquinas as part of the literal sense anticipates a similar interest in the modern era.

A second development is Aquinas's scholastic orientation. Aquinas was first and foremost an exegete and theologian, and he would at times employ Aristotelian logic to grapple with what Isaiah is teaching about God. For instance, as is common across Jewish and Christian commentators, the question emerges for Aquinas as to what it means when Isaiah 6 claims that Isaiah 'saw' God. If God is spirit, can he really be seen by human beings? In order to explain this, Aquinas employs the logic that only God sees himself and understands himself fully, and humans can only see God's essence after death in heaven. The prophet Isaiah, thus, must have 'seen' God in a mediated way, where God willed for an angel to use figurative expressions from the realm of the senses and creation (e.g. throne; kingship) whereby something of God could be understood, even if God in his essence was not actually seen (§206-12). This use of philosophical logic at the service of exegetical and theological enquiry is a distinctive of Aquinas within the commentary tradition.

Medieval rabbinic commentary

Although allegory dominates Jewish interpretation before and after the medieval period, an era of literal, historical interpretation among Jewish commentators represents a significant moment in Isaiah's reception. The best-known medieval commentator is Ibn Ezra, a nomadic Jew who eventually took up residence in Italy during a time when he wrote his commentary on Isaiah. Most modern commentators refer to him as the first to appeal to multiple authors behind Isaiah. A recent study by Kim Philips (2015) has advanced our understanding of Ibn Ezra's approach to Isaiah and why he appeals to multiple authors. Philips argues that Ibn Ezra's understanding of the Servant Songs (esp. 49.7-8; 53.12) is the key that unlocks Ibn Ezra's logic for why the author of Isaiah 40—66 is a prophet in Babylon. In 49.7, the 'servant' is described as a 'servant of rulers'. Ultimately, however, the rulers will pay homage to this Servant. For Ibn Ezra, it makes most sense to interpret the speaker as a prophet in exile whom Babylonian and Persian rulers will acknowledge after God restores Jerusalem (Friedländer 1873: 224). In Isaiah 53, after explaining the entire passage as if it refers to Israel (the common view of the time), he suggests that it is better to understand the individual as the prophet in Babylonian exile (Friedländer 1873: 246–7). The thematic interconnectivity between the Servant Songs and chapters 40—66 led Ibn Ezra to interpret Isaiah 40—66 as deriving from a Babylonian prophet who spoke of a return from exile (40—51) and of a greater eschatological, messianic era to come (52—66).

Isaiah in the Reformation

The Reformation ushered in a resurgence in commentary writing as the Reformers sought to expound the Scriptures from the original languages of Greek and Hebrew. The best-known Reformers, Martin Luther and John Calvin, both gave lectures on Isaiah which were turned into commentaries. We will consider their work before briefly noting the contribution of Campegius Vitringa.

Martin Luther

A decade after Martin Luther nailed his theses to the door of the castle church in Wittenberg, seeking reform within the Church, he was lecturing on Isaiah in that city (1528–9). The result of these lectures was a commentary published in 1532. He begins by identifying the knowledge of grammar and the historical context of the prophet as most important for understanding Isaiah. This, however, does not mean he thinks we are to read the prophet Isaiah in an eighth-century vacuum, for the chief aim of the prophets is to 'keep the people in eager anticipation of the coming Christ' (1969: 3). The prophets, in speaking about the physical kingdom of Israel, were also spiritually bearing witness to Christ: 'For this reason we must pay more attention to the designs and intentions of the prophets than to their words' (1969: 4). The intentions Luther has in mind are to prepare the hearer for Christ. In this way, although Luther attends to the grammar and historical dynamics of Isaiah's time, he often directs his gaze directly to how a passage figuratively speaks of Christ and the Church.

Luther's interpretation of Isaiah 6.1–3 provides a useful sample of his approach. Luther begins with attending to the literal sense. In verse 1, there is a vision of God filling the Temple with the train of his robe. Luther interprets this as a critique of the Jews who 'thought that God was enclosed in the temple and the mercy seat and was held there by their righteousness' (1969: 69). If just God's hem fills the Temple, how much greater is God than the Temple! He then moves in a christological direction by stating that the Temple and sacrificial system were 'only established with a view to the coming of Christ', so Isaiah is helping the Jews see that their current views of the physical Temple are 'only a fringe' of the glory of God to come. Similarly, the declaration that the whole earth is full of God's glory in verse 3 pushes Jews beyond the vision of their temple to giving God 'the confession which is due Him and which is paid Him in all the earth' (1969: 71). The Temple is merely preparatory for the greater recognition of God's glory that will be apparent in Christ. Although the literal sense guides Luther's main exposition, which culminates with how the passage in chapter 6 prepares for Christ, he appends an allegory to this chapter, explaining his comments on the figures in Isaiah's vision:

Lord sitting in glory	Christ at right hand of Father
Temple	Church or heaven
Seraphim	Apostles and preachers of the word
Two wings	Two Testaments
Veiled faces	Life of the godly hidden in Christ

Luther at times criticizes allegory, yet he resorts to it often in the commentary due to his interest in promoting a reading of Isaiah that leads a reader to Christ.

A second example of Luther's approach comes from Isaiah 40.2. When Isaiah announces in this verse that 'her [Jerusalem's] warfare has ended', he foretells the end of our anxious concern about satisfying God through obeying the law (1972: 5). Now, the Spirit and the word are the means of satisfying God for everyone. This 'spiritual' reading provides an opportunity to teach a doctrine central to Luther's theology – the distinction between law and gospel.

For Luther, then, the literal sense (with a reading of the text as it prepares for Christ and the new era of the gospel) and allegory (where words stand for something that is not apparent on the surface) promote an understanding of Isaiah that enabled those during the time of the Reformation to profitably read Isaiah as Christian Scripture.

John Calvin

Five hundred miles south of Wittenberg and 20 years later, John Calvin set out to teach through Isaiah in Geneva (late 1540s). The by-product was a commentary on Isaiah (2010, originally published 1559) that still is in high demand today. The difference between Calvin and Luther is most apparent in how closely Calvin stays to the literal and historical meaning of Isaiah, yet it would be a mistake to think Calvin did not include Christology as a component in the historical understanding of these texts.

In Calvin's exposition of Isaiah 6 he makes a number of points in a similar way to Luther. They both interpret the glory of God filling the earth as a critique of Jews who confine God to the Temple, and they both utilize the touching of a piece of coal to the prophet's lips and the accompanying word ('your iniquity is atoned for') as an occasion to teach that sacrament and word belong together. Yet, in Calvin, there is no hint of allegory as one finds in Luther on Isaiah 6. Calvin's preference for reading a text in association with Christ and the Church is to detect the 'doctrine' being taught in the passage and then trace the doctrine's relevance from Isaiah's time to the time of Christ and the Church. For instance, when Isaiah receives the call to 'harden the heart of this people' (see 6.9–10), Calvin begins by describing how Isaiah should expect a stubborn response from the Jews at the time of Isaiah to the prophet's message. He then extends this as a 'doctrine' that anticipates the future kingdom of Christ and the experience of all future ministers, as is also taught in the New Testament (John 12.39; Acts 28.27; Rom. 11.8). Similarly, the announcement that this hardening will last until the complete destruction of the land (Isa. 6.11) applies both to Isaiah's time and also 'to us; for this punishment has been pronounced against all who obstinately disobey God' (2010: 1/222). Yet again, for Calvin, the prospect of life for the decimated stump of 6.12 reveals a 'doctrine' that is

> not peculiar to a single age ... for it frequently happens that the Church, amidst the numerous afflictions which she endures, appears to have no strength, and is supposed to be utterly ruined. That energy lies hidden in the word of the Lord, by which alone the Church is sustained.
> (2010: 1/225)

Isaiah 40 provides yet another example of Calvin attending to doctrine taught by Isaiah's literal sense that finds resonance in the life of Israel as well as the time of Christ, the Church, and the second coming. With the announcement of 'Comfort ye' (40.1), Isaiah the prophet addresses the Jews who would soon be in exile, while also 'lay[ing] down a perpetual doctrine, which must not be limited to a single period' (2010: 3/197). It would be a mistake, according to Calvin, to believe that the 'good news' for the distressed begins in Christ's coming to the world; instead, it starts with the comfort for exiles as seen in Daniel, then the post-exilic reformers (Ezra, Nehemiah) and prophets (Haggai, Zechariah, Malachi), then Christ himself, and ultimately all who continue to declare the good news.

Like the interpreters before him, Calvin attended to the historical and spiritual dimensions of the text. Yet, Calvin stands out for how carefully he attends to the plain meaning of Isaiah and for how he does not leave this literal sense behind as he reads forward through to exile and post-exile and to Christ and the Church. Allegory has no place in Calvin. In fact, Calvin's commitment to the literal meaning of Isaiah is the reason why his commentary on Isaiah is the most highly regarded pre-modern commentary among modern scholars today (e.g. Childs 2004: 207–29).

Campegius Vitringa

After Calvin, another notable commentator is the Reformed Dutch scholar Campegius Vitringa, who published a two-volume commentary on Isaiah in 1722. Vitringa's commentary is one of the most impressive commentaries of any era. He translates Isaiah from Hebrew into Latin, engages with 94 secondary sources, including Jewish exegetes such as Ibn Ezra and David Qimchi, attends to the grammatical logic of the prophetic text, grapples with the spiritual and literal meaning, and reflects upon pastoral application. Charles Telfer's (2016) study of Vitringa's interpretative method in his commentary on Isaiah helpfully corrects mischaracterizations of Vitringa as excessively rationalistic and historical. Telfer convincingly demonstrates that Vitringa was between Calvin, who was bound to the literal, historical sense of Isaiah, and Johannes Cocceius, who was uncontrollably allegorical. Vitringa attempted to walk a fine line as he attended copiously to the literal sense while favouring a reading that leads to the spiritual sense.

Conclusion

If I were to 'test' what you had learned from this chapter, I would be interested to know if you could write a sentence or two in response to the following questions:

1 Why are the Dead Sea Scrolls so important for the study of Isaiah?
2 What 'narrative' does Isaiah provide that helped the apostles speak about Christ in the New Testament?
3 In what sense was Isaiah used 'apologetically' by the likes of Justin Martyr and Eusebius?
4 If you were to create a spectrum from literal to allegorical, where would you place the following figures on the spectrum: Jerome, Aquinas, Luther, and Calvin?

Whether you could pass my test or not is really secondary. My primary hope is that you see yourself as part of a long tradition of those who are reading Isaiah, a tradition within which one must ask: 'Am I considering the literal-historical meaning of this passage?' 'How does this passage direct me to Christ?' 'How should I understand Isaiah today?' Along with having these questions in mind as you read Isaiah, I hope you might be keen to consult some of the pre-modern commentaries yourself, as so many such commentaries are now available in English.

3
Interpreting Isaiah in the modern era

In the wake of the Reformation, a new era of humanism came to the fore. The greatest early champion of wedding humanism with the study of the Bible was a Jewish immigrant in Holland who had been banished from the synagogue across the Jewish world. Benedict Spinoza wrote his *Theological-Political Treatise* (1670) with the explicit aim of replacing superstition with 'the natural light of reason' when it comes to religion in general and interpreting the Bible in particular. He states (2007: 98):

> I hold that the method of interpreting Scripture does not differ from the [correct] method of interpreting nature, but rather is wholly consonant with it . . . to interpret Scripture, we need to assemble a genuine history of it and to deduce the thinking of the Bible's authors by valid inferences from this history.

Spinoza was ahead of his time, but within a few centuries his humanistic impulses came to dominate the interpretation of the Bible. Below, we offer the story of the scholarly interpretation of Isaiah from Spinoza up to the present day.

Breaking Isaiah into pieces (eighteenth to mid twentieth centuries)

For most of the eighteenth through to the mid nineteenth century, the academic study of Isaiah did not align with Spinoza's template. Bishop Robert Lowth (1868, original 1778) wrote a majestic commentary tapping into Isaiah's poetic nature. Georg Seiler (1792: 12) was so in awe of Isaiah, who spoke from the Assyrian era through exile to the messianic age, that he declared Isaiah to be 'one of the most exquisite books of Scripture'.[1] Heim and Hoffmann (1839) meshed the teachings of Calvin, Luther, and other Reformers on Isaiah into a commentary. Isaiah at this time was viewed as one book by one author. Yet a ripple that began with Eichhorn (1780) and Döderlein (1789), who argued that Isaiah consisted of two books, grew into a wave through the popular work of Ewald (1875–81) and Kuenen (1877). Isaiah was not one book by a single author. Instead, Isaiah was two books by numerous authors.

Two books

Ewald's approach is illustrative of the interest in interpreting Isaiah without a 'special hermeneutic'.[2] First, Ewald begins with passages that he deems to imply an eighth-century BC context. He argues that there were six phases in which Isaiah son of Amoz of the eighth century organized and published his messages, the final results being Isaiah 1—23 and 28—33. Second, Ewald examined the passages in those collections that were exilic and post-exilic in context, such as those referring to Babylon or to the reality of exile. He posits that a few anonymous prophets wrote oracles against Babylon in Isaiah 13.2—14.23 and 21.1–10 near the time of the overthrow of Babylon. Then, 'the Great Anonymous Prophet', who was in exile in Egypt under the influence of Jeremiah's disciples, wrote Isaiah 40.1—63.6 (63.7—66.24 was a later appendix). Finally, several other anonymous prophets wrote Isaiah 34—35 and 24—27, with 36—39 being added at some point along the way.

This modus operandi of Ewald came to typify a new era in the study of Isaiah. Gone were the days when Isaiah would be received as a prophet who speaks to generations far in advance through divine foreknowledge, as Jesus ben Sira, Josephus and the pre-modern interpreters (except for Ibn Ezra) supposed. As Kuenen (1877: 319) says:

> In [Josephus's] days criticism had not yet been born, and exegesis was in its infancy. What was permissible to [Josephus] is no longer allowed . . . the author of Isa. xl. ff. wrote shortly before the termination of the Babylonian captivity.

Thus, working from the premise that prophets spoke to contemporaries, Ewald and Kuenen created a wave that would forever affect the reading of Isaiah.

---

1 My translation of 'einer der vortreslichsten Bücher der heiligen Schrift'.
2 A special hermeneutic speaks to whether the Bible should be read differently from other books due to its 'special' character.

Three books

If Eichhorn and Döderlein were the ripple and Ewald and Kuenen the wave, then Bernhard Duhm was the tidal wave. Although numerous studies on Isaiah arose at the same time that upheld the critical view (e.g. Cheyne; G. A. Smith; W. Robertson Smith), Duhm's approach in *Das Buch Jesaia* (1922, original 1892) had the greatest impact due to his 'three book' hypothesis: the book of Isaiah (chs 1—39); Deutero-Isaiah (chs 40—55); and Trito-Isaiah (chs 56—66). Previously, Isaiah 40—66 was understood as one book (Second Isaiah), but Duhm identified a shift in context between 40—55 and 56—66. According to Duhm, Deutero-Isaiah wrote during exile (540s BC) in Phoenicia, and Trito-Isaiah wrote in Jerusalem just before the time of Nehemiah (*c.* 465 BC). The three-book theory proved convincing for many scholars.

Duhm's three-book theory is more complicated than the idea that three authors wrote three separate books. Duhm detected materials that he believed were added into these books very late in the process, even into the first century BC. So, with Duhm, the modern approach to Isaiah shifted from a two-book to a three-book theory.

Chronological rearrangement

At the centre of the view that Isaiah consists of three books that contain oracles from many eras is a prioritization of history above the canonical arrangement of these texts. So, at the close of the nineteenth century and into the twentieth century, scholars began rearranging texts into chronological order. For instance, in 1899, Frank Sanders and Charles Kent (1899: v) state: 'One who merely reads in course a certain number of chapters each day is largely cut off from a true appreciation of the part that the prophet played in the progress of revelation.' What is needed, then, is not to read the book of Isaiah from start to finish, but to arrange the passages from all of the Latter Prophets into historical timelines. Sanders and Kent examine Isaiah's prophecies beginning with his call (ch. 6), confrontations with Judah over its sin (chs 2—4; 5.1-24; 9.8–10.4; 5.25–30), and the Syro-Ephraimite crisis (7.1—9.7; ch. 17; ch. 1). After discussing Micah's prophecies, they return to Isaiah's prophecies from the time of Sargon (21.11–17; 20.1–6; 15.1—16.14; 19.1–25), Sennacherib's invasion (chs 28—32; 22.15–25), promises (chs 10—12; 14.24–27; 17.12–14), and the crisis in Jerusalem (22.1–14; chs 33; 36; 37). They then examine Jeremiah and Ezekiel before considering 'the great prophet of the exile' whose writings we find in Isaiah 40—48 and 49—55. Finally, after examining Malachi, Sanders and Kent conclude that Isaiah 56—59, 34—35, 60.1—63.7, and 65—66 find their homes in the eras of Ezra and Nehemiah.

Reactions

Commentaries (Gray 1912; Marti 1900; Orelli 1904) and works on the prophets (Davidson 1904; Driver 1904) continued along the lines of dividing and rearranging according to history through the mid twentieth century. Before we transition to the next phase in Isaiah's interpretation, it is worth noting two reactions to the critical approaches to Isaiah.

Authorship and faith

Since the long-held Christian tradition was to view Isaiah as the only author of the book, the multiple-authorship approach received a range of responses from faith communities. On the one hand, some believers espoused the critical approach to Isaiah and did not believe it was at odds with religious belief. For instance, Davidson (1904: 271) asserts: 'we ought to repudiate and resent the attempts that are made to make this question one of religious belief', for what is most important is that God's word came through prophets – whether it is Isaiah or not is of no consequence (1904: 271–2). Even the prominent conservative commentator Franz Delitzsch (1890: 39) changed his mind in the fourth edition of his commentary on Isaiah where he adopts a multiple-authorship view, amid a lingering hesitancy: 'It seems to me even probable, and almost certain, that this [multiple authorship] may be so; but indubitably certain it is not, in my opinion, and I shall not die without getting over this hesitancy.' For these authors, the careful reading of Isaiah led them to recognize different historical eras being addressed in the different parts of Isaiah and hence different prophets behind the book.

On the other hand, some sectors of Christianity voiced strong resistance to this approach. In 1909 the Pontifical Bible Commission issued a statement that rejected the notion that the book has multiple authors. As a result, some Roman Catholic interpreters sought to interpret Isaiah within the parameters of this statement. As a way to affirm Isaianic authorship yet benefit from the insights of the historical-critical approach, Johann Fischer (1937, 1939) argues that a single prophet would address future contexts in spirit, so he attends to the Assyrian context in 1—39, the Babylonian context in 40—55, and the post-exilic context in 56—66.

Within Protestant circles, Edward Kissane (1941, 1943) argued that the prophet Isaiah is the author of Isaiah 1—39, and that Isaiah 40—66 is a rearticulation of the ideas of Isaiah by a prophet from the time of exile. Going further, O. T. Allis (1951) and Edward J. Young (1958) sought to defend Isaianic authorship for the entire book in line with the earliest traditions, due to their view of the nature of prophecy and in view of the unity across both parts of the book.

Today, Christian communities differ in response to the issue of multiple authorship. I encourage generosity on this matter, having served and worshipped with colleagues of genuine faith on both sides of this topic.

Literary fragmentation

Another early reaction to the critical approach to Isaiah is a lament over how the fragmenting of Isaiah ruined its literary message. Already in 1891 – prior to Duhm's commentary! – Stanley Leathes (1891: 63–4) could lament: 'It is the fashion now to conceive of four or five Isaiahs; but who ever heard of four or five Miltons? . . . this passion for disintegration destroys the material.' In 1928 Charles Torrey (1928: 13) – who held to the multiple authorship of Isaiah – asserts with regard to Isaiah 40—66 that 'Instead of a comprehensive unit, the best scholarship of the present day offers us here only an incomprehensible scrap-heap'. He proceeds to argue that Isaiah 34—35 and 40—66 is a strategic arrangement of 27 poems composed by an author in Israel from the fifth century BC to convey a single theme: 'the hope of Israel, the people chosen of God to save the world' (1928: 53–4). In the same year, Karl Ellinger (1928) argued that Isaiah 56—66 was the work of a single author at the end of the sixth century BC that a redactor finalized with a few additions in the fifth century. In James Muilenburg's (1956: 382) commentary, he declares Isaiah 40—55 to be 'the noblest literary monument bequeathed to us from Semitic antiquity' and reads large sections of Isaiah as 'wholes'. These early quests to reassemble the pieces of each part of the book anticipated the next major phase in the critical study of Isaiah.

Reassembling Isaiah (mid twentieth to twenty-first centuries)

Reassembly describes the second phase of scholarship on Isaiah in the modern era, one that continues to this day.

In the 1950s a series of studies by Leon Liebreich (1954, 1956a, 1956b) initiated a shift in attention to how the pieces fit together across Isaiah 1—66. In 1954, in a move away from isolating texts in their historical eras, he devoted a study to the purpose of Isaiah 6's location between chapters 1—5 and 7—8. In 1956 he expanded his study to the entire book, noticing many linguistic and conceptual associations between the beginnings and endings of the sections across the book (esp. 1 and 39; 40 and 66; 1 and 65—66). Liebreich, who held to a multiple authorship view, did not attempt to explain who was responsible for these connections, but these linguistic affinities suggested that a compiler intended for the book to be read as a whole. Two prominent theories emerged after Liebreich that attempted to explain the historical process by which the many strands in Isaiah came together as a whole.

One theory may be referred to as the *combination* view. It argues that the core of First Isaiah and Second Isaiah were independent of one another and unrelated, but they were combined together by Trito-Isaiah in the post-exilic era (after 445 BC). Rolf Rendtorff (1984), for instance, argues that the entire book is built around Isaiah 40—55, with the editor (Third Isaiah) adding chapters 12 and 35 into 1—39 to help First Isaiah relate to Second Isaiah. Third Isaiah then wrote 56—66 to integrate the two 'books', as one finds, for instance, 56.1 using 'righteousness' both morally, as it is in First Isaiah, and salvifically, as it is used in Second Isaiah.

Adopting a similar approach, Jacques Vermeylen (1989) suggests that a post-exilic redactor (Third Isaiah) was reading both First Isaiah, with its prophecies of Jerusalem's fall, and Second Isaiah, with its prophecies of Jerusalem's restoration. Since chapters 1—2 already anticipated the judgement and restoration of Zion, Third Isaiah found it fitting to combine together First and Second Isaiah. In order to solidify a sense of unity between these books, the redactor (Third Isaiah) added materials into both 1—39 and 40—55 and wrote Isaiah 56—66 in the light of Isaiah 1—2 as a grand conclusion that would bring closure to this united corpus.

A second theory may be called the *organic growth* view. In this theory, Second Isaiah is an organic, intentional continuation of First Isaiah; the two are integrally interconnected. Hugh Williamson (1994) offers the most complete defence of this view. He begins with several passages that are firmly dated to the prophet Isaiah and demonstrates how the language of these passages clearly influenced Second Isaiah. For instance, among numerous examples, he demonstrates that expressions such as 'high and exalted' (6.1; 52.13) and 'the Holy One of Israel' (12x in 1—39; 11x in 40—55) from First Isaiah also occur in Second Isaiah. Next, he argues that the prophet Isaiah's pattern of writing his words as a witness for future generations (8.16–18; 30.8–9) probably influenced Second Isaiah, who viewed the time of exile as the moment of Isaiah's anticipated work of salvation. So, Second Isaiah 'regarded his own work as an integral continuation of the work of Isaiah' (1994: 113). Finally, he sets out to show how Second Isaiah added elements into Isaiah 2—12 (esp. ch. 12), 13—27 (esp. chs 13—14), and 28—39 (ch. 33). So, Isaiah 40—55 is an integral extension of the developing message of First Isaiah.

Jacob Stromberg, a student of Williamson, extended the organic growth view to include chapters 56—66 (Third Isaiah). After explaining the composite nature of Isaiah 56—66, Stromberg (2011) identifies 56.1–8 and chapters 65—66 as the final additions to Third Isaiah. As the latest additions, he traces allusions from those passages back to Isaiah 1—55. Next, he works through Isaiah 1—39 and 40—55, looking for redactional insertions by the final editor of Third Isaiah throughout the entire book. The combination of Williamson and Stromberg results in the depiction of an organic growth in the Isaiah tradition that began with the eighth-century prophet Isaiah, extends into exile through the work of Deutero-Isaiah and ultimately comes to a conclusion when Trito-Isaiah reaches its final form.

While the previous eras of scholarship slotted passages from the book of Isaiah into various historical eras, this next phase of *reassembling* Isaiah attempts to explain the historical process by which these historically distinct texts came to be part of a larger book. This pattern of diachronic study continues to this day. Commentators who align with this tradition include the likes of Blenkinsopp, Wildberger, Berges, Williamson, and Westermann.

Engaging Isaiah (late twentieth century to present)

During the twentieth century, as diachronic analyses continued, the hegemony of the scientific, historical approach over Isaiah loosened due to several newer approaches: the canonical approach; the literary approach; and experientialist approaches.

The canonical approach

Brevard Childs' (1979) monumental *Introduction to the Old Testament as Scripture* ushered in a new approach – the canonical approach. Although Childs acknowledged tremendous gains from the historical-critical approach and embraced these findings, he believed that its nearly exclusive focus on stages of development within Hebrew thought and stages of book composition resulted in a neglect of how the Church and synagogue interpreted these books. Old Testament books, such as Isaiah, have been read in their final form as authoritative, religious books that shaped the religious community. For this reason, Childs was interested in how the final form of the book of Isaiah creates a theological context for interpreting the various parts of the book. In the final form of Isaiah, 'Chapters 40ff. are now understood as a prophetic word of promise offered to Israel by the eighth-century prophet, Isaiah of Jerusalem' (Childs 1979: 325). In the canonical presentation, the historical origins of 40—66 have dissipated and now the book of Isaiah itself provides a context for how 40—66 are to be understood. By not tying these texts exclusively to one specific historical moment, the book of Isaiah speaks as God's word to the future for all of time. For this reason, Childs took great interest in how Isaiah had been interpreted as Christian Scripture throughout the ages, eventually writing a book on the topic (2004).

Christopher Seitz, a former student of Childs, is the foremost champion of his mentor's canonical vision. In an essay on making sense of the whole of Isaiah (1988: 105), Seitz states that a significant 'implication of the term "canonical" is that the intention of the final shape of the Book of Isaiah, while difficult to perceive, is greater than the sum of all previous intentions of the text'. Seitz describes his own commentary on Isaiah 1—39 as an argument that Isaiah 'is both an intelligible and an intended result of the efforts of those who gave shape to the present form of the book' (1993: xi–xii).

Not only does the canonical approach advocate for reading books in their final form, but there is also theological interest in how biblical books bear a discrete witness to God's work in Christ. As Childs opens his commentary on Isaiah (2001: 4–5), he acknowledges that 'As a Christian interpreter, I confess with the church that the Old and New Testaments, in their distinct canonical forms, together form a theological whole'. Although most of Childs' commentary focuses on reading texts in Isaiah in conversation with historical criticism, he does on occasion engage with distinctly Christian readings of passages such as the sign of Immanuel and the Suffering Servant. The canonical approach was carving out a place for the consideration of the theological witness of Isaiah within the field of OT studies and creating a place for pre-modern interpreters in contemporary discussion. My volume on the biblical theology of Isaiah could not have been conceived were it not for the canonical approach (Abernethy 2016).

Through the work of Childs and Seitz, there is now a place at the table in scholarship for those most interested in the final form of Isaiah and its theological, religious message for the community of faith. It should be noted, however, that several evangelical scholars were already writing commentaries that attended to the whole of Isaiah and its theological message (Motyer 1993; Oswalt 1986, 1998). The major difference between their work and that of the canonical approach is that Motyer and Oswalt established the unity of Isaiah in a single human author while Childs and Seitz do not.

The literary approach

Another approach that pushed against the hegemony of historicism in Isaiah studies is the literary approach. Edgar Conrad (1991) championed a radical shift away from historical-critical readings towards a literary reading of the final form of Isaiah. Conrad's interest in the final form is exclusively literary and focuses on the 'literary world of the text itself' (1991: 30) instead of the world behind the text. He attends to literary features such as repetition, the implied reader, and even genres that contribute to a unified reading of Isaiah as a literary whole. Around the same time, Barry Webb (1990) offered a sequential reading of Isaiah as a complete literary work. He concluded that Zion's transformation through judgement, along with the accompanying motif of the remnant, is the central literary message of the book. Building on their work, Katheryn Pfisterer Darr (1994), attending to family, and then Abernethy (2014), focusing on food and drink, offer sequential readings of Isaiah with an eye towards how a respective theme develops across the book.

Literary theory has also manifested itself in the form of intertextuality. In 1997 Patricia Tull Willey published her study on how Isaiah 40—55 'recollects' existing texts such as Lamentations, Jeremiah 30—31, Nahum, the Psalms, and the Pentateuch as it offers a message to exiles. In the same year, Benjamin Sommer's work on allusion and influence in Isaiah 40—66 and other biblical texts appeared. A few years later Richard Schultz (1999), a pupil of Brevard Childs, published a methodological treatment of verbal quotations in the prophets, particularly within Isaiah. There have been subsequent studies on intertextual associations within Isaiah (*intra*textuality) and between Isaiah and other biblical books (e.g. Hibbard and Kim 2013).

The long-recognized poetic brilliance throughout Isaiah, especially in 40—55, has resulted in the use of many other literary theories in the study of the book. Hyun Chul Paul Kim (2003) attends to ambiguity and tension as he reads texts from Second Isaiah where Israel and the nations intersect. Katie Heffelfinger (2011) reads Isaiah 40—55 as lyric poetry, with its inherent ambiguity and with God as the chief speaker. J. Blake Couey (2015) devotes a monograph to the poetry of 'First Isaiah'. Brittany Kim (2018) applies metaphor theory to the theme of Israel's household across the book.

Thus, in this movement, gains from the field of literary criticism are being applied to the book of Isaiah, as it is certainly remarkable literature.

Experientialists

The final approach to Isaiah that is not bound by the historical-critical approach could be described as *experiential*. By *experiential*, we mean interpreters who have a significant interest in how the book of Isaiah interacts with the experiences of readers today. Patricia K. Tull (2009) and Ellen Davis (2009) bring Isaiah into conversation with agricultural concerns. Louis Stulman and Hyun Chul Paul Kim (2010) promote the need to read the prophets, including Isaiah, through the lens of disaster and survival literature in view of post-colonial studies. Mark Gray (2006) offers readings of Isaiah 1 and 58 so as to bring Isaiah's vision of justice into conversation with the realities of violence and injustice today. Francis Landy (2001, 2002) is perhaps the greatest representative of the experiential approach, as his interdisciplinary essays on Isaiah engage the realities of death in Isaiah 28, the challenge of reading Isaiah 53 as a Jew, and issues of gender and sexuality, such as when Isaiah has intercourse with the prophetess (Isa. 8.1–4).

There have also been numerous feminist interpretations of Isaiah. Nancy C. Lee (2015) attempts to identify the voice of female prophetic poetry in Isaiah 5.1–7; 9.3–7; 12.1–3, and numerous texts from 40—55. Irmtraud Fischer (2012) surveys the female figures in Isaiah (e.g. the prophetess; the women of Jerusalem), along with the use of female metaphors for Zion and God. Katheryn Pfisterer Darr (1987, 1994) probes the portrayal of women both in her work on family in Isaiah and also in an essay on the blending of warrior and female imagery in Isaiah 42.

By way of summary, there are two common threads between the canonical, literary and experiential approaches. First, they all see a need for more tools in the study of Isaiah than those of historical criticism. For some, especially in the canonical approach, these new tools are viewed as an addition to historical criticism. For others, especially Conrad, the new tools are meant to replace historical criticism. Second, they all desire to engage with Isaiah in its final form, whether with canonical, literary, or experiential questions at hand. This expansion of the field of Isaiah studies has ushered in an exciting new era of interdisciplinary engagement in the study of this great book.

Conclusion, assessment, and a path forward

In the modern era, the academic study of Isaiah has had three major phases. At the turn of the nineteenth to the twentieth century, the dominant concern was to extract sections (e.g. 1—39; 40—55; 56—66) and passages (e.g. 13.1—14.23; 24—27) from their literary contexts in the book of Isaiah and rearrange them into a historical timeline – from the life of the prophet Isaiah, to later pre-exilic times, to early and late exile, and throughout the Persian and Greek eras. After this season of fragmentation and rearranging, there was a shift to redaction history in the mid twentieth century that continues to the present day. This agenda is largely historical, aiming to uncover how and why the various sections and passages in Isaiah came together over the course of four centuries. As redaction criticism continues with its diachronic quest, several approaches that move beyond the historicist agenda have carved out space for themselves in the field of academic studies. The canonical approach seeks to recover reading Isaiah as religious communities received it: as the religious community's literature, to be read in its final form. The literary approach employs a range of literary theories (e.g. reader response, genre, sequential reading, intertextuality, poetry, metaphor theory) in the service of reading the book of Isaiah as literature. The experientialist approaches bring personal and social dynamics into conversation with Isaiah. Although the dance is awkward at times, dancers with a variety of styles are now on the dance floor together and in some instances these dancers are picking up moves from one another.

Where do these two chapters on the history of interpretation leave us? At a minimum, this survey should help you understand why commentators focus on given issues. Another benefit of this survey is to enable you to detect how you have already been influenced by these research traditions. Does your previous exposure to Isaiah fit more in the pre-modern or modern approaches? Are you driven mostly by historical, literary, canonical, or experiential interests in your reading? Or a combination? Are you wondering how Isaiah speaks of Christ or what it meant originally? You are not an 'island', so the very philosophical currents that gave rise to these various approaches have also had an influence on you.

My own interests are primarily in how to best read Isaiah as Christian Scripture. A key issue is whether or not the methods of 'natural history' (historical criticism) are the best tools for interpreting a divinely inspired book. There is little doubt, though, that the book of Isaiah addresses historical audiences through the language and concepts of the time. So, attention to the social and cultural background of Isaiah – including its language – is a non-negotiable.

I am cautious, however, perhaps even concerned, about placing too much weight upon the importance of the historical-critical method when it comes to understanding Isaiah for several reasons. First, we must acknowledge how *limited* our confidence can be in the results of historical-critical enquiry. There remains no consensus about the historical location of the so-called 'Second Isaiah'. Is he in Egypt (Ewald 1875–81), Phoenicia or Lebanon (Duhm 1922), Babylon (Williamson 1994), or Jerusalem (Barstad 1989; Tiemeyer 2010)? There is also little agreement about the macro-structure of the book. Is the first half 1—39 (Duhm 1922) or 1—33 (Brownlee 1964; Evans 1988)? Does the second part end at chapter 49 (Liebreich 1954), 54 (Sweeney 1996), 55 (Muilenburg 1956), or 66 (Torrey 1928)? There is even greater disagreement on dates of the minute details of individual passages. For instance, Hayes and Irvine (1987) date all texts (except for 34—35) in 'First Isaiah' to the prophet Isaiah, while Vermeylen (1977–8) finds nearly 18 different redactional layers across Isaiah 1—35. A text like Isaiah 2.2–4 is pre-exilic for some and for others an expression of Israel's theocratic hopes in the Persian period. Assigning dates at the micro-level can feel like a free-for-all, and beginning students and senior scholars alike can find themselves dizzy in the whirlwind of conjecture.

A second reason for caution is that the historical-critical method cannot be the *exclusive* method for interpreting Isaiah. For one, what if the *aims* of Isaiah differ from the *aims* of historical-critical enquiry? In other words, if historical-critical methods are designed to answer a certain set of questions, what if those are answers that Isaiah cannot provide or, worse yet, what if Isaiah seeks to answer a different set of questions from those which the historical-critical method can address? The issue is that we need a method, or set of methods, that aligns with the nature of what we are studying. The danger here is that we might end up watering the leaves of a tree when it is the roots that need the water. We may end up being trained as engineers to disassemble and reassemble a car, although we never actually learned how to drive it. Even if the historical-critical method gives rise to a range of intriguing questions and intellectual investigations, not to mention its illumination of philological and cultural aspects of the text, other methods are needed for those seeking to read Isaiah.

What is more, if the book of Isaiah is divinely inspired, should Isaiah only be read like any other book? Pre-modern interpreters, with their concern for attending to the literal and spiritual elements of the text, seem to be on a better path than the modern, secular academy when it comes to having a method that aligns with the nature of the object under study (see Carter 2018). What the pre-modern commentators lacked, however, were some of the benefits of attending to the literal, historical sense of the text that the modern era has recovered. Recovering a sense of the theological dimension of Isaiah entails a willingness to engage with what these texts are saying about God and how they attempt to shape their original hearers, along with being open to the possibility that God intended to communicate through these texts in ways that were unknown to the original human author and only are able to be seen in the hindsight of redemptive history and the placement of Isaiah within a two-testament witness to Christ.

The key issue, then, is what approach to Isaiah will help us as readers to best align with the nature of the book of Isaiah and for what purpose. This leads to the beauty of the Discovering Biblical Texts series, with its demands that we attend to the historical, the literary, and the reception-historical components of interpretation. As for the 'historical', there is good reason why Isaiah has always been read in view of the historical contexts it evokes. Although I am not sure that studies which divide Isaiah into its compositional history are all that useful for religious readers, we must affirm the importance of attending to how Isaiah itself summons historical attention. As for the 'literary', it seems self-evident that the final form of Isaiah presents itself to us as a literary whole that must be read as literature. As for 'reception', we learn to ask important theological questions while reading Isaiah and to recognize the importance and validity of pondering how Isaiah can and should be read today.

Our set of questions stemming from Chapter 2 finds enrichment here at the close of Chapter 3.

1 Am I considering the literal-historical meaning of this passage? What historical vantage point does the book invite me to adopt when reading the passage? How do literary tools and a growing pool of historical knowledge enable me to better detect the literal-historical meaning of the passage?
2 How does this passage direct me to Christ? How does the canonical nature of Isaiah provide a context for detecting how Isaiah bears witness to Christ and addresses the Church?
3 How should I understand Isaiah today? How does Isaiah intersect with questions about justice, gender, the environment, and more?

In the light of our prioritization of the final form of Isaiah, the main concern in the rest of this volume will be to engage with the book of Isaiah in the light of how it is inviting us to read it in its final form. Chapter 4 will set forth the (hi)story the book of Isaiah tells, a metahistory from the Assyrian, Babylonian, and Persian eras to the new heavens and new earth. Chapters 5–9 will then examine five central themes that span the book of Isaiah, utilizing insights from literary, historical, and reception-historical studies. By engaging the book of Isaiah through a wide range of methods, we are in the best position to attend to the literal-historical sense of Isaiah and also to discern the theological witness of the text.

4

The history Isaiah tells

Martin Luther (1969: 3) opens his commentary on Isaiah by stating: 'Two things are necessary to explain the prophet. The first is knowledge of grammar . . . The second is more necessary, namely, a knowledge of historical background.'

For Luther, Isaiah's primary task was to prepare the people of his time and later times for the advent of Christ. In order to discern what the prophet was doing, understanding the historical eras behind the book was essential. For Luther, this meant a general grasp of the time frame a passage calls to mind. So, when Isaiah 7 anticipates the fall of Aram and Israel at the hands of Assyria, Luther (1969: 82) notes that 'From this chapter to the thirtieth the prophet always has Assyria in view'. In chapter 40, Luther points out that the second half of the book concerns prophecies about Christ the King and also about Cyrus and Babylonian captivity (1972: 3). Although Luther does not mention specific historical details about every verse, it is a general sense of the historical vantage point of various parts of the book that is most necessary for reading Isaiah.

If Luther had lived another 350 years, he would have probably nailed a few more theses to the doors of Protestant universities to decry how some historical study today obscures rather than illuminates a reading of Isaiah as God's word for the people of God. Driven by a desire to situate passages and verses within historical eras, Ewald, Duhm, and countless others took to extracting passages and verses from their *literary book* context and atomized them within purported *historical* contexts ranging from the eighth century to the first century BC (see Chapter 3 above). My sense is that Luther – and most pre-critical commentators – would have mourned the loss of historical movement across the book caused by such fragmentation. The canonical approach seeks to recover what such fragmentation lost, while not dismissing the contributions of historical-critical studies. Childs (1979: 46–106, 311–38) and Seitz (2007: 94–5, 181–2, 250), among others, declared that the *history that the final form of Isaiah tells* is most important for a religious reading of the book. Instead of attempting to reconstruct what is going on behind the scenes in given passages or playing the sleuth to discover redactional layers, the starting point of a canonical reading is to allow the biblical book – in this case Isaiah – and its part in a two-testament canon to provide the historical frame of reference for reading the book.

Isaiah offers us a theological history, a history that invites us as readers to find our place and identities amid God's mission in the world. Only a few chapters in Isaiah are written in the narrative genre (chs 6—7; 20; 36—39), so I am not suggesting that Isaiah is a story in the way that 1 Samuel is. Instead, the organization of the book at the grand scale offers a semblance of a historical movement. Grasping this historical narrative is perhaps the most important key to effectively reading the parts and the entirety of the book of Isaiah. As we will see, this is not a secular history – this is a history of a God dedicated to transforming a people, a city, and a world gone awry amid some incredibly turbulent times through some surprising means. Below, we begin by framing this history in the light of judgement and salvation before sketching four major phases of historical progression within the book. The chapter will conclude by pondering how we might find our place within this story.

A story of judgement and salvation

One unique feature in prophetic literature is the juxtaposition of messages of condemnation and hope.[1] For the prophets, judgement and salvation are two sides of the same coin, so learning to read Isaiah with an eye towards how judgement and salvation co-exist is vital. The opening of Isaiah, 1.1—2.5, establishes this pattern from the start.

In Isaiah 1.5 God asks Judah:

Why do you seek further beatings?
Why do you continue to rebel?

The people have already been struck once, and verses 7–9 show that Judah finds itself decimated, although the city of Jerusalem remains like a solitary hut in a field. More than likely, the siege of Judah by the Assyrian king Sennacherib in 701 BC stands in the background as the 'strike' alluded to in 1.5. If the people of Judah continue to rebel against God, they are in danger of being struck again. Sure, they are ramping up their efforts to appease God through sacrifice, worship services, prayers, and other religious activities (1.10–15), but these will not remedy their standing with God, for oppression and injustice towards the

---

1 A classic treatment of judgement and energizing hope in the prophets is Brueggemann 2001.

vulnerable have created a barrier between them and God (1.15–17). This stinging indictment culminates with a choice: the repentant will experience forgiveness and eat the good of the land in salvation (1.18–19) and those who ignore God will be devoured by the sword (1.20). They can either eat or be eaten.

Isaiah 1.21–26 tells a similar story of judgement and salvation. Zion, a formerly faithful city, is now unfaithful to God because its leaders turn a blind eye to the pleas of orphans and widows in exchange for bribes (1.21–23). Due to this state of affairs, God will purify Zion through judgement (1.24–25). The result is that 'afterwards you shall be called the city of righteousness, the faithful city' (1.26).

Immediately after chapter 1, with its stinging indictments and largely negative character, a vision of Zion's glory occurs at the start of chapter 2:

> In days to come
>> the mountain of the LORD's house
> shall be established as the highest of the mountains,
>> and shall be raised above the hills;
> all the nations shall stream to it.
>> Many peoples shall come and say,
> 'Come, let us go up to the mountain of the LORD,
>> to the house of the God of Jacob;
> that he may teach us his ways
>> and that we may walk in his paths.'
> For out of Zion shall go forth instruction,
>> and the word of the LORD from Jerusalem.
> He shall judge between the nations,
>> and shall arbitrate for many peoples;
> they shall beat their swords into ploughshares,
>> and their spears into pruning-hooks;
> nation shall not lift up sword against nation,
>> neither shall they learn war any more.
> (2.2–4)

This vision fills out the era of salvation hinted at in chapter 1. Once Zion becomes a faithful city after judgement (1.26), this will have an impact on the entire world. Zion will become an international capital city (2.2) to which the nations stream to receive instruction from God, the King (2.3). The result will be peace across the world (2.4).

Table 1 The pattern of judgement and salvation across Isaiah 1—12

Judgement/ Salvation	Salvation	Judgement	Salvation	Judgement	Salvation	Judgement	Salvation
ch. 1	2.2–5	2.6—4.1	4.2–6	5.1—8.23	9.1–7	9.8—10.33	chs 11—12

These opening chapters invite us into a story of judgement and salvation that continues across the entire book of Isaiah. For instance, this pattern is prominent across chapters 1—12 (see Table 1).

A similar schema of alternating judgement and salvation recurs throughout Isaiah 13—27, 28—35, 36—39, 40—48, 49—55, and 56—66. Even on a grander scale, one detects a predominant tenor of judgement in chapters 1—39, of salvation in 40—55, and a mixture of judgement and salvation in 56—66.

So, what is the pay-off of being alert to whether a passage is expressing judgement or hope? By recognizing whether a passage you are reading is expressing indictment and judgement or hope and salvation, you are in a position to detect what a passage or portion of the book is seeking to convey. When reading a passage of indictment and judgement, we should become alert to how the passage seeks to (1) unmask and name the sin that we and our communities are blinded to, (2) declare that God will not stand idly by as sin wreaks havoc – judgement will come, and (3) propel us towards repentance. When reading a passage of hope and salvation, we should be alert to how the passage aims to (1) energize those in despair through hope, (2) incentivize the faithful to endure and the rebellious to repent, and (3) offer a vision of God's ideal future so as to motivate those in the present to live in such ways now (cf. 2.2–5).

Along with asking, 'Is this a passage of judgement or salvation?', it is also vital to consider why the two are side by side throughout the book. What we find is that the book of Isaiah invites us into a story, a history within which God will act in judgement and salvation. As we will see below, only on rare occasions do we receive explicit historical references to Assyria, Babylon, or the name of a king. Instead, much like the Psalms, the generic nature of these prophecies suggests that they were preserved out of the conviction that future recipients of these messages would find relevance in these words from God far beyond the original context of these passages. After all, future hearers and readers are part of the same history within which God will continue to confront sin and act in judgement and to comfort the afflicted and act in salvation.

The metanarrative of Isaiah

If judgement and salvation is the rhythm of Isaiah's story, the metanarrative of Isaiah provides a landscape for its movements. Isaiah is not organized in an entirely chronological fashion, so we can detect various phases in Isaiah's story amid the different sections of Isaiah. The book of Isaiah's metahistorical vision unfolds in four phases.

- *Phase 1.* The Holy One judges Israel, Zion, and the nations through Assyria and Babylon.
- *Phase 2.* The Holy One uses King Cyrus of Persia to rebuild Jerusalem and send exiles home.
- *Phase 3.* The Holy One uses the Suffering Servant to spiritually restore and reconstitute God's people.
- *Phase 4.* The Holy One comes in final judgement and final salvation to make a new world for his servants.

Although these four phases align in general with the major parts of the book (Phase 1: 1—39; Phase 2: 40—48; Phase 3: 49—55; Phase 4: 56—66), there are elements from all four phases interspersed throughout multiple sections of the book. Below, I offer a sketch of each of these phases.[2] Although I do not expect a reader to retain all of the specifics in each phase, my hope is that you will walk away with a grasp of the big picture of each. We will return to these four phases in Chapters 5–9 when we trace key themes across Isaiah.

Phase 1: Judgement through Assyria and Babylon

The first phase of Isaiah's metahistory is a vision of the Holy One judging Israel, Zion, and the nations through Assyria and Babylon. Phase 1 finds expression throughout most of Isaiah 1—39. The general schema that emerges for Phase 1 is laid out in the diagram on page 43.

The superscription (1.1) situates Isaiah's message during the era of four eighth-century Judean kings: Uzziah, Jotham, Ahaz, and Hezekiah. These

---

2 See Steck 2000: 20–65, who observes the metahistorical character of Isaiah, yet leaves this underdeveloped amid his explanation of redaction history. Most similar to my concern here is Seitz (1988: 105–25), whose lists of phases differ from my own (he excludes Cyrus and the Servant from these phases), yet with whom I share a similar conviction that Isaiah tells a story of world history, with its various phases interspersed with elements from the other parts of the book so as to create unity across the whole.

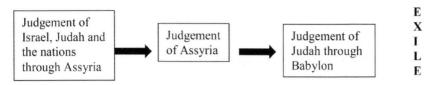

kings appear by name (except for Jotham) in chronological order across Isaiah 1—39, resulting in a semblance of chronology through the first half of the book.[3] King Uzziah's death (6.1; 735 BC) marks the occasion when Isaiah sees the Holy King. The Holy King reveals his plan to decimate a hardened nation through multiple rounds of military invasion until all that is left is a holy seed (6.9–13). In chapter 7, Israel and Aram join forces to wage war against King Ahaz in Jerusalem, threatening to overthrow Judah's king. Israel and Aram, however, would not be God's agents of judgement anticipated in chapter 6; instead, Isaiah announces that the king of Assyria would be God's tool for judging Aram, Israel, and even Judah (7.17, 20; 8.7; 733–732 BC). After King Ahaz's death (14.28), narratives about King Hezekiah conclude the first half of the book in chapters 36—39. We are told that King Sennacherib of Assyria's campaign against Judah (36.1; 701 BC) culminates with a siege of Zion. God miraculously delivers Zion from the Assyrian siege (chs 36—37), but the Hezekiah narratives end with the expectation that Babylon would bring a decisive blow to Zion, taking the house of David and the royal treasury into exile (ch. 39). Thus, references to Judah's kings in 1.1 and then across Isaiah 1—39 establish an arc that stretches from the revelation that the Holy King will judge his people, to the identification of Assyria as God's tool for doing so during the time of Ahaz and Hezekiah, and ultimately to the prediction that Babylon would finish what Assyria had started.

Also, the organizations of the two major subsections of Isaiah 1—39 (1—27; 28—35) establish the schema that begins with judgement via Assyria too. Isaiah 1—27 opens in Isaiah 1—12 with decrees of divine judgement through Assyria for Judah and Israel due to their injustice and pride (1—10.4). The jurisdiction of judgement expands, however, by announcing that Assyria too would be judged (10.5–34). This paves the way for the Oracles Against the Nations that present surrounding nations as objects of the Holy One's

---

3   It is unlikely that every passage, except for 34—35, in Isaiah 1—39 is arranged chronologically, through Hayes and Irvine (1987) argue for this.

judgement through Assyria and then Babylon (chs 13—23). Chapters 24—27 extend the anticipation of judgement and salvation eschatologically beyond Phase 1 of Isaiah's history. Although shorter, Isaiah 28—35 displays a similar sequence, as judgement begins with Ephraim and Judah (28—32) and extends to Assyria (30.31; 31.8) and Zion's foes from the nations (33.1–4). Chapters 34—35, like chapters 24—27, extend the anticipation of divine judgement and salvation eschatologically. The historical narratives in chapters 36—39 put flesh on the era of Assyrian incursion, and clarify that although Assyria was not the death knell for Judah, Babylon would be.

After Isaiah 1—39, no king from the superscription is mentioned by name, nor is Assyria. This does not automatically mean that Isaiah 1—39 and 40—66 were different 'books'; instead, this is simply an indication that Isaiah 1—39 tells only a part of the wider metahistory that Isaiah presents. Phase 1 is an era when God is judging Israel, Judah, and surrounding nations through Assyria and ultimately Babylon, who will bring about the exile of Jerusalem's kings. Although adumbrations of Phases 2, 3, and 4 surface in 1—39, Phase 1 must occur first before there can be any talk of Zion's restoration. Israel, Judah, surrounding nations, and the vehicles of judgement (Assyria; Babylon) must face the wrath of the Holy One.

Excursus on the Assyrian era

During the first half of King Uzziah's reign, the kingdom of Judah, along with its sister Israel, experienced peace and prosperity, yet both of these nations were engulfed in idolatry, injustice, and pride. For this reason, God raised up prophets like Amos and Hosea and then Isaiah and Micah to confront Judah and Israel for their sins and to announce that Assyria would bring God's judgement against them. When reading these eighth-century prophets, knowledge of Assyria and its involvement with Israel and Judah is vital.

The ancient empire of Assyria returned to its former glory as a world empire under Tiglath-pileser III (745–727 BC) – referred to as Pul in 2 Kings 15.19. Most likely, this is the 'king of Assyria' mentioned in Isaiah 7.17, 20; 8.7. Tiglath-pileser III's records speak of a campaign to Philistia in 734 BC during which he devastated many cities in Israel and 'spared only Samaria' and 'overthrew Pekah their king' (Younger 2003b). In another inscription, Tiglath-pileser III records his campaigns to overthrow Damascus (733–732 BC), and in the process he took thousands of exiles from Israel (Younger 2003a). These records align with the immediate circumstances of the Aram–Israelite threat to Judah that the prophet declared would be spoiled by the king of Assyria in Isaiah 7.

Over a decade after Aram and Israel came against Judah, Assyria would deal a decisive blow against Israel and its capital Samaria (722/721 BC; cf. 2 Kings 17). Shalmaneser V began the conquest of Samaria, and Sargon II would finish it. The Nimrud Prism captures this fall in Sargon's records:

> [The inhabitants of Sa]merina, who agreed [and plotted] with a king [hostile to] me, not to do service and not to bring tribute [to Aššur] and who did battle, I fought against them with the power of the great gods, my lords. I counted as spoil 27,280 people, together with their chariots, and gods, in which they trusted. I formed a unit with 200 of [their] chariots for my royal force. I settled the rest of them in the midst of Assyria. I repopulated Samerina more than before. I brought into it people from countries conquered by my hands.
> (Younger 2003c)

The exile of Israel and its repopulation by non-Jews took place right in the backyard of Judah, during the time of Isaiah and King Ahaz.

It is during the reign of King Hezekiah that Assyria's impact on Judah is felt most acutely. An incursion commissioned by King Sargon II of Assyria was so monumental that Isaiah 20 dates an oracle of Isaiah to that time (713 BC). The most devastating campaign, however, is recounted in Isaiah 36—37, when Sennacherib (701 BC) campaigns through Judah and begins to besiege Jerusalem.[4] Isaiah 36.1 reads: 'In the fourteenth year of King Hezekiah, King Sennacherib of Assyria came up against all the fortified cities of Judah and captured them.' Behind this single verse looms a dark, dark day for Judah. The Sennacherib Prism (also known as the Taylor Prism) fills in the picture:

> As for Hezekiah, the Judean, I besieged forty-six of his fortified walled cities and surrounding smaller towns, which were without number. Using packed-down ramps and applying battering rams, infantry attacks by mines, breeches, and siege machines, I conquered (them). I took

---

4 For an archaeological overview of Sennacherib's invasion and sieges on Lachish and Jerusalem, see Ussishkin (2013).

out 200,150 people, young and old, male and female, horses, mules, donkeys, camels, cattle, and sheep, without number, and counted them as spoil. He himself, I locked up within Jerusalem, his royal city, like a bird in a cage.
(Cogan 2003b: 303)

For Sennacherib, the campaign into Judah was so significant that an artistic relief recounting the conquest of Lachish (a Judean city) graced the wall of his palace. Isaiah 36.2—37.38 picks up where Sennacherib's Prism leaves off. Hezekiah turns to the Lord first through Isaiah and then through his own prayer, and God ultimately delivers Zion from Assyria's siege.

Phase 2: Cyrus to the rescue!

Already within Isaiah 1—39, there are expectations that after judgement Zion would be restored. Visions of Zion's glory juxtapose with the demise of Jerusalem (e.g. 3.1—4.1 and 4.2–6; 30.1–17 and 30.18–33; 32.9–14 and 32.15–20) and the falls of Assyria (e.g. 10.5–19 and 10.20–27) and Babylon (e.g. ch. 13 and 14.1–2). As it turns out, just as Zion's judgement would involve multiple stages (Assyria, then Babylon, then eschatological judgement), so too would Zion's salvation and restoration. In Isaiah 36—37, Zion's miraculous deliverance by the hand of God from Assyria (701 BC) would only be a moment in the providential outworking of God's salvation. Within 120 years, Zion would fall to Babylon as was anticipated in chapter 39. What comes next for Zion? Phase 2 in the history Isaiah tells unfolds in Isaiah 40—48: the Holy One will use King Cyrus of Persia to rebuild Jerusalem and send exiles home.

Exile led to a spiritual crisis. Is Israel's God weaker than the gods of Babylon? Has God given up on his people Israel? How can God save face for allowing his people to have such a shameful existence, with no temple, no king, and no land? Isaiah 40—48 declares that God will do something to recover the glory of his name among his people and among the nations. Yes, Babylon had taken his people into exile, yet God would show that Babylon and its gods are nothing compared to him, the Holy One of Israel, the King of Jacob. God would show his incomparability by predicting in advance that he would deliver his people from Babylon through Persia's king, Cyrus.

There are at least five different passages in Isaiah 40—48 that speak of God's plans to use Cyrus (41.2–5, 25–28; 44.24–28; 45.1–13; 46.9–13) to bring

Babylon to shame and to restore Zion.[5] In Isaiah 41.2, God invites the nations into his courtroom and asks:

Who has roused ['*ûr*] a victor from the east,
    summoned him to his service?
He delivers up nations to him,
    and tramples kings under foot;
he makes them like dust with his sword,
    like driven stubble with his bow.

As if in a courtroom, the nations see evidence that God's power is far greater than anticipated. The God of Israel is arousing a victor from the east – not from Israel – to accomplish his purposes. Although some old traditions identify the 'victor' ('righteous one') as Abraham,[6] Isaiah eventually specifies that Cyrus is this individual. The nations will turn to idols as they fear this rising threat from the east (41.5–7), but the captive people of Israel need not fear, for their redeemer is the Holy One of Israel (41.8–20), the One who chose them and will uphold them. In fact, to prove his superiority over all other gods, the Holy One is foretelling what is to come through Cyrus:

I stirred up ['*ûr*] one from the north, and he has come,
    from the rising of the sun he was summoned by name.[7]
He shall trample on rulers as on mortar,
    as the potter treads clay.
(41.25)

The name of the one stirred up ('*ûr*) is not specified in chapter 41, nor is it made clear how this one will benefit Israel. Yet, God claims responsibility for the success of this victor, and Israel is to bear witness to the fact that God has declared in advance what this one will do.

---

5   Most modern scholars agree with this list, although Blenkinsopp (2002: 210) would add 42.1–4. Admittedly, there is ambiguity, particularly in chapter 41, that allows the referent to coordinate with Cyrus at first reference, yet transcend Cyrus to point to God's ability to bring about further restoration for Zion after Cyrus.

6   Jerome (2015: 550) notes that some Jews identify the person as Abraham. Jerome (2015: 550) and Eusebius (2013: 208) both interpret the referent as Christ. Calvin (2010: 3/246) interprets the figure as Abraham, an example of encouragement for the exiles.

7   The NRSV translation 'summoned by name' favours the tradition in the Septuagint, while the Masoretic and Qumran traditions read: 'He will call by my name.' Since Cyrus never calls on the name of the LORD, this leads Gary Smith to rule out Cyrus as a referent (2009: 148). For a mediating position, see Oswalt 1998: 97 n. 88, 103.

At the end of chapters 44—45, both the name of the one stirred up and how he will benefit Israel are specified. God, Israel's redeemer and the creator of heaven and earth, is the one

> who says of Cyrus, 'He is my shepherd,
>   and he shall carry out all my purpose';
> and who says of Jerusalem, 'It shall be rebuilt',
>   and of the temple, 'Your foundation shall be laid.'
> (44.28)

Shockingly, Cyrus, the Persian king, is designated as God's 'shepherd' – a term previously used to describe King David (cf. Ps. 78.70–72). Cyrus would carry out God's purpose of rebuilding Jerusalem and the Temple, the city David established and the temple Solomon originally built. The surprising language continues into chapter 45 where Cyrus is described as God's 'anointed' (i.e. Messiah; 45.1). God's choice of Cyrus is 'for the sake of [God's] servant Jacob, and Israel [his] chosen' (45.4), and his work through Cyrus will make it clear across the globe that 'there is none besides' the LORD (45.6).

This emphasis on displaying God's supremacy over all other gods due to his work through Cyrus continues into chapter 46. Unlike other gods who need humans to carry them, God is the one who carries his people. There is no one like God (46.9), and God's purposes will surely come to pass because he summons

> a bird of prey from the east,
>   the man for my purpose from a far country.
> I have spoken, and I will bring it to pass;
>   I have planned, and I will do it.
> (46.11)[8]

This one from the east (cf. 41.2) who carries out God's plans is none other than King Cyrus.

As God uses Cyrus to enable the return of exiles and the rebuilding of Jerusalem, the prophet exhorts the people:

---

8   Jerome (2015: 600) notes that the Jews interpret this passage as referring to Cyrus, but he opts for interpreting it as Christ, as does Eusebius (2013: 234). Calvin (2010: 3/442) interprets this passage as referring to Cyrus.

Go out from Babylon, flee from Chaldea,
   declare this with a shout of joy, proclaim it,
send it forth to the end of the earth;
     say, 'The LORD has redeemed his servant Jacob!'
(48.20)

Thus, Phase 2 focuses on God recovering the glory of his name and displaying his supremacy over all gods by foretelling that he would use Cyrus to redeem his people from Babylon and mobilize them to return to Jerusalem and rebuild.

The significance of Phase 2 in the history Isaiah tells finds resonance elsewhere in the Old Testament. Ezra opens with language similar to that of Isaiah by stating that 'the LORD stirred up the spirit of King Cyrus' (1.1; cf. Isa. 41.2, 25) to claim that God has given him the task of rebuilding God's house in Jerusalem (Ezra 1.2–3; cf. Isa. 44.28—45.6). Second Chronicles concludes its retelling of Israel's history with the same decree by Cyrus to rebuild the temple (2 Chron. 36.22–23). These accounts in Ezra and Chronicles appeal to a prophetic view of history where God is recognized as the one responsible for Cyrus's decree. Remarkably, archaeologists discovered 'the Cyrus Cylinder', which chronicles how Cyrus viewed himself as an agent of deity to re-establish ruined sanctuaries in Mesopotamia and beyond (Cogan 2003a).[9]

Lest one be mistaken, God's act to restore Zion through Cyrus is not due to any merit on the part of Israel. Just as Sennacherib's campaign did not result in Judah returning to God (Isa. 1.5), so exile to Babylon was not necessarily a 'come to Jesus' moment. Israel remains 'deaf' and 'blind' (42.18–19). Its people do not grasp that God himself was the one behind their desolation; he was punishing them for their sin (42.20–25). They are not calling on God (43.22), and they continue to burden him with their sin (43.24). What, then, motivates God to redeem exiled, perpetually sinful Israel by the work of Cyrus? God's inextinguishable love for Israel, whom he had chosen and redeemed, intertwines with his quest to display his incomparability to Israel and the nations:

For the sake of my servant Jacob,
   and Israel my chosen,
I call you [Cyrus] by your name . . .

---

9   The Cyrus Cylinder, now housed in the British Museum, London, is a baked-clay cylinder with an account of Cyrus of Persia's military victories and policies pertaining to Babylonia impressed into it.

I am the LORD, and there is no other;
>   besides me there is no god.
>   I arm you [Cyrus] . . .
so that they may know, from the rising of the sun
>   and from the west, that there is no one besides me;
>   I am the LORD, and there is no other.
(45.4, 5, 6)

As it pertains to Persia, there are indications from Isaiah 56—66 of Israel's existence back in Judah under Persian rule. In particular, God's reminder that efforts towards rebuilding the Temple do not compare to God's desire for a people who tremble at his word (66.1–2) could echo the historical realities hinted at in Ezra and Haggai. If so, the impact of Phase 2 in Isaiah's story extends into the final section of the book. Childs (2001: 444) seems to be correct, though, when he observes that the prophets' 'testimony to God's purpose with Israel functions in [Isaiah 56—66] apart from an individual historical identity, which is not given a specific historical context apart from its location within the narrative witness'. So, if post-exilic life after a return under Cyrus is the backdrop to how we are to read Isaiah 56—66, it must be remembered that this background is not very prominent.

Phase 3: The Servant reconstitutes God's people

The third phase in the history that Isaiah tells pertains to the Holy One's use of a Suffering Servant to spiritually restore and reconstitute God's people. Although the international character of God's people has been hinted at throughout the book (e.g. 2.2–4; 19.18–25; 25.6–8), Isaiah 49—55 speaks of a time when God will act through a Suffering Servant to create a faithful people for himself from Israel and all nations – a community of servants. As we will see, this message extends throughout 56—66.

Isaiah 49—55 alternates between passages about the Servant and Zion (Smith 2009: 54):

Servant poem 49.1–13
>   Salvation for Zion 49.14—50.3
Servant poem 50.4–11
>   Salvation for Zion 51.1—52.12
Servant poem 52.13—53.12
>   Salvation for Zion 54.1–17
Conclusion 55.1–13

This alternation provides a clue for grasping the message of 49—55. The work of God's servant will coordinate with the salvation of Zion.

Isaiah 49 opens with the Servant specifying the mission God has for him: 'to bring Jacob back to [God]' (49.5). The Servant's mission of restoring Israel to God extends to the nations, for God says: 'I will give you as a light to the nations' (49.6). The Servant's mission of reconciling Israel and the nations to God is met with great resistance. He feels as if his labour has been in vain (49.4), and God addresses him as one 'deeply despised, abhorred by the nations' (49.7). Although God assures the Servant of success, it is not clear by the end of 49.1-13 how the Servant will attain this. Already, though, it is apparent that the extent of the Servant's mission goes beyond that of Cyrus. Cyrus will help rebuild the Temple for Israel, but the Servant will spiritually reconstitute God's people to include those from the nations who will be reconciled to God.

The scene shifts in Isaiah 49.14—50.3 to Lady Zion. She feels forgotten by God (49.14) and is barren (49.21), yet God reassures her with a vision in which she will be overcome with amazement at all the children who return to her (49.21). This return is far grander than what Cyrus accomplishes, so we are left looking beyond the initial return from exile for a greater return of Zion's children.

A transition back to the Servant occurs in 50.4-11. Whereas 49.1-13 focuses particularly on the Servant's mission, it is the faithfulness of the Servant that is in view in 50.4-11. The Servant is one who is taught by God, with ears to hear and a tongue prepared to teach faithfully (50.4). He endures striking, beard-pulling, disgrace, and spitting, knowing that God will ultimately vindicate him (50.6-9). It is unclear how this faithful suffering will accomplish God's purposes, and the dots are not connected with hopes for Zion's restoration, but as we continue reading, answers begin to emerge.

Zion comes into view again in 51.1—52.12. Zion is a waste (51.3) and has drunk the wrath of God in judgement (51.17-20), but an era of salvation awaits! She will bloom like Eden (51.3), her oppressors will be done away with (51.22-23), and she will know the redemption of God (51.11; 52.9). In this depiction, Zion is both like the Servant and unlike the Servant. Like the Servant, Zion suffers at the hands of tormenters (51.23; cf. 50.6). Like the Servant, Zion awaits vindication (51.1; cf. 50.8-9). Unlike the Servant, however, Zion's suffering relates to being under God's wrath due to sin (51.17-20). Unlike the Servant, Zion takes no active role in God's saving purposes; instead, she is a recipient of God's saving intervention. Zion's redemption depends upon 'the arm of the LORD' – the very arm that led Israel out of Egypt (51.9-10). And the grand hope is that the LORD will lay bare his holy arm before all the nations as the good news comes to Zion that 'your God reigns!' (52.7-10).

Although 51.1—52.12 provides no specifics as to what the manifestation of God's arm would entail, a surprise comes as the scene shifts to the final Servant Song (52.13—53.12). It turns out that the revelation of 'the arm of the LORD' is wrapped up in God's unexpected use of a Suffering Servant:

> Who has believed what we have heard?
> And to whom has the arm of the LORD been revealed?
> (53.1)

The report of God's bearing his arm through a Suffering Servant is met with disbelief. By all external indications, this Servant has no special place in God's plans; he is disfigured (52.14), unattractive (53.2), downcast and sorrowful (53.3), despised (53.3), wounded (53.5), oppressed (53.7), and seemingly rejected by God (53.4). Shockingly, however, the Servant's mission of restoring Israel and the nations to God comes about through his suffering (49.5-7; 50.4-9). His suffering brings healing (53.5) for the lambs that had gone astray (53.6). His life becomes the means of repairing a rupture between God and humanity (53.10), and those who accept this news of the Servant's work will become the offspring of the Servant (53.10). Through the Servant's suffering, the people of God are reconstituted as the servants of God who have been put right with God through the Servant.

In chapter 54, we return to Lady Zion and her children. Lady Zion, once barren, is now rejoicing and spreading her tent across the nations to make room for her children (54.1-3). Yes, God had been angry with Zion for a moment, but now in a display of unending compassion Zion is transformed into a bejewelled city (54.4-12). So, who are Zion's children? Several clues indicate that Zion's children are none other than the offspring of the Suffering Servant. A first clue is that Zion's children are described as those 'taught by the LORD' (54.13). This corresponds closely with 50.4, where the servant says: 'The LORD God has given me a tongue of those who are taught' (my translation). Just as the servant has been taught by God, and is therefore able to teach others, so Zion's children will also be taught by God. The second, and most obvious clue, is the reference to the security of Zion as 'the heritage of the servants of the LORD' (54.17). In Isaiah 40—53, 'servant' only occurs in the singular, but after chapter 53 it only occurs in the plural (54.17; 56.6; 63.17; 65.8, 9, 13, 14, 15; 66.14).[10] Zion's children are the servants of the LORD, those from Israel and the nations who have been reconciled to God through the Suffering Servant.

---

10   See Beuken (1990) on the development of this in chapters 56—66.

The topic of reconstituting the people of God as including the nations and those who turn to God, through the work of the Servant, extends through chapters 55—66. To partake in Zion's glory through the work of the Servant, the thirsty must come to the waters and turn to God (ch. 55). Those who were previously considered outsiders, such as foreigners and eunuchs, will have a place in God's heritage as his servants if they bind themselves to God (56.1-8). Indeed, even as idolatry and injustice continue in Israel (56.9—59.15), the repentant (59.20) will indeed partake of Zion's glories with those from among the nations who worship God (66.21).

Thus, Phase 3 in Isaiah's story looks beyond Phase 2's return of exiles to rebuild the Temple under Cyrus. Phase 3 anticipates a time of greater glory for Zion when the Servant's suffering will produce a new community of servants; a people from Israel and the nations who believe this report of God baring his arm through a Suffering Servant and then turn to God in faithfulness.

Phase 4: The endgame

Phase 4 in Isaiah's story expresses the endgame, when the recurring history of divine judgement and salvation reaches its culmination. Isaiah 1—27 intermingles promises of salvation (2.2-4; 4.2-6; 9.1-7; chs 11—12; 14.1; 19.19-25) amid expectations of judgement for Israel, Judah, and the nations (1—23), yet these declarations of coming judgement and salvation peak in chapters 24—27. There God's judgement stretches across the globe and even into the heavenly host (24; 27.1), and his salvation results in all nations streaming to Zion to feast before God as King (e.g. 25.6-8). Within Isaiah 28—35, expectations of judgement and restoration for Ephraim, Jerusalem, and the nations (28—33) reach their height in the gruesome slaughter of all nations, typified by Edom, and even the withering of the host of heaven (ch. 34), and the transformation of the wilderness into a majestic landscape when God comes to liberate the captives for a return to Zion (ch. 35).

The movement towards the endgame also manifests itself across Isaiah 40—66. Yes, God would deliver those in exile through Cyrus to restore Zion (Phase 2), but a far greater renewal of Zion would unfold through the Suffering Servant (Phase 3). Vistas into Zion's glory when God returns within 40—55 (e.g. 40.1-11; 51.3, 11; 52.7-10; 54) take on a new frame of reference in view of chapters 56—66. Although the Suffering Servant created a new community which is prepared to inhabit Zion, it is apparent that the offspring of the Servant, the servants, will live during a time when religious leaders cast them off (65.5), when injustice and idolatry continue (58.1—59.15), and when Zion's greater glory awaits (chs 60—62; 65—66).

It is in chapters 56—66 where the servants of the Lord – those from Israel and the nations who are reconciled to God through the Servant – are admonished to remain faithful as they await the endgame. The faithless are warned that the Lord will come as a warrior to judge (59.15b–20; 63.1–6; 66.6, 15–16, 24), but the servants – the repentant (59.20) – are to hold on to the hope that Zion will be glorious once again (60—62; 66.18–21), that God is creating a new heaven and a new earth for his servants (65.17–25).

Thus, at an unspecified time after God's astonishing work through the servant, there will be a judgement of the wicked on a scale far grander than what Judah and the nations experienced through Assyria and then Babylon. There will also be a salvific transformation more far-reaching and more enduring than Zion's deliverance during the time of Sennacherib (36—37) and Cyrus's decree for exiles to return to rebuild Zion (44—45). Isaiah's vision of history understands these earlier moments of judgement and salvation as evidence of a God who can be expected to continue such judgements and salvations until everything is made new.

The structure of Isaiah

As noted above, the four phases of the (hi)story Isaiah tells correspond generally to but are not an exact match with the structure of the book. Here is a general outline:

1 The Holy One judges Zion and the nations through Assyria and then Babylon (Isa. 1—39)
    (a) Isaiah 1—27
        (i) Judgement and hope for Zion and David (chs 1—12)
        (ii) Judgement and hope for surrounding nations (chs 13—23)
        (iii) Eschatological judgement and hope (chs 24—27)
    (b) Isaiah 28—35
        (i) Woes against Israel and Judah and hope for a new day (chs 28—33)
        (ii) Eschatological judgement and hope (chs 34—35)
    (c) Isaiah 36—39 Bridge: historical salvation and judgement for Zion and David

2 Salvation for exiled Zion and its inhabitants (Isa. 40—55)
    (a) God's sovereign use of Cyrus to rebuild Zion (chs 40—48)

(b) A greater reconstitution of Zion's inhabitants through the Servant (chs 49—55)

3 Awaiting eschatological judgement and salvation in Zion (Isa. 56—66)
    A. Faithful outsiders to be in God's service upon salvation (56.1-8)
        B. Faithless insiders to be judged and the faithful will be saved (56.9—59.8)
            C. Prayer for forgiveness and restoration (59.9-15a)
                D. The Warrior King judges the wicked and redeems the repentant (59.15b-21)
                    E. Zion's international renown amid King YHWH's glory and that of his Messenger (60—62)
                D^1. The Warrior King judges and saves the nations (63.1-6)
              C^1. Prayer for forgiveness and restoration (63.7—64.12(11))
            B^2. Faithless insiders to be judged and the faithful will be saved (65.1—66.17)
    A^1. Faithful outsiders to be in God's service upon salvation and judgement in Zion (66.18-24)[11]

Let me clarify how the book of Isaiah's structure corresponds with the four phases of Isaiah's historical narrative. To begin, although the prominent tenor of Isaiah 1—39 is that of judgement during the Assyrian and Babylonian contexts, its two major subsections offer an eschatological movement. By placing chapters 24—27 after the declarations of judgement against Israel and the nations by Assyria and Babylon in 1—23, and chapters 34—35 after the woes of judgement against Israel, a reader has the end point of the book in view throughout: worship at Zion in the wake of eschatological judgement and salvation. The same can be said for the vistas of hope interspersed throughout Isaiah 1—39. So, Phase 1 and Phase 4 in Isaiah's story correlate both throughout the book and in view of the general movement from the beginning to the end of the book of Isaiah. Additionally, Isaiah 40—55 almost exclusively presents Phases 2 and 3 of the story, with a focus on a two-phase restoration of Zion, through Cyrus and then through the Suffering Servant. Finally, it should be apparent how the impulse of judgement and salvation undergirds much of the book. As we work our way through key themes in Isaiah in the rest of this

---

11   This is an adaptation of Goldingay's outline of Isaiah 56—66 (2014: 2).

volume (holiness; Zion; Davidic kingship; the Servant; justice; worship), a greater grasp of the book's story and structure will emerge.

Your place in Isaiah's story

As we saw in Chapter 2, from the time of Qumran to the New Testament and throughout the history of the Church, readers have drawn upon Isaiah as a frame of reference that casts light on where they fit within God's purposes in the world. Here are a few words of guidance as you consider your place in the story.

If you profess that Jesus is the Suffering Servant and that he is the surprising means by which you have been united to God, then you can see yourself in the light of Phase 3 in Isaiah's story. You are among the servants of the LORD who are exhorted to live faithfully as you await final judgement and salvation.

If you are not of Jewish descent, the story of Isaiah invites you to discern how you have been incorporated into an expanded (inclusive of nations) yet narrowed (the faithful remnant) people of God who are anchored directly within God's plans for Israel.

If the points above are true of you, it might be tempting to conclude that Phase 1 has nothing to do with you, assuming that as a servant of the LORD the stinging indictments and warnings of judgement are inapplicable. It is vital to acknowledge the typological nature of Isaiah's history. Up until the new heavens and the new earth, one can expect that God will continue to act in judgement and salvation, holding all to account. We can observe how God has consistently brought down proud nations, whether Israel, Judah, Assyria, Babylon, Persia, Greece, Rome, or beyond. If God was willing to hold his 'insider' nation, Judah-Israel, accountable, then the Church of God should heed God's words of indictment against Israel and take warning from Israel's experiences of judgement. The consistency of God's work across time does not leave the Church exempt from his indictments and judgement; instead, the God who confronts and judges his people throughout time continues to do the same with the Church today. The Church itself should wrestle with the question of whether it, like Israel, will only survive as a faithful remnant in the end. After all, didn't Jesus warn that the kingdom of God is like a field with wheat and weeds intermingled (Matt. 13.24–30)? Don't the letters to the churches in Revelation 2—3 warn of the judgements of God and promise deliverance for those who endure?

A final word of advice is in order. It may also be tempting to simply glean from Isaiah an ahistorical template of sin, judgement, and salvation, as is common in Christian articulations of the story of God reconciling sinful humanity to himself through Christ. The story Isaiah tells, however, invites us to marvel at God's acts throughout history – his acts in actually using nations to judge his people; his acts of speaking to his people through the prophets during eras of hardening and despair; his acts of raising up a pagan king to send his people back to the land; and more. By anchoring the story Isaiah provides us in the history it tells, the people of God are prepared to detect this same God of judgement and salvation at work during the time of Rome when the Son was nailed to a cross and the stone rolled away. We are prepared to expect this same God to continue his works of salvation and judgement in our world today, in our nations today, and in our churches today until the consummation of all things in the new heaven and new earth.

In the light of this advice, as you read Isaiah, may God help you, indeed help us, find our place in his story, the (hi)story Isaiah tells.

Conclusion

The aim of this chapter was to offer a sketch of the history Isaiah tells. We began by establishing that Isaiah tells a metahistory of divine judgement and salvation. Next, we identified four phases in Isaiah's story: (1) judgement through Assyria and Babylon; (2) restoration of Jerusalem through Cyrus; (3) reconstitution of God's people through the Servant; (4) ultimate judgement and salvation. Finally, we reflected on how to find our place in Isaiah. In the remaining chapters, important themes in Isaiah's story that are only mentioned briefly above will receive extended attention.

5
Holy, holy, holy

On 1 January 1808, the United States Congress issued a decree to abolish the African Slave Trade. On this date, in Philadelphia, a black minister, Revd Absalom Jones, took to the pulpit in the African Episcopal Church. His text was Exodus 3.7–8. His message was that the same God who saw the afflictions of the Israelites in Egypt and delivered them had done so once again for the African people. After a series of exhortations, Revd Jones closed his sermon with a moving prayer. His final words were (2010: 75): 'And now, O Lord, we desire, with angels and arch-angels, and all the company of heaven, evermore to praise thee, saying, Holy, holy, holy, Lord God Almighty: the whole earth is full of thy glory. Amen.'

There is a gap of 2,500 years between Isaiah 6 and AD 1808, so how have the declarations of the seraphim in Isaiah 6.3 become the go-to words for Revd Jones in prayer? This chapter offers a sketch of the importance of holiness in Isaiah and explores its influence upon countless generations. As we will see, God's all-encompassing holiness in Isaiah invites future generations to live before a God who is always worthy to be praised with the words 'Holy, holy, holy; the whole earth is full of your glory' (see 6.3).

The holy in Isaiah

Holiness is a central attribute of God in Isaiah. Isaiah 6 offers an invaluable vantage point on how we are to understand 'holiness' in the book. A close reading of the declaration 'Holy, holy, holy' within Isaiah 6 will set the stage for reflections on holiness across the book.

Isaiah 6

It is 740 BC, a long-tenured king of Judah named Uzziah has died, and Isaiah reports: 'I saw the Lord sitting on a throne, high and lofty' (6.1). He does not use the Tetragrammaton (YHWH) to identify the one on the throne, but instead uses 'Lord' (*'ădōnāy*) to emphasize the royalty of God in this vision. Since 'sitting on a throne' signifies official business in Ancient Israel (e.g. 1 Kings

2.19; 22.10), Isaiah recognizes that God's rule has not been interrupted by Uzziah's death. The unending Ruler continues to exercise his power. Further descriptions of the Lord highlight his vastness; the throne is 'high and lofty' and 'the hem of his robe filled the temple'. Height indicates prestige and stature (cf. Isa. 2.12–17). 'Fullness', when describing God, can refer to God's being present (cf. Exod. 40.34–35; 1 Kings 8.10), but in Isaiah 6.1 it most likely emphasizes God's vastness (cf. 11.9). The hem of his robe on its own fills the Temple, so his vastness pushes beyond the limits of the known world. What is this exalted Lord about to do?

Before articulating the plans of the King (6.8–13), verses 2–7 depict what is transpiring around his throne. Elsewhere in Scripture, 'cherubim' (Exod. 25.18–20) are the angelic beings that flank God's throne, but Isaiah describes them as 'seraphim' – a term that derives from a root meaning 'burning'. Throughout the Old Testament, seraphim are always agents of divine judgement (Num. 21.6, 8; Isa. 14.29; 30.6), so terror certainly infuses Isaiah's experience as he sees these burning angelic beings. These seraphim have six wings, and what they are doing with their wings is significant, yet ambiguous. The ambiguity stems from the Hebrew, which we might translate woodenly as: 'with two each one was covering *his face*, with two each one was covering *his feet*, and with two each one was flying' (6.2, my translation). The crux is in identifying *his* – does 'his' refer to each seraph or to God? Are the seraphim covering their own faces and feet or God's face and feet? The Old Greek interprets this as pertaining to each seraph, as do most modern interpreters – the seraphim cover their own faces and feet while flying. Jerome (2015: 152) believed the Hebrew indicates that the seraphim were covering the face and feet of God, to shield God from sight. In either case, the emphasis is on God's otherness, his inapproachability, whether the seraphim shield themselves or others from gazing on God.

The first spoken words in this chapter are not God's or Isaiah's but rather the seraphim's. Their words give us an inside look at their response to such a God. The seraphim were calling to one another, over and over again:

Holy, holy, holy is the LORD of hosts;
the whole earth is full of his glory.
(6.3)

What does 'holy' (*qādôš*) mean? Why is it listed three times? In my experience with churchgoers, a popular definition of 'holy' is 'to be set apart'. The problem with this definition is that it can leave God out of the equation.

I can set a basketball apart from other basketballs, but this does not make it holy. You can isolate yourself from the entire world, but this does not make you or anyone else holy. I could describe a student as set apart, but this does not mean I think he or she is holy. Holiness belongs exclusively to God, as it expresses God's distinctness from all that is not God. Anything other than God that is said to be holy is so because its holiness stems from being associated with God.

The threefold use of 'holy' is significant. Often scholars (Motyer 1993: 76; Oswalt 1986: 181) are content to label such repetition as a 'superlative', conveying God's incomparable holiness. Yet, we need to ask how triplets operate within the Hebrew Bible – do they always convey something as superlative? David Reimer (2012) analyses all four occasions where there are triplets (6.3; Jer. 7.4; 22.9; Ezek. 21.27(23 MT)). He reaches the reasonable conclusion that the triplet brings emphasis, and what that emphasis entails must be determined in its particular literary context.

There are several shades of colour to holiness in Isaiah 6. First, God's holiness is apparent in God's *unbounded royal glory*. We saw this when Isaiah tells us that merely the hem of his robe 'filled' the Temple (6.1) – how vast must the Lord on the throne be if just his hem fills the Temple! Of utmost significance, however, is the second line in 6.3 which fleshes out the declaration that God is 'holy, holy, holy': 'the whole earth is full of his glory'. Throughout Isaiah (e.g. 8.7), and across the Old Testament (Ps. 24), glory is often affiliated with kingship (Williamson 2018: 59–60). The seraphim, from their heavenly vantage point, recognize that God's royal reach extends across every square inch of the known world. His glory is not limited to the Temple or to Israel, but fills the whole earth! This uncontainable, never-lacking glory of God is part of what makes him holy, holy, holy.

Second, God's holiness creates *danger for those misaligned with God*. Isaiah's response to the vision captures this: 'Woe is me! I am lost, for I am a man of unclean lips, and I live among a people of unclean lips; yet my eyes have seen the King, the LORD of hosts!' (6.5). The result of seeing the King who was sitting on the throne (6.1) is an unshakable awareness by Isaiah of his unclean lips and his people's unclean lips. Why this focus on lips? On the one hand, unclean lips probably calls to mind speech about God that does not align with a heart and life of the kind that God seeks. Later in the book, Isaiah confronts the people who 'draw near with their mouths and honour [God] with their lips' even though their hearts are far from him (29.13; cf. 5.19; 30.11; Williamson 2018: 65). On the other hand, 'unclean lips' represent sin in general, for verse 7 speaks of Isaiah's 'sin' and 'guilt' being dealt with; surely, the sins removed from him include, yet go beyond, the sins of speech. In view of the cache of sins confronted in chapters 1—5, pride, idolatry, and injustice would come to mind. Oswalt is most likely right that in the backdrop of Isaiah's response is a recognition that 'the primary mark of God's holiness is his moral and ethical purity' (1986: 33). Thus, there is a disconnect between what the people profess about God and how they are living; their lives and hearts misalign with what is befitting of a people whose God is holy, holy, holy. This creates danger for Isaiah and God's people, and, as one sees in 6.8–13, this will result in the laying waste of Israel and Judah until a holy seed emerges.

Third, God's holiness is manifest in his *forgiveness and transformation*. The God who is 'holy, holy, holy' does not reveal himself to Isaiah simply to make him grovel in the dust. One arm of God's holiness exposes danger and the other arm offers a remedy. A seraph touches Isaiah's mouth and states: 'See, this has touched your lips, your guilt is taken away and your sin atoned for' (6.7 NIV). This symbolic act signifies a new status for Isaiah before God, that of being forgiven and exempt from the danger of judgement. By touching Isaiah's lips – the lips Isaiah confessed as being unclean in verse 5 – God prepares Isaiah for the role of serving as God's mouthpiece to the people. This experience of forgiveness coordinates with the hope at the end of the chapter that the purging fire of the Holy One will result in a transformed remnant, a holy seed. The remnant will be far different from the people of Isaiah's time: they will be holy; they will live in a way that aligns with who God is and what he deserves.

Thus, the threefold repetition of 'holy' in 6.3 is a clue to the reader about what the chapter seeks to emphasize. This account is a vista into a transcendent realm, a realm where the Divine King reigns and where seraphim declare his glory. The scene around 6.3 fills in the picture of what God's holiness entails – unbounded royal glory, danger for the sinner, and forgiveness and transformation. As the seraphim declare that God is 'holy, holy, holy', it might be tempting for us to assume that our immediate task is to join the seraphim in their declarations. Isaiah, however, does not. Although he certainly agrees with the chorus of the seraphim, this vision and their declaration lead Isaiah to tremble and confess. What we have, then, may be two responses to the holy Lord; the seraphim shield themselves and shout forth, and Isaiah confesses his sin. Perhaps Isaiah 6 offers two sanctioned responses, with readers invited to learn from both. This is a holy God whose glory is manifest across the globe; a holy God whose utter distinctness presents danger; a holy God who extends grace to restore his people. Declaring his holy glory and confessing sin can both be fitting responses depending on the person and circumstances. Since this vision is in time ('the year King Uzziah died'), yet transcends time and space as it is set in the heavenly realms, readers inside and outside Israel and throughout time can detect in this vision an enduring reality that continually summons a response to the holy, holy, holy Lord.

The Holy One of Israel: transcendence and immanence

The title 'the Holy One of Israel' occurs 25 times across Isaiah – that is nearly 80 per cent of all occurrences in the Old Testament.[1] When the title 'the Holy One of Israel' occurs in Isaiah, it serves as an occasion to bring the transcendence of God (God's 'beyondness') together with his immanence, his nearness.

For one, the combination of 'the Holy One' with 'Israel' evokes a recognition that the transcendent one is uniquely bound to Israel. As Walter Brueggemann (1998: 7) states, '[The title "Holy One of Israel"] acknowledges at the same time that (a) Yahweh is indeed linked intimately to Israel, but (b) Yahweh is holy, that is, awesome, unapproachable, and not to be presumed upon.' Or as Alec Motyer (1993: 44) puts it, God has 'drawn near to and in a real sense become the possession of Israel, he is "Israel's Holy One"'. Amid all that is going awry in Israel, the title is a constant reminder that the Holy One has been and remains the God who stands in close relationship to Israel.

Additionally, the title 'Holy One of Israel', with its ability to capture the intersection between the Holy God and his people, provides a potent backdrop for exposing Israel's sin. Israel has 'despised' the Holy One of Israel and his word (1.4; 5.24; 30.12). The people mock claims that the Holy One of Israel is offering counsel (5.19). They are unwilling to look to the Holy One in trust for their salvation (30.15). Instead of looking to the counsel of the Holy One of Israel (31.1), they are turning to foreign alliances for military support. The Holy One of Israel is truly that – the incomparable, unmatchable God who is committed to and available to Israel – yet Israel turns away from this God who has drawn near. This title for God makes Israel's sin all the more gut-wrenching when it is used amid indictments.

---

1   Isa. 1.4; 5.19, 24; 10.20; 12.6; 17.7; 29.19; 30.11, 12, 15; 31.1; 37.23; 41.14, 16, 20; 43.3, 14; 45.11; 47.4; 48.17; 49.7; 54.5; 55.5; 60.9, 14. The title 'Holy One' (without 'of Israel') occurs several times: 10.17, 23; 40.25; 49.7. Outside Isaiah, 'the Holy One of Israel' occurs in 2 Kings 19.22 (same as Isa. 37.23); Jer. 50.29; 51.5; Pss. 71.22; 78.41; 89.19. The title 'Holy One' appears in Job 6.10; Prov. 9.10?; 30.3; Ezek. 39.7; Hos. 11.9; 12.1?; Hab. 1.12; 3.3.

Furthermore, the title 'Holy One of Israel' regularly parallels some of the most powerful designations of God as saviour.[2] In six verses, all in Isaiah 40—55, 'redeemer' parallels 'the Holy One of Israel' (41.14; 43.14; 47.4; 48.17; 49.7; 54.5). For instance, in 43.14–15, we read:

Thus says the LORD,
    your Redeemer, the Holy One of Israel:
For your sake I will send to Babylon
    and break down all the bars,
    and the shouting of the Chaldeans will be turned to
        lamentation.
I am the LORD, your Holy One,
    the Creator of Israel, your King.
    (43.14–15)

By combining 'Redeemer', a term that calls to mind the role of a relative who can acquire what a family might otherwise lose (e.g. land) due to poverty (cf. Ruth), and 'the Holy One of Israel', the personal and the transcendent intersect to assure those in exile that God cares for them and is powerful enough to deliver. Along with 'redeemer', 'the Holy One of Israel' parallels references to him as saviour (43.3) and maker (17.7; 41.20; 54.5). In fact, it is the Holy One of Israel who beautifies Zion (55.5; 60.9).

Thus, referring to God as 'the Holy One of Israel' is not meant to conjure up an image of an austere, unapproachable God (like the Wizard of Oz). Instead, the appellation 'the Holy One of Israel' reminds all who hear that the wholly Other is the One who has chosen to come near to his people. This accentuates the travesty of Israel's rebellion against God – the Holy One of Israel is their covenant God, yet they despise him and do not turn to him. This also illuminates the wonder that the one who made the people of Israel and will redeem them is the Holy One of Israel.

Given the prominence of 'the Holy One of Israel' in Isaiah (x25) in comparison to the rest of the Old Testament (x6), we may probe why this is the case. Many point to Isaiah's encounter with the holy, holy, holy Lord in Isaiah 6 as the reason. Otto, in his classic work, *The Idea of the Holy* (1958: 75–6), states:

---

2   See also Williamson 2001.

The note struck in the vision of his call is the keynote of his entire prophecy. And nothing is in this regard more significant than the fact that it is in Isaiah that the expression 'the Holy One of Israel' first becomes established as the expression, *par excellence*, for the deity over all others by its mysterious potency.

Along similar lines is the following comment by John Oswalt (1986: 33):

It cannot be an accident that Isaiah's favorite appellation for God is 'the Holy One of Israel'. Above everything else the realization which struck the prophet in his call experience (ch. 6) was the realization of the terrifying 'otherness' of God.

Motyer (1993: 44, italics original) also points to Isaiah's vision as the reason for this appellation in Isaiah: '*The Holy One of Israel* may well have been coined by Isaiah as a title for the Lord to express the revelation granted to him in his inaugural vision.'

Although it is possible that the call experience is the reason why holiness is so integral to the book, Hugh Williamson (2001, 2008) raises several historical observations that complicate the picture. If the book of Isaiah is a composite of many sources from Isaiah of Jerusalem (eighth century BC) through to the post-exilic Persian period, Williamson argues that only four out of the 26 uses of 'the Holy One of Israel' derive from the prophet Isaiah himself (30.11, 12, 15; 31.1). Four other occurrences (1.4; 5.24; 10.17; 37.23) are added in the later pre-exilic times, but the bulk of the book's uses of 'the Holy One of Israel' derive from so-called Second Isaiah during the time of exile (12.6; 17.7; 29.19, 23; 41.14, 16, 20; 43.3, 14; 45.11; 47.4; 48.17; 49.7; 54.5; 55.5). Although there are two occurrences in Third Isaiah (60.9, 14), these are in texts most closely connected to Second Isaiah, and no other occurrences appear in chapters 56—66 or even 24—27 and 34—35, texts often attributed to Third Isaiah. He argues, then, that Second Isaiah was influenced by the account of Isaiah 6 and the eighth-century Isaiah's sparing uses of the title so that Second Isaiah is responsible for imprinting 'the Holy One of Israel' across the book. Whether or not one agrees with Williamson, the encounter between the holy, holy, holy Lord and Isaiah – through the experience of the prophet himself and/or a response of later writers to the recounting of this event in Isaiah 6 – shapes the theological outlook of the entire book.

Holiness in the story of Isaiah

We can now ask: where does 'holiness' fit into the (hi)story Isaiah tells, as recounted in Chapter 4?

In Phase 1 of Isaiah's story, Israel's rejection of the Holy One of Israel is the basis for the holy, holy, holy Lord bringing judgement against the nation through Assyria and then Babylon. The opening five chapters of Isaiah, consisting largely of indictments against Israel and Judah, are framed by nearly identical statements (Liebreich 1954). The people of Israel have 'despised the Holy One of Israel' (1.4); they 'have despised the word of the Holy One of Israel' (5.24). All of Israel's sins between this frame – injustice, pride, idolatry, and more – are perceived as a despising of the Holy One of Israel. As a result, chapters 1—5 prepare readers for the vision of the holy, holy, holy Lord and the revelation of his plan to bring desolation across the land, as predicted in chapter 6.[3] Chapters 28—33 also express Israel's sin with an eye towards how the people refuse the word of the Holy One (30.12) and do not depend on the Lord (30.15; 31.1). Not only are Israel and Judah affronting the Holy One of Israel, but so is Assyria! Sennacherib's mob, as they mock Hezekiah's trust in the Lord, are in fact mocking, reviling, and lifting their eyes with pride 'against the Holy One of Israel' (37.23). The prophet even declares that Israel's Holy One will become a flame that burns Assyria to the ground (10.17). Thus, judgement is coming against Israel, Judah, and even Assyria under the sovereign decree of the holy, holy, holy Lord because of their rejection of the Holy One of Israel.

In Phase 2, the Holy One of Israel directs the redemption of the exiles and rebuilding of Jerusalem through his sovereign use of King Cyrus of Persia. Within Isaiah 40—48, there is a declaration (also quoted above):

Thus says the LORD,
   your Redeemer, the Holy One of Israel:
For your sake I will send to Babylon
   and break down all the bars,
   and the shouting of the Chaldeans will be turned to
      lamentation.
I am the LORD, your Holy One,
   the Creator of Israel, your King.
(43.14–15)

---

3 For more on the interplay between Isa. 6 and Isa. 1, see Beuken 2004.

The Holy One of Israel will act to redeem his people out of Babylon! Although Cyrus is not mentioned explicitly in 43.14–15, Cyrus's role in fulfilling God's plan to redeem his people from Babylonian exile is certainly in view (Blenkinsopp 2000: 227). This becomes explicit as Cyrus is mentioned by name in 44.28 and 45.1. This fall of Babylon again intersects with the Holy One in chapter 47. As Babylon is stripped of her glory (47.1–3), the prophet interjects: 'Our Redeemer – the LORD of hosts is his name – is the Holy One of Israel' (47.4). Exile is not Israel's final word. The Holy One of Israel will bring down Babylon through Cyrus and redeem his people that they might return to Jerusalem to rebuild.

In Phase 3, the Holy One of Israel chooses the Suffering Servant so that all nations might become Zion's children. In Isaiah 49.1–7, God encourages his Servant – who feels like his labour has been in vain – by showing him that his mission is to become a light of salvation to the nations (49.6). What is more, there is another word of encouragement for this Servant:

Thus says the LORD,
    the Redeemer of Israel and his Holy One,
to one deeply despised, abhorred by the nations,
    the slave of rulers,
'Kings shall see and stand up,
    princes, and they shall prostrate themselves,
because of the LORD, who is faithful,
    the Holy One of Israel, who has chosen you.'
(49.7)

The Holy One receives mention twice in this verse. The Holy One of Israel has a word for this despised, internationally abhorred servant. The Holy One of Israel has chosen the Servant, so, by implication, though he is lowly at the moment, his destiny is international renown. In Isaiah 51—53, the hope that the Lord will 'lay bare his holy arm before all nations' (see 52.10) finds expression in the unexpected revelation of God's arm in the Servant's suffering (53.1), repairing the breach between God and his servants by making the servant a reparation offering (53.10). For this reason, when barren Zion swells with a new population of children – the servants of the LORD (54.17) – she can break forth in joy because 'your husband, your maker, the Lord of Hosts is his name; your redeemer is the Holy One of Israel' (54.5, my translation).

As for Phase 4, it is admittedly difficult at times to determine whether the book's vision of the future pertains to the return from exile or to a greater, eschatological restoration. In Isaiah 1—12, judgement by the holy, holy, holy

Lord will result in the creation of a 'holy seed' (6.13). This resonates with the hope that on the day of salvation the remnant in Zion will be called 'holy' (4.3; cf. 62.12). What is more, an eschatological hymn of thanksgiving concludes chapters 1—12 with a call for daughter Zion to rejoice 'because great in your midst is the Holy One of Israel' (12.6). These opening 12 chapters look beyond judgement by the holy, holy, holy Lord to a time when a holy people will inhabit Zion with the Holy One of Israel dwelling in their midst. Elsewhere in the book, the main intersection between holiness and eschatological hope centres upon Zion, God's 'holy mountain'. On this holy mountain, there will be peace (11.9; 65.25), foreigners will be welcome (56.7), and those abroad will stream there to worship God (27.13; 66.20).

Where do we fit in this story? If we locate ourselves within the story between Phases 3 and 4, between when the Holy One of Israel revealed his holy arm through Jesus the Suffering Servant and when the Holy One of Israel will dwell on his holy mountain amid a holy remnant in the end of time, what guidance do we have for persevering in the meantime? Isaiah 57.15 offers a wonderful vantage point:

> For thus says the high and lofty one
>   who inhabits [šākan] eternity, whose name is Holy:
> I dwell [šākan] in the high and holy place,
>   and also with those who are contrite and humble in spirit,
> to revive the spirit of the humble,
>   and to revive the heart of the contrite.

In language reminiscent of the vision in Isaiah 6, God is described as 'high and lofty' (rām weniśśā') and as 'holy' in 57.15. The focus is particularly upon where he dwells, as the verb occurs twice. What the NRSV translates as 'inhabits' is the same verb (šākan) as the one translated as 'I dwell' a few words later. The one named Holy 'dwells for ever' and 'dwells in a high and holy place'. Time and place have no hold on the Holy One; his reign is unending and spans far beyond the geographical limits of any other. Yet, as we have seen throughout this chapter, God's transcendence intersects with his immanence, with God drawing near. In the second half of this verse, the one named Holy is said to take up residence with the contrite and humble in spirit to revive them. These are humble and contrite servants of the Lord, who will find the Holy One himself dwelling among them to strengthen them as they await the era of peace on God's holy mountain. We find our place in the story as those who find God dwelling among us, the humble and contrite, as we await the end of the story.

Holy, holy, holy in reception

The effects issuing forth from the message of holiness in Isaiah throughout history are profound. Our focus below is on the reception of the vision of the holy, holy, holy Lord in Isaiah 6 within Christian tradition.[4]

New Testament

Within the New Testament, the vision in Isaiah 6 figures prominently in John 12 and Revelation 4. In John 12, the apostle alludes to Isaiah's claim that he saw the Lord (Isa. 6.1) when he says: 'Isaiah said these things [quotations from Isa. 53.1 and 6.10] because he saw his [Jesus'] glory and spoke of him' (John 12.41 ESV). John is claiming that Isaiah saw Jesus on the throne in Isaiah 6.[5] In Revelation 4, John peers into a heavenly scene where the heavenly creatures from Isaiah 6 and Ezekiel 1 merge. Four living creatures, with eyes all around and with six wings, gather around one seated on the throne and say without ceasing:

> Holy, holy, holy,
> the Lord God the Almighty,
>   who was and is and is to come.
> (Rev. 4.8)

Obviously, the first half of this refrain is verbatim what the seraphim say in Isaiah 6.3. Since the angelic beings sing this 'without ceasing' and because they praise a God 'who was and is and is to come', the coordination between Revelation 4.8 and Isaiah 6.3 presents this chorus as a perpetually appropriate song of praise to the one eternally on the heavenly throne. These uses in John 12 and Revelation 4 introduce the two predominate interests of pre-modern Christian interpreters: pondering Isaiah's vision of Christ and also utilizing 'holy, holy, holy' as a sacred, liturgical script for the Church.

Christological and Trinitarian revelation

From New Testament times through to Calvin, reading Isaiah 6 regularly involved christological and Trinitarian reflection. Eusebius (c. AD 337–9) reads Isaiah 6 as a vision of the future (2013: 29–30). Since the unbegotten God cannot be seen with physical eyes, Isaiah sees a heavenly vision of the

---

4   Although the topic of hardening from Isa. 6.8–13 is also significant in Christian tradition, the focus of this chapter is on the vision of God and the declaration that he is holy, holy, holy.

5   See Brendsell 2014.

only begotten Son with spiritual eyes. The response of the seraphim, when they cry 'Holy, holy, holy is the LORD of hosts; the whole earth is full of his glory', portrays their wonder at 'the descent of the glory of the Word of God from on high . . . [for] not only was heaven *full of his glory*, but it flooded even as far as the *earth*'. These seraphim 'were expressing great admiration in foreknowledge of what was to be subsequently accomplished in prophecies after the first advent of our Savior' when Gentiles and the entire world hear of Christ's glory.

Jerome (*c.* AD 408–10) also ponders what it means when Isaiah said 'I saw the Lord' (2015: 151, 153). He notes that John (12.41) reveals that Isaiah saw the Son, but in Acts 28.25–27 Paul claims that it was the Holy Spirit who spoke to Isaiah. This does not mean, however, that the Son and Holy Spirit are 'seeable' while the Father is unable to be seen. Instead, no persons of the Godhead can be seen in their nature, so Isaiah's vision was a spiritual vision in his mind whereby God allowed himself to be seen in such a way that the Son was 'seen in the majesty of the one reigning' (the Father) and the Holy Spirit spoke from their shared substance. Additionally, the threefold use of 'holy' 'show[s] the mystery of the Trinity in one divine nature'. Furthermore, the declaration that God's glory fills the earth anticipates the incarnation of the Son to save the world.[6]

Thomas Aquinas (*c.* AD 1148) engages extensively with what it means that Isaiah saw God. Leaning upon Dionysius (a convert to Christianity mentioned in Acts 17.34 who later became bishop in Athens), Aquinas reasons that those living on earth can only see God through 'similitudes of his goodness, whether in sensible things or images' (2017: §209). If Moses could only receive God's revelation through angelic mediation, then Isaiah's vision must have been mediated by angels through figurative language, whereby something of God could be understood even if Isaiah does not see God in his essence (2017: §210). This vision of God on his throne reveals his immovability and glory. When the seraphim proclaim 'Holy, holy, holy', they praise the Trinity through the threefold repetition. Yet, since the Trinity consists of one substance though three persons, 'the Lord of hosts' signifies the unity of the Godhead (2017: §219). Although Aquinas shows interest in a Trinitarian reading like Jerome, he does not interpret the glory of God filling the entire earth as a reference to Christ's incarnation. Instead, God's glory across the globe refers to God's providential generosity to every person on earth (2017: §219).

---

6 Cyril of Alexandria (420s AD; 2008: 1/146) aligns closely with Jerome's interpretation of Isaiah 6.

John Calvin (AD 1559) continues the tradition of probing what it meant for Isaiah to see God. If God is spirit, how can a human see him? Calvin's response is worth quoting:

> But we ought to be aware that, when God exhibited himself to the view of the Fathers, he never appeared such as he actually is, but such as the capacity of men could receive. Though men may be said to creep on the ground, or at least dwell far below the heavens, there is no absurdity in supposing that God comes down to them in such a manner as to cause some kind of mirror to reflect the rays of his glory. There was, therefore, exhibited to Isaiah such a form as enabled him, according to his capacity, to perceive the inconceivable majesty of God.
> (2010: 1/200)

As he continues, he indicates that he agrees that the refrain 'Holy, holy, holy' refers to praise of the Trinity. Yet, if he were to try to prove the doctrine of the Trinity to a heretic, he would not appeal to this passage, for threefold repetition may indicate perfection (2010: 1/205).

Assessment of pre-modern interpretation

How do we 'moderns' assess the work of these pre-modern commentators? Two axioms are important here: (1) interpretations of Isaiah 6 are theologically deficient if one disregards how God intended to speak into *an original historical situation* by means of the human author; (2) interpretations of Isaiah 6 are theologically deficient if we never read it in view of the *christological and Trinitarian vantage point* available to the Church today.

For those of us training or trained in biblical studies, we are moulded to seek to grasp what the original human author meant and what the original audience understood. A theological basis for this is the conviction that God spoke in ways the people of the time would have been able to understand (Axiom 1). This would caution against a reading that supposes Isaiah and the people of the time had a developed doctrine of the Trinity. It seems unlikely that when Isaiah wrote 'Holy, holy, holy' or when his audience read these words they understood each mention of 'holy' as referring to each of the three persons of the Trinity. As Reimer (2012) argues, the triplet brings emphasis to 'holy' in this passage. This grounding in how it would have probably been understood preserves the text's aims of expressing how wholly 'other' God is; he is the sovereign King whose presence puts the sinner in danger and yet extends grace.

On the other hand, the pre-modern Christian reception of Isaiah 6.3 pushes us to move beyond the modern interest in coolly explaining the text historically, for God's very person and being should be at the centre of interpretation. In other words, interpreting Scripture is an opportunity to consider and worship the God to whom the text bears witness. Isaiah 6.3 bears witness to a God who eternally exists as one God in three persons, whether Isaiah knew it or not. On this side of Pentecost, Christians who ponder their God should do so in view of the Triune God. Even if the threefold use of 'holy' does not prove the doctrine of the Trinity, the emphasis on God's revelation as holy leads us to recognize this text's witness to the Triune God as 'holy, holy, holy'. Consider how Peter's response to the Son is similar to Isaiah's: 'he fell down at Jesus' knees, saying, "Go away from me, Lord, for I am a sinful man!"' (Luke 5.8). Jesus responds by telling him not to fear and commissions him (5.9–10), just as Isaiah receives his commission after encountering God in Isaiah 6. Or in the case of John 12.41, the apostle interprets God's revelation in Isaiah 6.1 as an instance where Isaiah saw the Son. If, as Aquinas and others argue, God is not seen in his essence in Isaiah 6 but instead is portrayed through a figurative vision so as to reveal something of the divine glory to Isaiah, one need not believe that Isaiah walked away from the vision with a clear recognition of the Trinity. Instead, Isaiah's vision of God is a genuine revelation of the grandeur and total otherness of the One whom we now profess to be the Triune God. For this reason, we can ultimately receive this as directing our gaze to the total otherness of the Trinity, even if we take a slightly different route to get there from that of the pre-moderns. Thus, our theology would be deficient if what the seraphim declare about the one on the throne cannot also be equally sung of the Three-in-One:

Holy, holy, holy! Lord God Almighty . . .
God in three persons, blessed Trinity.[7]

Liturgy of the holy

Isaiah 6 and Revelation 4 both present heavenly beings who praise the Lord by declaring 'Holy, holy, holy'. Shortly after the New Testament era, Clement of Rome (Coxe 1885) exhorts the church of Corinth saying:

Let our glorying and our confidence be in him; let us submit ourselves to his will; let us consider the whole multitude of his angels, how they

---

7 From a hymn by Reginald Heber (1783–1826).

stand by and serve his will. For the scripture saith, Ten thousand times ten thousand stood beside him, and thousands of thousands served him; and they cried, Holy, holy, holy Lord of Sabaoth! All creation is full of his glory.

(*1 Clement* 34.5–6)

The Church, then, according to Clement, should look to the language of the angels for guidance in praising God. Strikingly, although he clearly recalls Revelation 4—5 by mentioning the thousands of angels (5.11), he uses Isaiah 6.3 ('All creation is full of his glory') instead of Revelation 4.8 ('who was and is and is to come') in the second half of the refrain. This preference for looking to angels for guidance is also reflected in works attributed to Dionysius. In his *Celestial Hierarchies* 7.4 (1897) he reasons that, since only angels have unmediated access to God, we who are lower in the hierarchy are to learn from angels 'that frequent and most august hymn of God, "Holy, Holy, Holy, Lord of Sabaoth, the whole earth is full of His glory"'. Again, as with Clement, it is the language of Isaiah 6.3, not Revelation 4.8, that is presented as exemplary for the Church.

In an exhaustive study of the reception of the Sanctus in liturgical tradition,[8] Bryan Spinks (1991) traces how the refrain 'Holy, holy, holy is the Lord God Almighty; the whole earth is full of his glory' became a central fixture in the Orthodox, Roman Catholic, and Protestant liturgies for the Eucharist. Here is a sample from the Book of Common Prayer that would have been used at the time of Revd Absalom Jones at every communion service, just before the words of institution:

Priest: It is very meet, right, and our bounden duty, that we should at all times, and in all places, give thanks unto thee, O Lord, [*Holy Father,] Almighty, Everlasting God.

Priest and People: Therefore with Angels and Archangels, and with all the company of heaven we laud and magnify Thy glorious Name; evermore praising Thee and saying, Holy, Holy, Holy, Lord God of hosts, heaven and earth are full of Thy glory: Glory be to Thee, O Lord Most High. Amen.

(Communion Service, Book of Common Prayer, 1789)

---

8   The Sanctus (Latin, 'holy') refers to the refrain from Isa. 6.3 when it occurs within a liturgy.

It is striking that in all liturgical traditions the Sanctus is either said or sung by *both* priest and people. This underscores a recognition that the heavenly hymn was understood to be an opportunity for all people on earth to join in the heavenly anthem in praise to God.

Another development of the Sanctus is in the Latin hymn Te Deum, dating to the fourth century AD. It has been put to music by many Baroque and Classical composers. It opens with the following words:

> We praise Thee, O God: we acknowledge Thee to be the Lord.
> All the earth doth worship Thee, the Father everlasting.
> To Thee all Angels cry aloud: the Heavens and all the powers
>   therein.
> To Thee Cherubim and Seraphim continually do cry:
> 'Holy, Holy, Holy, Lord God of Sabaoth;
> Heaven and earth are full of the Majesty of Thy Glory.'
> (Morning Prayer, Book of Common Prayer, 1789)

This hymn has been a go-to song and prayer to nourish the saints throughout the generations of the Church. It became a regular element in the daily prayer of the faithful.

Within the Protestant hymn tradition, 'Holy, Holy, Holy, Lord God Almighty' written by Reginald Heber (1783–1826) has put the Sanctus on the lips of the Church for over 200 years. There is a clear Trinitarian direction in the praise ('God in three persons, blessed Trinity'). In fact, this hymn was written for Trinity Sunday. One cannot say whether Heber saw the threefold repetition of 'holy' as a Trinitarian statement, but this hymn certainly aligns with the trajectory of Christian interpretation that appropriates Isaiah 6.3 in view of Trinitarian ontology.

Thus, the reception of Isaiah 6 in both pre-modern Christian interpretation and worship contexts offers a useful, perhaps essential, partner for the modern interpreter. It heightens our awareness of how the heavenly nature of the vision in Isaiah 6, anchored as it is in the eighth century BC, prompts those well after that time to join in a transcendent, transhistorical reality of angelic praise of an eternally triune God who is holy, holy, holy.

Conclusion

Let's return to Revd Jones and 1808. As an Episcopal priest, there is little doubt that he was influenced by the Book of Common Prayer. For good reason the Book of Common Prayer, and then Revd Jones at the end of his prayer, drew upon Isaiah 6.3. The scene in a heavenly realm invites generation after generation to recognize that, regardless of time, place, or race, those upon the earth can join in with the company of heaven praising God who sits on the throne. The vision of God as holy, holy, holy in Isaiah 6 not only leaves an indelible imprint on the Church but also influences the book of Isaiah's depiction of God throughout as the Holy One of Israel.

6

Zion

'What is Zion?' is a question I hear every semester from students. If holiness is the most important attribute of God in the book of Isaiah, then Zion is the most important motif. By the end of this chapter, you should be able to answer the question 'What is Zion?' and be alert to how Zion fits into the story Isaiah tells; as a result, you will be positioned to read Isaiah more profitably.

What is Zion?

Answering 'What is Zion' is akin to enquiring about Buckingham Palace. You could begin with the *physical* – bring up Buckingham Palace on a digital map and then view a few images of the palace. Yet, one must move beyond the physical to its *symbolic* (ideological) nature, for the palace represents the British monarchy. So, when a headline reads 'Prince Harry Criticizes Buckingham Palace', anyone in the UK would know that Prince Harry is not upset with the location or physical structure of the palace itself; instead, he has issues with how the monarchy is conducting itself. Or, if a headline were to read 'Protests at Buckingham Palace', we would know that both the physical location and the symbolism of the monarchy are in view; the protestors chose this location because it represents the locale of the monarchy. In a similar fashion, answering 'What is Zion?' requires us to be mindful of the physical and symbolic dimensions of Zion, as one seeks to decipher its meaning in each occurrence.

Physical Zion

Within the Old Testament, the term 'Zion' occurs 154 times, yet all but six of the occurrences appear in books referred to as prophetic or poetic books in English Bible divisions.[1] The vast majority of the mentions of Zion come from Isaiah (47 times) and the Psalms (38 times). It seems, then, that the term 'Zion'

---

1   The six exceptions are 2 Sam. 5.7 // 1 Chron. 11.5; 1 Kings 8.1 // 2 Chron. 5.2; 2 Kings 19.21, 31.

is most at home in the figurative literature of the prophets and poets, yet there is a physical, material base that informs these uses.

Zion is first mentioned in 2 Samuel 5.7, referring to a walled city that David captures from the Jebusites. In the previous verse, the same city is referred to as Jerusalem (2 Sam. 5.6), so it is important to not drive a wedge between the referent of these two terms. For this reason, we will speak of Zion-Jerusalem. This city comes to be referred to as 'the city of David' (2 Sam. 5.7; 1 Kings 8.1).

Zion-Jerusalem sits nestled in the Judean hill country, approximately 15 miles west of the northern tip of the Dead Sea. It is shaped like a thumb, sloping down to the south from an elevation of 740 metres and with valleys to the east and west. The Mount of Olives stands to the east across the Kidron Valley, some 50 metres higher than Zion. In size, Zion at the time of David was only about 12 acres – approximately the size of 12 US football fields or the size of four cricket fields (pitches).[2] This puts a population of around 1,000 people living in the city at the time of David. The city was insulated from the coastal plain and Jordan Valley, providing a natural barrier from invading armies, yet the surrounding valleys enabled travel for merchants and pilgrims.

Although 'Zion' can refer to Jerusalem as a whole, there are other mounts within Jerusalem too. Of particular importance is Mount Moriah, where the Temple was built during the time of Solomon, extending David's city to the north towards a higher elevation of 770 metres and approximately 60 acres. By the time of Solomon, the city was slightly larger than St James's Park in London (57 acres) and the grounds of the White House in Washington DC (52 acres). By the time of Isaiah, Zion had expanded significantly beyond David's city to approximately 150 acres and a population of around 12,000.

In the book of Isaiah, the physical city of Zion-Jerusalem is often not far from view. The book presents itself as a vision 'concerning Judah and Jerusalem' on two occasions (1.1; 2.1). 'Jerusalem' occurs in 49 verses, 'Zion' in 47, and terms for mountain (26 times) and city (28 times) refer to Zion-Jerusalem throughout the book. The book opens with daughter Zion left like a booth in a cucumber field, depicting Zion as standing – albeit barely – as the cities around have been ravaged (1.7–8). What is more, the two major blocks of historical narrative in

---

2   There is some debate over how to calculate the population in Jerusalem. King (1992: 753) notes that though the Jebusite city was 12 acres, it was 15 acres with 2,000 inhabitants under David. Solomon expanded it to 32 acres with 4,500 to 5,000 inhabitants, and Hezekiah had a city of 125 acres with a population of 25,000. These figures are based on there being between 150 and 200 inhabitants per acre. I have drawn instead on calculations from Knight (2011: 168) as recent scholars opt for a lower population-to-acre ratio (80 people per acre).

Isaiah deal with foreign nations coming against Jerusalem (e.g. 7.1–17; chs 36—39). Although there may be times when the symbolic ideals connected to Zion render its physical reality of secondary importance, physical Zion-Jerusalem is regularly in view within the book of Isaiah.

So, Zion-Jerusalem is not a fictional city like Cair Paravel in the Chronicles of Narnia. Zion-Jerusalem is an actual city of modest size and modest elevation in the hill country of Ancient Judah. Yet, although there were many cities on small hills in Ancient Israel and cities larger in size and population and higher in elevation, the symbolic value of Zion causes this city to rise to the fore within the book of Isaiah. To this we now turn.

Symbolic Zion

While the term 'Zion' refers to a particular location, it is infused with layer on layer of symbolic meaning, just as Buckingham Palace symbolizes a great deal about the British monarchy and Commonwealth. When it comes to Zion, four areas of symbolic value are essential to keep in mind: God's presence; Davidic kingship; the inhabitants; a microcosm for Judah and the world. It is rare for all four areas of symbolism to be equally prominent in a given passage, so a reader must discern what areas are being called to mind in a particular text.

God's royal presence in Zion

Today, mountains evoke in us a sense of awe in view of their natural beauty. My wife and I once had such a great time hiking in the mountains of Colorado and enjoying their beauty that I declared: 'I want to live here!' Although the Ancient Israelites certainly enjoyed mountainous beauty, there would have been something else at the forefront of their minds when seeing a mountain. Mountains were the meeting place between heaven and earth, between God and humanity (see Clifford 1972). This is why 'high places' are mentioned throughout the Old Testament as places of idolatrous worship. God met with Moses at Mount Sinai, and after David captured Zion it came to be the dwelling place of Israel's God. David brings the ark of the covenant to Zion (2 Sam. 6), and his son, Solomon, fulfils David's desire to build God a permanent residence in Zion. After the Temple was complete, the glory cloud of God's presence filled the Temple (1 Kings 8.11). God declares: 'I have consecrated this house that you have built, by putting my name there for ever. My eyes and my heart will be there for all time' (9.3 ESV). The promise of God's presence in Zion gave way to a Zion theology (Ollenburger 1987), with psalms like Psalm 46 that delight in the city of God, for

God is in the midst of the city; it shall not be moved;
  God will help it when the morning comes.
(Ps. 46.5)

Psalm 48 celebrates:

Great is the LORD and greatly to be praised
  in the city of our God.
His holy mountain, beautiful in elevation,
  is the joy of all the earth.
Mount Zion, in the far north,
  the city of the great King.
(48.1–2)

As we noted above, an ancient reader would obviously know that Zion is just a small mount, but its elevation in the minds of those in Israel derives from the fact that the God of the entire world dwells there. So, a pre-eminent idea that Zion evokes is God's dwelling place.

Throughout Isaiah, Zion continually calls to mind God's royal presence.[3] A few examples from across the book will make this clear. As part of the book's dual introduction, Isaiah 2.2–4 envisages how Zion is God's royal residence:

In days to come
  the mountain of the LORD's house
shall be established as the highest of the mountains,
  and shall be raised above the hills;
all the nations shall stream to it.
  Many peoples shall come and say,
'Come, let us go up to the mountain of the LORD,
  to the house of the God of Jacob;
that he may teach us his ways
  and that we may walk in his paths.'
For out of Zion shall go forth instruction,
  and the word of the LORD from Jerusalem.
He shall judge between the nations,

---

3 The most overt passages that speak of God's presence in Zion-Jerusalem are Isa. 2.2–4; 4.2–6; 6.1; 8.18; 12.1–6; 18.7; 24.23; 25.6; 26.1; 27.13; 33.20; 35.3–4; 40.9–11; 44.28; 52.7–10; 56.7; 57.13; 60.14; 66.20.

and shall arbitrate for many peoples;
they shall beat their swords into ploughshares,
    and their spears into pruning-hooks;
nation shall not lift up sword against nation,
    neither shall they learn war any more.

This announcement centres on Zion being a mountain where the LORD has taken up residence – Zion is 'the mountain of the LORD's house' (2.2). Just as Psalm 48 could extol the elevation of Zion, even though it was in actuality a small mountain, so Isaiah 2.2 envisages a time when Zion will be the 'highest' of mountains. The term 'highest' might better be rendered 'at the head of' or 'pre-eminent'. Geological transformation is not in view; instead, since mountains are the dwelling place of the gods, the claim here is that Zion – as the home of God – will be chief among all mountains because it is YHWH himself who dwells here. The supremacy of God will become known across the globe and therefore Zion, as his dwelling, will be supreme. Marvin Sweeney (2014: 180) captures this quite well when he states:

> the book of Isaiah is fundamentally concerned with Zion or the city of Jerusalem, insofar as Jerusalem is the site of YHWH's holy temple, which in turn symbolizes YHWH's role as the sovereign creator of the entire universe, including Israel, Judah, and the nations at large.

Since Zion is the locale of God, the nations will stream to Zion to receive his instruction and judgements over international disputes.

A strategically crafted hymn concludes Isaiah 1—12 with a call of praise to Zion:

Sing praises to the LORD, for he has done gloriously;
    let this be known in all the earth.
Shout aloud and sing for joy, O royal Zion,
    for great in your midst is the Holy One of Israel.
(12.5–6)

The holy, holy, holy Lord of Isaiah 6.1-5 will ultimately reside in the midst of Zion, resulting in praise to God resounding across the globe from the inhabitants of Zion that the Holy One of Israel is great in their midst.

Another example of Isaiah's grand hopes of God's glorious presence in Zion is apparent in the similarities between how Isaiah 27 and 66 conclude their portions of the book. In Isaiah 24—27, God's judgement of heaven and earth stems from the fact that 'the LORD of hosts will reign on Mount Zion' (24.23). This King will hold a feast for all peoples on this very mountain (25.6–8). The section culminates with all who have been scattered returning to 'worship the LORD on the holy mountain at Jerusalem' (27.13). Similarly, Isaiah 60 prepares for Isaiah 66, as the glory of God residing in Jerusalem (60.1–3) attracts those from all nations to stream to Zion to worship the LORD whose glory is there (66.18–23).

Thus, throughout Isaiah, Zion-Jerusalem is the locale of the Divine King's presence.

Zion as the headquarters of Davidic kingship

Zion-Jerusalem also is the capital city of the Davidic king. Since David captured and established Zion, it is called 'the city of David' 40 times in the Old Testament.[4] David founded the city (2 Sam. 5) to be the religious and political capital of Judah. Although the northern kingdom ('Israel') had multiple capitals, Jerusalem is the sole capital of the Davidic kings of Judah. However, there are only a few passages in Isaiah where Davidic kingship comes into view in association with Zion-Jerusalem. The most overt promises about a future Davidic ruler in Isaiah do not mention Zion as the locus of his reign (9.1–7; 11.1–10; 16.4–5), although this is probably implied. The most overt depiction of Davidic rule in Zion comes in the historical narratives in Isaiah 7 and 36—39.

In Isaiah 7, Rezin of Aram (Syria) and Pekah of Israel (the northern kingdom) come to wage war against Jerusalem. Word reaches the 'house of David' and King Ahaz shakes in fear (7.2). Rezin and Pekah approach Jerusalem for one primary reason. This is the headquarters of Judah, so, although the vast majority of Judah's population did not reside in Jerusalem, an assault against the city would enable a transfer of power. In particular, they hope to dethrone Ahaz and 'make the son of Tabeel king in it [Jerusalem]' (7.6). There is uncertainty over the identity of this 'son of Tabeel', but more than likely he is either from Phoenicia (Williamson 2018: 128–30) or Ammon (Blenkinsopp 2000: 230). A transition in leadership from a Davidic king in Jerusalem to an ally from a neighbouring country would be advantageous to the Aram–Israel coalition as Assyria's threat was looming on the horizon. Thus, these foreign powers have Jerusalem in their sights because this is where the house of David resides.

---

4   2 Sam. 5.7, 9; 6.10, 12; 1 Kings 2.10; 3.1; 9.24; 11.27, 43; 15.8, 21; 22.50; 2 Kings 8.24; 9.28; 12.21; 14.20; 15.7, 38; 16.20; 1 Chron. 11.5, 7; 13.13; 15.1, 29; 2 Chron. 5.2; 8.11; 9.31; 12.16; 14.1; 16.14; 21.1, 20; 24.16, 25; 27.9; 32.5, 30; 33.14; Neh. 3.15; 12.37.

In Isaiah 36—37, the Assyrian king Sennacherib has ravaged towns across the Levant and now has his eye on Jerusalem. So, his messenger brings a letter to King Hezekiah in Jerusalem. The messenger never once refers to Hezekiah as king – only by his first name – yet repeatedly speaks of Sennacherib as 'the great king' (36.4, 13), 'the king' (36.14), or 'the king of Assyria' (36.8, 15, 16, 18). By not referring to Hezekiah as king, the message to Hezekiah and the people of Jerusalem is that the Davidic king is nothing in comparison to Sennacherib, the Great King. After Hezekiah does not acquiesce to Assyria's demands of surrender, Sennacherib takes a different tack in his second letter, referring to him from the start as 'king of Judah' (37.10 ESV), perhaps to ingratiate himself with Hezekiah but also to lump Hezekiah in with the other kings who crumbled before Assyria (37.13). Will Hezekiah's fate be any different from those kings? As it turns out, the crux of this episode does not revolve around the Davidic king showing greater might than Sennacherib; instead, it is the LORD who shows himself to be the God of all the kingdoms of the earth (37.16) when he defeats Assyria. Thus, Jerusalem again becomes a focal point for foreign aggressors because it is the seat of Davidic kingship (Abernethy 2014: 101–4).

Chapter 39 also coordinates David and Zion in a unique fashion. Many interpreters speak of Isaiah 39 as promising Zion's exile to Babylon, but a close reading reveals that it is the exile of David's house that is in view. The treasures in the house of David will be 'carried to Babylon' and David's descendants will become eunuchs in the palace of the king of Babylon (39.6–7). Since the house of David was a major symbolic fixture in Jerusalem, the announcement that David's house would be exiled serves as a metonymy for Zion's destiny of exile.

Thus, close affiliations between Davidic kingship and Zion-Jerusalem surface in several of the major narratives in Isaiah. I am sceptical of those who read Davidic kingship into every mention of Zion, such that every promise of a glorious future for Zion implies the restoration of Davidic kingship. A careful reading of each text should look for explicit clues that Davidic kingship is evoked when Zion is mentioned.[5]

Zion and its inhabitants

Consider the following statements: 'Chicago is crazy about the Bears' (American Football team); 'London loves football, but Cardiff loves rugby.' In these examples, the cities are all depicted in a non-literal way. Cities

---

5 For an exemplary evaluation (with a negative conclusion) as to whether Davidic kingship is in view in Isa. 28.16, see Dekker 2007.

and towns are not actually avid sports fans, nor are they capable of love; but, of course, these sentences make sense to us because we know that the people of these cities and towns are in view. Similarly, throughout Isaiah, the motif of Zion-Jerusalem can call to mind the inhabitants who live there. In particular, since Zion is the dwelling place of God, these inhabitants signify God's people.

Isaiah 1 provides a clear example of this. Isaiah 1.21 reads: 'How the faithful city has become a whore!' Literally, cities are neither faithful nor whores. It is the inhabitants of the city, especially those who have judicial power, who are in view. These inhabitants once were faithful, promoting justice and righteousness, but now they turn a blind eye towards injustice if the price is right (1.21–23). Another example comes from Isaiah 51.16. It speaks of God

> stretching out the heavens
>> and laying the foundations of the earth,
>> and saying to Zion, 'You are my people.'

Clearly, Zion signifies God's people in this verse. Examples like this abound across Isaiah. We are told that there will be a remnant in Zion (4.3; cf. 1.9). God confronts the 'daughters of Zion' (3.16; cf. 32.9–14). God is a stumbling block and snare 'to the inhabitants of Jerusalem' (8.14). God speaks to his people: 'O my people, who dwell in Zion, be not afraid of the Assyrians' (10.24). The 'inhabitant of Zion' is to sing because of the greatness of the Holy One (12.6). The afflicted of God's people take refuge in Zion (14.32). There are also a range of promises that God's people will again dwell in Zion (e.g. 30.19; 44.26; 57.13). On these and other occasions (cf. 1.8–9, 21; 3.8; 51.3; 59.20; 60.14; 62.1, 12; 65.19), Zion is the habitation of God's people.

One of the more striking developments of the city as home for God's people is the personification of Zion as mother (Fischer 2012). In Isaiah 49.14–26, Lady Zion states that she has been forsaken by the LORD. God promises that her children will return. She will say:

> Who has borne me these?
> I was bereaved and barren,
>> exiled and put away –
>> so who has reared these?
> I was left all alone –
>> where then have these come from?
> (49.21)

A similar thread develops in Isaiah 54:

> Sing, O barren one who did not bear;
>> burst into song and shout,
>> you who have not been in labour!
> For the children of the desolate woman will be more
>> than the children of her that is married, says the LORD.
> Enlarge the site of your tent,
>> and let the curtains of your habitations be stretched out;
> do not hold back; lengthen your cords
>> and strengthen your stakes.
> For you will spread out to the right and to the left,
>> and your descendants will possess the nations
>> and will settle the desolate towns.
> (54.1–3)

Also, in chapter 66, Zion is a mother giving birth to children before experiencing labour pains – birthing an entire nation in one day (66.7–14).

Thus, since Zion is God's city, an extension of this is to speak of God's people as Zion's inhabitants, even personifying Zion as a mother and the inhabitants as her children.

Zion as microcosm

The notion of Zion as a microcosm is a bit less intuitive for modern readers. The idea is that Zion, in its small scale as a city (micro), is symbolic for the world as a whole (cosmos). This is most apparent in Isaiah 65.17–18:

> [17] For I am about to create new heavens
>> and a new earth;
> the former things shall not be remembered
>> or come to mind.
> [18] But be glad and rejoice for ever
>> in what I am creating;
> for I am about to create Jerusalem as a joy,
>> and its people as a delight.

The opening of verse 17 is well known, as it is repeated and developed in Revelation 21. Yet, God's creating a new heaven and a new earth is parallel to Jerusalem in Isaiah 65.18. The same verb 'to create' (*bārā'*) occurs in participle form with the first-person pronoun ('I') as subject in verses 17 and 18, yet there is a shift from 'new heavens and a new earth' in verse 17 to 'Jerusalem' in verse 18. This focus on God's creation of Jerusalem extends to verse 25, as it depicts future life in Jerusalem, on God's holy mountain: joy, no more lamenting, no dying before old age, building houses and orchards without dispossession, a close relationship with God, and an absence of conflict. Why is it that the passage focuses exclusively on Jerusalem when it opens with God declaring his plans to create a new heaven and earth? The reason is that Jerusalem can be seen as a microcosm for God's plans across the globe.[6] Elsewhere (Abernethy 2016: 176–7), I have described it this way:

> What if God said this? 'I'm going to make a new world. In Chicago there will no longer be a children's hospital, for there will be no more sick children. Everyone will be able to find fulfilling employment and enjoy the fruits of their labours, for those on the south side will have the same opportunities as those in the western suburbs. Fourth of July gatherings at Grant Park will no longer be a time of fear, for rivalries and violence will be no more'. In this hypothetical scenario God describes new life in Chicago as a sample of what life will be like throughout the entire world. In a similar way, by describing what life will be like in God's particular realm, Zion, one can conceptualize what new creation might entail for the entire world.

The illustration above, however, has its limits. The choice of Jerusalem is strategic [in Isaiah]. Could Samaria, Jericho, Bethlehem, Cairo, Damascus or Babylon have served this purpose of envisaging the new creation? No. Ever since David chose Jerusalem to be his capital and God inhabited the temple in Zion, Yahweh's presence as king has been inextricably tied to Zion. Yes, Zion is a symbol, even of the entire cosmos, but Zion is also an actual place in the 'theo-topological' outlook of Israel. It is a geographical reference point that is to orient the entire world around God's kingship. Or, as Levenson (1985: 116) puts it in his discussion of Zion, 'geography is simply a visible form of theology'. In Isaiah the realm of God's kingdom is universal, but the universal, cosmic scope of God's kingdom has a centre point in Zion. Zion, then, is not just an illustration

---

6 Levenson 1984; Berges 2002: 14–15. The claim that Jerusalem is a microcosm often stems from symbols of creation in the Temple (1 Kings 7.23–26) and parallels between creation and temple construction (Levenson 1985: 142–5). For Levenson (1985: 138), the tension between God's omnipresence and particular presence in the Temple leads him to state: 'the Temple is the epitome of the world, a concentrated form of its essence, a miniature of the cosmos.'

of God's plans for the rest of the world, but it is also a hub around which the rest of God's kingdom finds its orbit.

Isaiah 65.17–18 is a clear example of this notion of microcosm, and readers should pause to ask when they encounter a passage about Zion: in what way is the vision in Zion reflective of God's plans beyond Zion, for the entire world?

In summary, Zion-Jerusalem can signify a range of ideas: God's dwelling place; God's Davidic King; its inhabitants as God's people; the cosmos. By being alert to these categories, you are in a better position to answer the question 'What is Zion?' In any given text, some of these ideas are present while others are absent, some receive more priority, and others are secondary. As you develop discernment in how best to read individual texts pertaining to Zion, your reading of Isaiah as a whole will become more profitable. Yet, as we will see in the next section, a recognition of how Zion figures into the message and shape of the entire book – not just individual passages – is important as well.

Zion in the story of Isaiah

When scholars speak of the most prominent motif across the structure of Isaiah, Zion quickly rises to the fore, and for good reason. As many note, the superscription opening the book identifies its message as pertaining to 'Judah and Jerusalem' (1.2; 2.1). The dual introduction of the book (ch. 1; 2.1–5) presents Zion under divine judgement with the hope of its restoration (1.21–26, 27–28) and offers a vision of Zion becoming the international capital of the world (2.1–5). Each major section in Isaiah 1—39 culminates with rejoicing in Zion (12.1–6; 27.13; 35.9–11). Isaiah 36—39 serves as a hinge between the two halves of the book, as it depicts Zion's deliverance from Assyria (36—37) and the expectation of Zion's exile to Babylon (38—39). The second half of the book opens with comfort for Jerusalem (40.1–2) and the expectation that God would return to Zion (40.3–5, 9–11). The book concludes by depicting Zion's eschatological destiny in the new heaven and new earth (65.17–25), with Zion's judgement preparing the way for the international worship of God at Zion (66.15–24). So, at the most important points of the book, Zion is central.

William Dumbrell was one of the first to argue along these lines. He states (1985: 112): 'If the book is read as a unit there is an overmastering theme which may be said effectively to unite the whole. This is the theme of Yahweh's interest in and devotion to the city of Jerusalem.' Five years later Barry Webb (1990: 67) made a case for something similar: 'the transformation of Zion is the key to both the formal and thematic structure of the book as a whole.' He goes beyond Dumbrell, however, by tracing how the 'remnant' motif figures into Zion's transformation. Christopher Seitz (1991) develops more extensively and more historically how chapters 36—39 came to relate to Isaiah 1—35 and 40—55 and establish Zion's destiny as the heartbeat of the book. Antti Laato (1998: 124) focuses on how Jerusalem's deliverance from Assyria (chs 36—37) serves as a paradigm 'to convince the potential readers [in the Persian period] that the marvelous fate of Zion is more than merely utopian visions of the future'. Isaiah 40—55 applies this to the Babylonian era, and then Isaiah 56—66 extends the vision of Zion's deliverance to 'a future time when the people has become loyal to Yhwh' (Laato 1998: 169). Below, we will attempt to situate Zion within the four phases of the story Isaiah tells, as set forth in Chapter 4.

Phase 1: Zion under judgement by Assyria and Babylon

Isaiah 1.1 is a good indication of what is to come in the book: 'The vision of Isaiah son of Amoz, which he saw concerning Judah and Jerusalem . . .' In the book's opening chapter, the judgement of Zion is front and centre. Isaiah confronts an audience that has recently made it through a devastating campaign by Assyria:

> [7] Your country lies desolate,
>   your cities are burned with fire;
> in your very presence
>   aliens devour your land;
>   it is desolate, as overthrown by foreigners.
> [8] And daughter Zion is left
>   like a booth in a vineyard,
> like a shelter in a cucumber field,
>   like a besieged city.
> [9] If the LORD of hosts
>   had not left us a few survivors,
> we would have been like Sodom,
>   and become like Gomorrah.
> (1.7–9)

Across Judah, cities have been scorched and harvests have been confiscated (1.7), and only 'daughter Zion' is left (1.8). Her survival is purely due to God's grace in leaving a few survivors (1.9). The historical situation here aligns with the story of Sennacherib's campaign in 701 BC quite well, as one reads about in Isaiah 36—37 and the Sennacherib Prism. Many cities had been devastated by Sennacherib, yet God miraculously delivers Zion. Although one might have expected Zion to turn to God amid such devastation, it is apparent from the start of the book that she does not. God asks: 'Why do you seek further beatings? Why do you continue to rebel?' (1.5). She is in great danger if she continues to rebel against God.

Isaiah 1.21–26, a passage noted above, also presents Zion under judgement at the start of the book. Zion, who was once a faithful city, is now a whore and God will turn against her to purify her in judgement. The motif of Zion brings the chapter to a close in 1.27–28, which announces that Zion will be redeemed in righteousness, and her repentant people in justice. A different fate awaits the wicked.

From the start of the book, then, Zion is under the historical purview of God's judgement. Two related observations are essential for grasping the role of Zion in this part of Isaiah's story.

First, *God* is responsible for judging Zion *due to sin*, even if he uses a foreign nation to do so. In 1.21–26, the faithful city is now called a whore due to her injustices, so God says: 'Ah, I will pour out my wrath on my enemies, and avenge myself on my foes!' (1.24). The next line makes it clear that God's enemies are in fact his very people in Zion ('I will turn my hand against you', 1.25). The reason for Zion's judgement obviously is sin. In Isaiah 5.1–7, God announces that he will allow his vineyard to be trampled due to her injustice. God will humble Jerusalem due to her idols (10.11). He confronts the rulers of Jerusalem (28.14) who have made a covenant with death. God himself will camp against his city, Ariel, as a siege against his people (29.1–4). Thus, Zion is the object of *God's* judgement. What is implied in many places becomes explicit in 10.5–6, where God speaks of Assyria as 'the rod of my anger' and as the one sent by God himself to plunder his people. In 7.17, King Ahaz, in Jerusalem, is told: 'The LORD will bring on you and on your people and on your ancestral house such days as have not come since the day that Ephraim departed from Judah – the king of Assyria.' In fact, God will bring Assyria like flooding waters to reach up to the neck (i.e. Jerusalem) of Judah (8.7–8). Yet, although God's judgement of Jerusalem due to sin is to result in a pure Zion, it is apparent from the start of the book that even after devastation via Assyria Zion remains unrepentant and under divine judgement.

Second, there are *multiple phases* of God's judgement against Zion, first through Assyria and then through Babylon. God asks in 1.5: 'Why do you seek further beatings?' *Further* judgement is coming beyond Sennacherib's campaign. It becomes clear at the end of Isaiah 1—39 that Babylon would bring greater judgement against Zion, as it will take the house of David – and presumably all of Zion – captive (39.6–7). Multiple phases of judgement by God are also apparent in Isaiah 6.13, where God speaks of God's people being burned 'again' just like a tree that is cut down and then its stump is later set on fire. Assyria cuts down the tree, and then Babylon burns the stump. Thus, Zion figures into Isaiah's story in the sense that God will bring judgement against her due to sin *in multiple phases*, via Assyria and then Babylon.

Although the first part of Isaiah's story features Zion's judgement, God did remarkably deliver Zion in Isaiah 36—37 from Sennacherib, giving great hope that once again he would restore life to Jerusalem after its fall to Babylon.

Phase 2: Zion to be rebuilt by Cyrus

Zion's judgement via Assyria and Babylon is not the end for the city. Isaiah 40—48 depicts the start of God's restoration of Zion. As noted in Chapter 4, the expectation arises that God is raising up Cyrus to be his anointed agent (41.2, 25). The clearest articulation of God's purposes through Cyrus appears at the end of Isaiah 44:

> Thus says the LORD, your Redeemer . . .
> who says of Jerusalem, 'It shall be inhabited',
>   and of the cities of Judah, 'They shall be rebuilt',
>   and I will raise up their ruins' . . .
> who says of Cyrus, 'He is my shepherd,
>   and he shall carry out all my purpose';
> and who says of Jerusalem, 'It shall be rebuilt',
>   and of the temple, 'Your foundation shall be laid.'
> (44.24, 26, 28)

In a way similar to how 2 Chronicles ends, the expectation is that Cyrus will promote God's plans to rebuild God's temple in Jerusalem. The final line of Isaiah 44.28 brings a focus on the Temple being rebuilt. The habitation of God would again stand in Jerusalem due to God's purposes manifest through King Cyrus of Persia.

Phase 3: Zion and the Suffering Servant

Even as God initiates Zion's restoration through Cyrus in Isaiah 40—48, there is a lingering question about who are the rightful inhabitants of Zion.

Sure, there will be some returnees under Cyrus, but Isaiah 49—55 clarifies that the Suffering Servant will populate Zion with a community of servants.

In Isaiah 40—48, Israel-Jacob is portrayed as persisting in hardness towards God. This is why God can ask 'Who is blind but my servant [Israel]?' (42.19). He says:

> Bring forth the people who are blind, yet have eyes,
>   who are deaf, yet have ears!
> (43.8)

The people of Israel are burdening God with their sins (42.24). Yet, for his name's sake, he will enable them to return to Zion by blotting out their sin, and commission Cyrus to rebuild Jerusalem. Although God shows a particular commitment to Israel in this respect, there is a growing emphasis on the reconstitution of the inhabitants of Zion into a faithful community of servants, the offspring of the Suffering Servant.

Isaiah 49—54 alternates between passages regarding the Servant (49.1-13; 50.4-11; 52.13—53.12) and Zion (49.14—50.3; 51.1—52.12; 54). Central to all of the Zion passages is offspring. Isaiah 49.14—50.3 opens with Lady Zion stating: 'The LORD has forsaken me, my Lord has forgotten me.' God responds by assuring her: 'I have inscribed you on the palms of my hands; your walls are continually before me' (49.16). Of utmost importance is God's granting Zion assurance that her children will return. She will suddenly be surrounded by children who will complain that there is not enough room for them. Zion will be wondering in her heart:

> Who has borne me these?
> I was bereaved and barren,
>   exiled and put away –
>   so who has reared these?
> (49.21)

God will raise a signal, and royals will bring her sons and daughters home (49.22).

The second Zion passage (51.1—52.12) is also infused with hopes of Zion being reinhabited. It opens by calling to mind barren Sarah – this is the quarry from which Israel was hewn (Janzen 1986). God plans to comfort Zion, making her desert like a garden (51.1-3). The hope for Zion is that God's arm will awake and 'the ransomed of the LORD shall return, and come to Zion with singing' (51.11). Jerusalem is left without children (51.18, 20) in the aftermath of her judgement via exile, but she is to awake and clothe herself in beautiful garments (52.1-2), for God is not finished with Zion. The repopulation of Zion is not pictured until chapter 54. In Isaiah 54, the barren one is called to rejoice:

> Sing, O barren one who did not bear;
>> burst into song and shout,
>> you who have not been in labour!
> For the children of the desolate woman will be more
>> than the children of her that is married, says the LORD.
> Enlarge the site of your tent,
>> and let the curtains of your habitations be stretched out;
> do not hold back; lengthen your cords
>> and strengthen your stakes.
> For you will spread out to the right and to the left,
>> and your descendants will possess the nations
>> and will settle the desolate towns . . .
> All your children shall be taught by the LORD,
>> and great shall be the prosperity of your children . . .
> This is the heritage of the servants of the LORD
>> and their vindication from me, says the LORD.
> (54.1-3, 13, 17)

In this wondrous passage, Zion's children will not merely inhabit the city. Her tent will extend across the nations!

It is at this point, with chapter 54 in view, that we can ask how Zion's destiny intertwines with the servant passages. First, in Isaiah 49.1-13, the Servant takes on the task of reconciling not only Israel but also the *nations* to God himself (esp. 49.5-7). This certainly intertwines with the international constituency of Zion's children hinted at in 54.3 and develops further in Isaiah 56—66 (cf. 56.3-8; 60.3, 10; 66.18-23). Second, in the next Servant Song (50.4-11), the Servant is described in a way very similar to the children in 54.13. The Servant receives from God a 'tongue of those taught' and 'an ear to listen like those who are taught' (50.4, my translation). The same term from 50.4 for being taught (*limmûdîm*) describes Zion's children as being 'taught by the LORD' in 54.13. The inhabitants of Zion will be like God's Servant, taught by God himself. Third, the mention of Zion's children as the 'servants of the LORD' (54.17) is strategic. After Isaiah 52.13—53.12, the final Servant Song, the term 'servant' ('*ebed*) only occurs in the plural (56.6; 63.17; 65.9, 13, 14, 15; 66.14; cf. Beuken 1990), presenting the 'servants' as the offspring of the Servant. Isaiah 53 anticipates that after God makes the life of the Servant 'a guilt offering', the Servant will see 'offspring' (53.10). Apparently, the many whom the Servant justifies are the servants of the Lord whose heritage will be Zion.

So, in Isaiah 49—54, it becomes clear that God's plan for Zion involves more than the rebuilding of city and temple under Cyrus. As a far greater restoration of Zion awaits (see next section), the Suffering Servant reconstitutes Zion's inhabitants. The offspring of the Suffering Servant will populate Zion as her borders extend across the nations. This figures into an increasingly polemical message in 56—66; regardless of nationality, the servants of the LORD (56.6; ch. 65) will inherit the blessings of Zion's ultimate destiny.

Phase 4: Zion and eschatological judgement and salvation

With clarity emerging as to who are the ultimate inhabitants of Zion, the final phase of Isaiah's story depicts Zion's ultimate judgement and salvation. Although this culminates in Isaiah 56—66, the book points towards this final judgement and salvation along the way. Yes, God would judge Zion via Assyria and Babylon, but Zion will one day become the international capital of the world (2.2-4), the recipient of God's cleansing (4.2-6), and the site where God the King will not only judge the world (24.21-23) but also host a feast (25.6-8). Weeping will be absent from Zion (30.19), Zion will bloom like the wilderness (32.15; 35.1), and the redeemed will return (35.10). Isaiah 40—55 anticipates this too, as it opens with Zion receiving comfort because God himself would be returning to Zion with power and tenderness (40.9-11). This culminates with good news messengers declaring to Zion, 'Your God reigns' (52.7), for the watchmen will see God returning to Zion (52.8).

Isaiah 56—66 advances these hopes for Zion's eschatological judgement and salvation as it closes the book. At the centre of Isaiah 56—66 are chapters 60—62. In these chapters, God's light of glory shines so brightly in Zion that the entire world streams to Zion, bringing tribute and participating in the process of rebuilding the city. Yet, on either side of chapters 60—62 are dreadful portraits (59.16-20; 63.1-6) of judgement. God will come in wrath against the unrepentant in Zion (cf. 59.20) and among the nations. The entire book concludes with a similar coordination of fiery judgement and God's international glory in a redeemed Zion (66.15-24). What is more, as noted above, Isaiah 65.17–25 envisages the destiny of God's servants across all of the new creation in the light of Zion's destiny.

In summary, the story of Zion across Isaiah entails several significant movements. For one, Zion begins as a city under judgement (1.8; 1.21–24) and ends in glory (66.18–24). Judgement could have brought a final end to Zion, but the holy, redeeming God (see Chapter 5) did not forsake his people. Assyria and Babylon would judge Zion (Phase 1), but this was just a prelude for a far more glorious Zion. The city's initial rebuilding under Cyrus displayed God's faithfulness (Phase 2), yet God takes measures to prepare a new community, the offspring of the Suffering Servant (Phase 3), that will inhabit a greater Zion when God comes in glory to reside there (Phase 4).

Zion, Isaiah, and Christian reception

Within the Christian tradition, it is striking how naturally the Church adopts Zion as its own. There is a need to affirm that a Christian interpretation of Zion in Isaiah will often be metaphorical, allegorical, typological, or figural (pick your term of choice), but at the same time Christian reception reminds us not to disregard the historical and physical. Below, we begin by sketching three ways the Church has interpreted Zion in Isaiah figurally, and then offer two examples where retaining the literal character of Zion offers a balance to the figurative.

Zion as Christ, the Church, and heaven

Christian tradition has a long-standing pattern of interpreting Zion from Isaiah as figurative for Christ, the Church, and/or heaven. Let me illustrate each of these three.

Zion as Christ

Zion can call to mind the very presence and Temple of God, so it is a natural extension to interpret Zion as referring to Christ. Christ, in his earthly life, is God incarnate, the dwelling place of God on earth (John 1.14; Col. 2.9), and even speaks of his body as a temple that would be torn down and then rebuilt in three days (John 2.18–22). In this way, Jesus himself comes to represent what Zion, as God's dwelling place, had represented in the Old Testament. For this reason, passages speaking of Zion as God's habitation in Isaiah point forward to and teach of the God who would make his dwelling place in Christ.

An example of this comes from Thomas Aquinas (2017). As he explains Isaiah 2.3, where the nations say to one another 'Come, let us go up to the mountain of the LORD', he clarifies what 'the mountain of the LORD' is by saying 'that is, to Christ'.

Isaiah 26.1 is another occasion where Christian interpreters have equated Zion with Christ. Eusebius (2013: 127) states: '*The city of dominion is our salvation* . . . the Hebrew text unambiguously is speaking of *Jesus*, for we find the very same letters with which the name of our Savior is written in Hebrew.' Jerome (2015: 401) notes of this passage: '*the city of our strength* is *the Savior, that is, Jesus.*'

Thus, although it is more common for interpreters to speak of Zion as the Church or heaven, some passages about Zion are understood to be about Christ since he is the dwelling place of God.

Zion as the Church

In Isaiah, Zion frequently refers to God's people, so Christian tradition often views Zion as the Church, for the Church is now the dwelling place of God (1 Cor. 3.16–17; Eph. 2.19–22; 1 Pet. 2.5). This is the most common interpretation of Zion in Isaiah among ancient interpreters.

Jerome (2015: 90) interprets the promise that whorish Zion will one day be 'the city of the just one, the faithful city' (1.26) as speaking of the Church that would one day consist of Jew and Gentile. In chapter 8, he acknowledges (2015: 179) an 'analogical' interpretation that coordinates the attack of Jerusalem by enemies with the attack of heretics against the Church. In Isaiah 52, when the good news messenger declares to Zion 'Your God reigns', Jerome (2015: 660) interprets Zion as 'the church'.

Cyril of Alexandria (2008: 1/63), in commenting on Isaiah 2.2, states: 'We are told that Zion in Judah is situated on a mountain and has been built there. It is not, however, to be understood in a material manner, but spiritually in reference to the church.' The streaming of the nations to the Church through faith gives further proof that the mountain in 2.2 is in fact the Church (2008: 1/64).

Aquinas (2017) too displays this tradition of associating Zion with the Church. In Isaiah 2.2, while he applies the 'mountain of God' to Christ, he speaks of the 'house of the God of Jacob' as the Church. In 8.13, which speaks of God 'dwelling in Zion', Aquinas also clarifies that this refers to the Church. Throughout the splendid vision of God's glory in Zion in Isaiah 60, Aquinas refers to Jerusalem as the Church 13 times.

Calvin interprets Zion as the Church throughout his commentary. For instance, when Isaiah 25.6 speaks of a feast 'on this mountain', he clarifies

(2010: 2/197) that 'by this we must understand the Church; for nowhere else can anyone partake of this food'. In Isaiah 27.13, where returnees from exile stream to the holy mountain to worship God, Calvin states (2010: 2/266): 'Then were the people of God gathered, to flow together to Mount Zion, that is, to the Church.' In Isaiah 52.1 (2010: 4/93), Isaiah 'addresses the Church, which appeared to be in a benumbed and drowsy condition, and bids her "awake", that she may collect her strength and revive her courage'. These are just a few of hundreds of examples in Calvin's commentary on Isaiah where he speaks of Jerusalem and the Church in the same breath.

Zion as heaven

Viewing Zion as a heavenly reality is the final way Zion has been interpreted figuratively in Christian tradition. This is apparent in Revelation 21.1–2 due to its development of Isaiah 65.17–18. Although there is no mention of Jerusalem in the *heavens* in Isaiah 65, John sees 'the holy city, the new Jerusalem, coming down out of heaven from God' (Rev. 21.2). Again, in 21.10, we see 'the holy city Jerusalem coming down out of heaven from God'. Drawing upon Isaiah 60, where Zion basks in the light of God's glory and the nations stream there to glorify Zion with their gifts (cf. 66), Revelation 21 concludes by declaring that the Lamb will be the light of the city and kings will bring their glory to it (21.23–24). So, what in Isaiah is not explicitly 'heavenly' comes to be seen through a 'heavenly' lens in Revelation.

The interpretation of Zion as heavenly is readily apparent in two of the most important books in the history of the Church. In Augustine's *The City of God*, Zion, God's city, is a heavenly reality that takes on an earthly shape in the lives of the faithful remnant throughout all ages and will intermingle with the City of Humanity for as long as the City of Heaven sojourns on earth. In John Bunyan's *The Pilgrim's Progress*, its lead character, Christian, sets out on a journey from the City of Destruction to the Celestial City, Zion. When Christian finally enters the land of Beulah (Isa. 62.4), whose citizens are called '"The Holy People, The Redeemed of the LORD" . . . "Sought Out"' (62.12), fear seizes him as he must cross the river (death) to reach the heavenly city of Zion. Christian receives encouragement from Isaiah 43.2 ('When thou passest through the waters, I will be with thee; and through the rivers, they shall not overflow thee'). After crossing the river, Christian ascends the mighty hill, whose foundation is above the clouds (Isa. 2.2?) and enters into Mount Zion, the heavenly city. In the works of both Augustine and Bunyan, Zion readily infuses their Christian imaginations, whether to envisage God's will being done on earth as in heaven (Augustine) or to express heavenly hope (Bunyan).

Ancient commentators also appeal to Zion as a heavenly reality. On Isaiah 2, Eusebius (2013: 11) states:

> *The mountain of God* may be understood in various ways. Like the Jewish people who read the Scriptures literally, one could assume that it is the land of Palestine. But according to the deeper meaning, according to the final *word*, the high and heavenly and angelic *word* of God and the divine apostle of the 'heavenly' *Zion* teaches that it is 'the Jerusalem above, which is the mother of us all'.

He again finds a deeper meaning at the end of Isaiah, when those from among the nations will come to Zion, God's holy mountain, to worship through sacrifices (66.18–20). Eusebius (2013: 319) explains:

> All these things were spoken in a coarse and literal fashion, as was appropriate for the Jewish audience. But according to the deeper meaning, this phrase signifies their journey up through the air and on into heaven . . . And so they shall enter into the heavenly city of God, and so those who have been saved from every nation shall come to the heavenly Jerusalem, just as *the sons of Israel* ascended and were bringing *their sacrifices* up on the earth.

Jerome (2015: 873) interprets the journey to the 'holy mountain' in 66.19–20 as having two options – referring either to the Church of the present age or the Church in the age to come, the heavenly Jerusalem.

Frequently, in the Church's gospel hymns, it is heavenly Zion that is most common. For instance, one thinks of 'We're Marching to Zion' (Isaac Watts, 1640), which has had such an imprint within the African-American church tradition. Or, more contemporary, Sandra McCracken draws on Isaiah 25 in her song 'We Will Feast in the House of Zion' (2015).

Thus, as the Church now reads Israel's Scripture in a different key, the key of Christ, there is often a figural interpretation of Zion as bearing witness to Christ, the Church of God, and/or heaven, depending on a given passage.

Zion as historical, physical city

Although figural interpretation of Zion in Isaiah is affirmed in Christian reception, this does not mean Christian reception amounts to a wholesale replacement of the physicality of Zion with a spiritual, metaphorical reading. Interpreters frequently appeal to the physical nature of Zion. It may prove useful to illustrate how Christian interpretations have retained Zion's historicity by referencing two ends of the spectrum on this topic.

Minimalist

At one end of the spectrum, we have the bare minimum of what Christian reception affirms about the historicity of Zion when interpreting Isaiah. This has at least three layers.

For one, within history, God *rebuilt the Temple and Jerusalem under Cyrus* beginning in 539 BC. Jerome (2015: 585) argues against some Christian readers who read the Greek *kyrō* ('Cyrus') in 45.1 as *kyriō* ('Lord'), resulting in a reading that dismisses Cyrus in favour of Jesus Christ. He directs his readers to the histories of Xenophon and Josephus to read of how Cyrus fulfils these prophecies. Eusebius (2013: 226) also appeals to Josephus as confirmation that God's promises to use Cyrus to rebuild Jerusalem come true. Calvin (2010: 3/390–1) too marvelled at God's commitment to Jerusalem through his promise to use Cyrus in 44.28. These verses are written 'that they may rest assured that "Jerusalem" shall infallibly *be built*, and may learn from it how dear and precious they are to God, when they shall see the monarchy of all the east transferred to the Persians'. Thus, although Jerusalem's rebuilding through Cyrus comes before Christ, Christian interpretation affirms God's actions towards Zion *within history*.

The next layer of physicality that Christian interpreters affirm regarding Zion is that *Jesus came to physical Zion*. Due to the prophecies regarding Zion in Isaiah and elsewhere, Jesus could not have fulfilled his mission if he had only gone to Bethlehem, Nazareth, Capernaum, or any foreign city like Rome or Athens. It matters that Jesus came to Jerusalem, and interpreters regularly observe this. For Eusebius (2013: 11), because Isaiah's message was said to be 'for Judah and Jerusalem' (2.1), this finds fulfilment in Christ because 'the Christ of God walked about *Judea* and Galilee, and he was constantly in and out of *Jerusalem* "preaching the kingdom of God"'. Eusebius (2013: 289), in his comments on Isaiah 60.1 ('Shine, O Jerusalem, for your light has come'), notes that 'these things were partially but not entirely fulfilled at the first coming of our Savior' to Jerusalem. Jerome (2015: 95) observes how Jesus gave instruction in Jerusalem from the Temple, thereby confirming Isaiah 2.3 which states that God's word would come from Zion. In another passage, Jerome explains the exhortation for Zion to 'Arise, Arise, put on strength' in Isaiah 52.1. Although Jerusalem 'fell' when it rejected and 'laid hands on the Son of Man', this was not the end of Jerusalem's story. 'Having fallen at the passion of Christ, it was raised up at his resurrection, when many thousands of Jews became believers [cf. Acts 2.41; 4.4] and a remnant was saved [cf. Rom 11.5]' (2015: 653).

The final layer of historicity, related to the previous, is that *the Church came into existence in Jerusalem and began with Jews*. In view of Isaiah 2.2-3, Jerome (2015: 95) states: 'the church was founded first in Jerusalem, and then churches were planted in the whole world.' Similarly, throughout Eusebius, he draws upon the launch of the Church from a remnant of Jewish believers as evidence of the fulfilment of God's promises to Zion. Augustine (1887: 894) also affirms the importance of literal Jerusalem, for, quoting Isaiah 2.3 ('Out of Sion shall go forth the law and the word of God from Jerusalem'), he notes that this finds its realization when, after Christ's Ascension, the Holy Spirit fell upon Peter at Pentecost in Jerusalem, empowering him to proclaim God's word, resulting in thousands of conversions. When Calvin (2010: 4/269) comments on the hope that a redeemer would come to Zion (Isa. 59.20), he states: 'he could not be the redeemer of the world, without belonging to some Jews, whose fathers he had chosen, and to whom this promise was directly addressed.'

At a bare minimum, in my opinion, Christian reception summons attention to God's involvement with the historical, material Jerusalem when the Temple was rebuilt during the time of Persia, when Christ came to Zion in his first coming, and when the Church began in Jerusalem with Jews who launched it from Jerusalem before going across the globe.

Maximalist

At the other end of the spectrum, there are those who interpret promises regarding Zion as an expectation that physical, geographical Zion will again be restored. This is the expectation that ethnic Jews would return to their homeland with Zion as their restored capital. Although this is not a common view in the history of interpretation, it deserves mention as this view surfaces from time to time today.

Two striking examples from the early United States stand out. In the nineteenth century, John McDonald (1814) wrote *Isaiah's Message to the American Nation* based on Isaiah 18, a chapter known as being difficult to interpret. He argues that the USA is the nation beyond Cush that has the charge of bringing a powerful, smooth nation (the Jews) as a gift of tribute to the Lord at Mount Zion. So, the USA, in concert with other Christian nations, is to share the gospel with Jews and bring these Jews back to Jerusalem as a tribute offering to God himself. Around this same time, Ethan Smith (1825) (unrelated to Joseph Smith) based a similar appeal on Isaiah 18, yet he went a step further by arguing that Native Americans ('aborigines') are from the ten lost tribes of Israel. So, the United States is a nation chosen by God to share the gospel of the Saviour with these Jews (Native Americans) and return them to Zion as a gift of tribute to the Lord. This sort of thinking about the Native Americans reflects similar conceptions within Mormonism.

A similar brand of maximalist historicity for Zion in the light of Isaiah is readily apparent in the commentary of the famous dispensational preacher, H. A. Ironside. For instance, he states of Isaiah 2.2–4 (1952: 19):

> It tells in language too plain to be misunderstood, that in the last days GOD will again take up His ancient people, Israel, restoring them to their land, and making Jerusalem His throne-city, from which His laws will go forth to the ends of the earth.

It would be remiss, however, at this point not to mention how a materialist reading could go wrong. It would be wrong for any country, including the USA, to adopt an identity as being a new, physical-material Zion (Shalev 2013). Also, a commitment to a material Zion should not become grounds for endorsing a nationalism, particularly one that disadvantages other peoples, including the Palestinians, for it is Christ who is king of the land and Zion has always been seen as a hub for many nations (see Katanacho 2005, 2013).

Thus, as we have considered *how* Zion has been received within Christian tradition, interpreters should be engaging with both the figural and the historical. Figural readings will ask questions such as: 'In what respect might Zion refer to Christ?', 'How does Zion symbolize the Church?' and 'How can heavenly Zion serve as a frame of reference for understanding this passage?' Yet, a layer of historicity should influence our interpretations. At a minimum one should at least consider how Isaiah's messages regarding Zion relate to the exilic and post-exilic eras; Christ's ministry, death, and resurrection in Jerusalem; and the launch of the Church from there. Maximalist readings should provoke us to ponder if and how God may fulfil his promises to Zion in a physical, geographical fashion.

Conclusion

Hopefully this chapter has put you in a better position to answer the question 'What is Zion?' according to Isaiah. Any answer should be mindful of the physical reality of Zion and the ideals it symbolizes (divine presence; Davidic kingship; the people; the cosmos). Within the four phases of the story Isaiah tells, Zion is central. First, Zion experiences God's judgement via Assyria and then Babylon. Second, God commissions Cyrus to rebuild Jerusalem and its temple. Third, the Suffering Servant reconstitutes Zion's inhabitants. Finally, a greater judgement and restoration will come to Zion as God makes all things new. In the Christian reception of Isaiah's Zion, figurative readings of Zion as Christ, the Church, and heaven have abounded, yet the physicality of Zion is regularly in view when it comes to Cyrus's rebuilding of Jerusalem; Jesus' ministry, death, and resurrection there; and the launching of the Church by Jews in Jerusalem. Some have gone further by expecting a grand restoration of literal Zion in the future. Thus, interpreting Zion in Isaiah requires a great deal of discernment, as one deciphers the symbolic and physical dimensions of Zion in a given passage, keeps the entire book in mind, and factors in the vantage point Christians now have in this era of redemptive history.

7

The messianic King

'Isaiah is such an important book!' This is the sort of response I receive from churchgoers when they find out that my specialty is Isaiah. Typically, these folks have in mind the following verses:

> Look, the young woman is with child and shall bear a son, and shall name
> him Immanuel.
> (7.14)

> For a child has been born for us,
>   a son given to us;
> authority rests upon his shoulders;
>   and he is named
> Wonderful Counsellor, Mighty God,
>   Everlasting Father, Prince of Peace.
> (9.6)

> A shoot shall come out from the stump of Jesse . . .
> (11.1)

My guess is that most are familiar with these verses not because of a careful reading of the book of Isaiah but due to savouring them yearly through Handel's *Messiah* and Advent liturgies. As it turns out, there are only a few passages in Isaiah that explicitly promise a future Davidic King, a royal Messiah (9.6-7;[1] 11.1-10; 16.4-5; see also 7.14; 32.1).[2] The task before us is to consider how the historical and literary contexts of Isaiah enrich our

---

1   The versification differs between the Hebrew (8.23—9.6) and English (9.1-7). This is noted only here, and the English versification will be followed below.
2   See also Abernethy 2016 and Abernethy and Goswell 2020.

understanding of Isaiah's hopes for a royal messiah.[3] Then we will reflect on this theme in Christian reception.

Isaiah's messianic hopes in historical and literary contexts

Christians 'know' that verses like Isaiah 7.14, 9.6, and 11.1 apply to Jesus – after all, the Gospels, our hymns, and many apologists testify to this. Yet, by extracting these pieces (verses) from their puzzle (contexts) in Isaiah, the pieces themselves lose some of their hue and brightness. As a result, we see a portrait of Jesus that is more faded, less dazzling than it should be. There have been many studies on the most pertinent passages in Isaiah (e.g. Goswell 2013, 2014, 2015; Heskett 2007; Laato 1998; Schibler 1995; Wegner 1992; Williamson 1998), yet instead of taking a passage-by-passage approach I will offer four observations about how reading these key passages in their literary and historical contexts in Isaiah can enrich our reading.

Light in the darkness

'The people walking in darkness have seen a great light' (9.2 NIV). A week in the north woods of Michigan brought this metaphor to life for me. Without a torch, I had to stumble along a remote, mile-long path through the woods every evening in hopes of seeing the dim light of my cabin that would help guide me home. Isaiah's era was a time of darkness, yet there was light promised in a coming Davidic King.

The anticipation of 'great light' in Isaiah 9.1–7 follows a theme of darkness at the end of chapter 8. Although God offered himself as a sanctuary to those who would turn to him (8.14), the house of Israel did not revere God, so its destiny would be war and brokenness (8.10, 15). We read:

> They will pass through the land, greatly distressed and hungry; when they are hungry, they will be enraged and will curse their king and their gods. They will turn their faces upwards, or they will look to the earth, but will see only distress and darkness, the gloom of anguish; and they will be thrust into thick darkness.
> (8.21–22)

---

3   Although the term 'messiah' only occurs in Isaiah in relation to Cyrus, my use focuses on the concept, not the term. The royal messianic concept in Isaiah relates to the expectation that God will use a chosen, royal figure in a significant way to accomplish God's purposes in the future.

This is a vision of displacement and hunger, a time when an invading army has ravaged the land, as in the invasions of Tiglath-pileser III, Shalmaneser, Sargon or Sennacherib across Israel and Judah. Yet, as is so common in the prophets and the opening part of Isaiah (chs 1—12), doom and gloom give way to hope. 'The people walking in darkness have seen a great light' (9.2 NIV). Due to the placement of this light of hope (9.2) just after the darkness of judgement in chapter 8, we must interpret the messianic hopes in 9.1–7 as a reversal of despair and desolation in Israel. The promise of a coming king is a promise that God's judgement of Israel and Judah for their sins via Assyria and Babylon would not be his final word.

One finds a similar editorial practice of juxtaposing passages of despair and hope in a coming Davidic King in Isaiah 10 and 11 (Beuken 2002). Here the shared imagery is that of trees. In Isaiah 10, God depicts Assyria like an axe. Assyria is the axe that chopped down the nations, including Israel, yet Assyria fails to recognize that the one wielding the axe (God), not the axe itself (Assyria), gets the glory (10.15). Ultimately, Assyria will be chopped down by God:

> Look, the Sovereign, the LORD of hosts,
> will lop the boughs with terrifying power;
> the tallest trees will be cut down,
> and the lofty will be brought low.
> He will hack down the thickets of the forest with an axe,
> and Lebanon with its majestic trees will fall.
> (10.33–34)

The arboreal imagery is prominent: boughs (i.e. branches), trees, thickets, and majestic trees. As Osborne (2018: 118–21) demonstrates, the tree in the ancient world serves as an image of power and kingship. The fallen trees announce the fall of Assyria and its ruler. By way of contrast, Isaiah 11.1 opens with Judah's kings already having fallen (they are a 'stump') and offers hope that a 'shoot' will emerge: 'A shoot shall come out from the stump of Jesse' (11.1 NIV). Patricia K. Tull (2010: 226) captures well the shift from chapter 10 to 11: 'As the tree of Assyrian royalty falls, the Judean royal tree, though cut down, grows again.' Isaiah 1—39 ends with the expectation that the house of David will be in exile, with Hezekiah's descendants becoming eunuchs. All seems to be lost for the house of David. Nonetheless, hope emerges in 11.1. There is hope for the tree to come to life again. So, as the tall, lofty, majestic trees meet their fate at the end of chapter 10, a meagre, humble shoot from Jesse's stump will arise out of the ashes.

A third vantage point on the hope of Davidic kingship in the wake of disaster arises in Isaiah 16.4–5. Here, the scene is in Moab, and an invasion by an army has wreaked havoc, scattering many Moabites abroad. These Moabite refugees are to find shelter and refuge in God's temple-city which becomes their place of refuge. There the future Davidic King will serve 'as chief judicial officer' as he 'consider[s] pleas for the granting of asylum by foreign refugees' (Goswell 2014: 102). This is because there will one day be a throne in David's tent, God's sanctuary in Zion, from which justice will come forth (16.5). Thus, displacement, not simply among Israelites but even for Moab, serves as a backdrop for grasping the expectation of a coming Davidic King.

Through the strategic placement of these promises, therefore, hope for a Davidic King emerges out of a context of ashes. Yes, judgement against Israel will lead to darkness amid the invasions of Assyria and then Babylon, but light is on the horizon during an era when a Davidic King will reign (9.6–7). The mighty tree of Assyria will fall (10.33), yet a shoot of hope will spring forth from Jesse's house (11.1). As judgement spreads to the nations (e.g. Moab), hope can be found in the prospect of a Davidic King in Jerusalem (11.10; 16.5). When read within their immediate literary and historical contexts in Isaiah, the promises of a future King are set against a backdrop of darkness. Suffering and upheaval, anchored initially in the Assyrian and Babylonian eras, in Israel and abroad, will not be God's final word. A *great* light will dawn; a Davidic King will reign on the throne.

A king of justice

It is common to hear in the Church: 'The Old Testament expected the Davidic Messiah to come as a military conqueror.' There are only a few passages in the Old Testament that speak of the future King as an agent of war (e.g. Num. 24.17), but one of the most common characteristics of the coming King is that he will uphold justice and righteousness within society (Abernethy and Goswell 2020). In Isaiah, every passage that promises a future Davidic King focuses on his role as an agent of justice (see esp. Schibler 1995; Williamson 1998). All of Chapter 9 in this volume will address justice and righteousness in the book of Isaiah, so my comments here about justice and righteousness await further development in that chapter.

In Isaiah 9.1–7, the expectation is that a 'son' will rule on the throne of David. We read:

> His authority shall grow continually,
>> and there shall be endless peace
> for the throne of David and his kingdom.
>> He will establish and uphold it
> with justice and with righteousness
>> from this time onward and for evermore.
> The zeal of the LORD of hosts will do this.
> (9.7)

The first half of verse 7 describes two characteristics of the King's future reign – ever-increasing authority and endless peace. The second half of the verse clarifies why the Davidic King's reign will be expanding and peaceful – because the kingdom's foundation will be justice and righteousness. In contrast to the society of Isaiah's time, where orphans and widows were neglected (1.17, 21–23), where the rich confiscated the land of the poor (3.14), and where there was outcry instead of justice (5.7), the future Davidic King will reign in justice and righteousness.

Isaiah 11 is similar to Isaiah 9 in its emphasis upon justice and peace when it comes to the Davidic King. The shoot from Jesse's stump will be endowed by the Spirit with Solomonesque wisdom (11.2–3a). As a result, the Davidic King will be empowered to establish justice:

> He shall not judge by what his eyes see,
>> or decide by what his ears hear;
> but with righteousness he shall judge the poor,
>> and decide with equity for the meek of the earth;
> he shall strike the earth with the rod of his mouth,
>> and with the breath of his lips he shall kill the wicked.
> Righteousness shall be the belt around his waist,
>> and faithfulness the belt around his loins.
> (11.3b–5)

Interwoven across these verses is a focus on how the King will bring about justice in society. He will have a perception that is not swayed by smooth talkers or schemers; instead, the justice he brings about for the poor and afflicted will be righteous and equitable. Isaiah 11 hopes for a time when a shoot from David will fulfil this sacred duty of upholding justice. This will lead to a time of peace, depicted poetically as a time when hostile animals will dwell in harmony with one another (11.6–9).

Isaiah 16.5 also features the characteristics of justice and righteousness. We read:

> then a throne shall be established in steadfast love
>> in the tent of David,
>> and on it shall sit in faithfulness
> a judge who seeks justice
>> and is swift to do what is right.
> (my own translation)

In this verse a cluster of terms that promote faithfulness occur: 'steadfast love' (*ḥesed*), 'faithfulness' (*'emet*), 'judge' (*špt*), 'justice' (*mišpāṭ*), and righteousness (*ṣedeq*). All the characteristics stem from the character of God himself, and the expectation is that God will establish a Davidic King who will promote these realities in contrast to the experiences of oppression and injustice of the time.

The final passage to note is Isaiah 32.1. Although it could be more of a proverbial statement rather than a promise of a coming messianic King (Williamson 1998: 62–72), it underscores how central justice is to the King's job description.

> See, a king will reign in righteousness,
>> and princes will rule with justice.
> (32.1)

This passage expresses an ideal that contrasts with the rulers at the time of Isaiah. The people of Zion flourish and find security when kings reign with righteousness and justice.

Today, at least in the USA, I do not think of the president as responsible for justice; instead, my mind drifts to the Supreme Court and judges when it comes to ensuring justice across the country. In the ancient world, however, a chief task of the king was to establish justice. In the Code of Hammurabi, King Hammurabi explains that the gods put him in place to establish justice in Babylon. The same is the case throughout the Old Testament, from Israel's request for a king ('Now appoint for us a king to judge us like all the nations', 1 Sam. 8.5 ESV), to descriptions of David's reign ('And David administered justice and equity to all his people', 2 Sam. 8.15 ESV), to Solomon's decision-making ('Give to your servant a listening heart to judge the people, to discern between good and evil, for who is able to judge your people?', 1 Kings 3.9, my translation; cf. 3.28; 10.9), and even to the hopes of the prophets (e.g. Jer. 23.5–6; 33.15; Ezek. 34.16, 23; Mic. 5.1). In the key royal messianic texts of Isaiah (9.6–7; 11.1–10; 16.4–5; 32.1), the primary mission of the Davidic King is to serve as God's agent in establishing justice and righteousness within a world previously marked by injustice.

Fulfilment, canon, and *sensus plenior*

One question that arises pertains to the referent(s) of these passages. This is particularly the case with 'Immanuel'. Up to this point, we have set Isaiah 7.14 to the side in our discussion of texts that expect a future Davidic King. As detailed in Chapter 4, Isaiah 7 is set during a time when two nations to the north – Israel and Aram – come against Ahaz, king of Judah, in the 730s BC. In this fear-inducing situation, God invites Ahaz to request a sign, but the king refuses the invitation. As a result, God offers his own sign:

> Therefore the Lord himself will give you a sign. Look, the young woman is with child and shall bear a son, and shall name him Immanuel. He shall eat curds and honey by the time he knows how to refuse the evil and choose the good. For before the child knows how to refuse the evil and choose the good, the land before whose two kings you are in dread will be deserted. The LORD will bring on you and on your people and on your ancestral house such days as have not come since the day that Ephraim departed from Judah – the king of Assyria.
> (7.14–17)

The first thing to observe is that the 'sign' (7.14) clearly relates to the immediate context that Ahaz is facing. The 'child', Immanuel, will still be young when the lands of Israel and Aram are deserted, presumably due to an invasion by the king of Assyria (7.16–17).

Debate revolves around the identities of the young woman and her child.[4] The 'young woman' seems to be someone known both to Isaiah and King Ahaz, but who is she? The Hebrew word *'almâ* is a general term that refers to a 'young woman', so the choice of this term does not specify whether she is a virgin or not.[5] If this *'almâ* is a virgin, the assumption is that she would conceive via intercourse with a man. Some scholars speculate that she is one of Ahaz's wives (Wildberger 1991: 310; Williamson 1998: 104–10), yet it proves

---

4   For an excellent overview of many issues in Isa. 7.14, see Willis 1978.
5   See scholarly discussions in Walton 1987; Wegner 2011; Wenham 1972.

difficult to reconcile this with the age of Hezekiah. Others suggest that this is Isaiah's wife (8.3; Roberts 2015: 119), but referring to her as the *'almâ* is strange, especially when she is referred to as 'the prophetess' in 8.3. Within the context of Isaiah 7—8, parentage is always explicit when Isaiah's children are in view – 'Go out to meet Ahaz, you and your son Shear-jashub' (7.3); 'And I went to the prophetess, and she conceived and bore a son. Then the LORD said to me, Name him Maher-shalal-hash-baz' (8.3) – so the ambiguity as to the parentage of Immanuel points away from Isaiah's wife as the *'almâ*. The identity of the *'almâ* is ambiguous in the final form of the text, and, as will be suggested below, this ambiguity seems purposeful.

The significance of the child in this sign relates to his name and also to his age. As for his name, Immanuel means 'God with us' in Hebrew. This is a theophoric name, a name that includes a mention of God. Examples of this are Isaiah ('YHWH saves'), Ezekiel ('God is strong'), Elimelek ('God is King'), and Uzziah ('YHWH is strong'). Just as Isaiah, Ezekiel, Elimelek, and Uzziah are not YHWH or God – even though their names contain God's name – so a natural reading of the mother calling her son 'Immanuel' is not meant as an ontological description of the son (i.e. that the son is divine), at least not in the first level of reading. Instead, by bearing this name, the son will remind those during this tumultuous time that God is with his people. This reminder occurs again in 8.8 and 10, as God with Us proves to be an important promise during the time of turmoil amid Assyrian invasion.

As for his age, the repetition of 'by the time / before he knows how to refuse the evil and choose the good' (see 7.15, 16) anchors the sign in the early years of the child's life. Whether this refers to a time when the child can choose between good and bad food (Roberts 2015: 119; Williamson 2018: 164–7) or can be held accountable for moral choices (Oswalt 1986: 214), the message is clear. Within only a few years after the child is born, the two threatening nations will be dismantled by Assyria (7.16–17). The 'son' is not active in this passage; instead, his name ('God with us') and age (within a few years of his birth) express the idea that God will make good on his promise to deliver his people from the threat of Israel and Aram, even if their Davidic king has proven to be faithless.

The question, then, naturally arising for Christian readers is: 'If the young woman and son were alive during the time of Isaiah and Ahaz, then how can Isaiah 7.14 *also* find fulfilment in Mary and Jesus, as Matthew 1.22–23 claims?' As you will see below, Jews throughout the centuries have forced Christians to wrestle with how Isaiah 7.14 can speak of Jesus while also addressing the original context. And Jews have a strong basis in the text itself for not letting

Christians ignore the plain meaning of this passage which relates to the eighth-century context. Two comments will suffice at this point.

First, the intentional ambiguity in Isaiah 7 and its canonical placement as part of Isaiah 7—11 invites a reading of Isaiah 7 that points beyond its initial context. Brevard Childs (2001: 63, 80–1), Hugh Williamson (1998: 103–9), and R. Clements (1990) helpfully observe how Isaiah 7.14 takes on a wider vantage point relating to Davidic kingship than it would have taken if read as an isolated text. One begins by recognizing that Isaiah 7.14 is part of a rebuke given to 'the house of David' (7.13) due to Ahaz's faithlessness. Even if the son (*bēn*) 'Immanuel' is not explicitly said to be a replacement for Ahaz, the positioning of the announcement that a child (*yeled*) will be given in 9.6 (MT 9.5), just after Isaiah 7—8, opens up a reading where the coming Davidic King in 9.1–7 comes to be seen as God's light who will shine after the darkness of invasion by Assyria. This, of course, continues in the corresponding hope in Isaiah 11.1–10. The result is a reading where Immanuel's initial referent, a child born during the crisis with Israel and Aram, extends into a promise that intertwines with hope in a coming Davidic King.

Second, when it comes to Isaiah 7.14, one may appeal to *sensus plenior* (Latin, 'fuller sense'). *Sensus plenior* claims that there is a fuller meaning in the text than what an original human author knew, although organically connected. God may have led Isaiah to use an ambiguous term like *'almâ*, a term that can include a virgin, and then led the LXX translators to translate it as *parthénos* ('virgin'). This prepared the way for a retrospective recognition that the miraculous conception and virginal birth was anticipated in advance by God in Isaiah 7.14. What is more, the theophoric name Immanuel (meaning 'God with us') did not initially describe the ontological nature of the 'son' born in the eighth-century BC context. Yet, through divine inspiration, God had more meaning in mind, which would become apparent after the Virgin Mary conceives while still a virgin and births a son whose theophoric name describes his very person, God with us. God seems to have infused these texts with ambiguity in terms of referent (Who is the *'almâ*? Who is the son?) and directs editors to strategically situate Isaiah chapter 7, 9.1–7, and 11.1–10 so as to create a surplus of expectation that found fulfilment in the coming of Jesus and awaits further fulfilment in his Church and second coming.

The messianic King in Isaiah's story

As has been our pattern in previous chapters, we can now consider how hopes in a messianic king figure into the four phases of Isaiah's story (see Chapter 4).

In Phase 1 of Isaiah's story, the Holy One will judge Israel, Zion, and the nations through Assyria and Babylon. The kings of Judah are not exempt from this judgement. King Ahaz (ch. 7) serves as an example of the 'hardening' anticipated in Isaiah 6. Judah's king, most likely Hezekiah, is confronted and warned for forging alliances with Egypt (Isa. 30—31). The judgement of Judah's kings intertwines so closely with the punishment awaiting Zion that Isaiah 39 predicts the exile of Zion by focusing on the destiny of the Davidic King. Speaking to Hezekiah, Isaiah declares: 'Some of your own sons who are born to you shall be taken away; they shall be eunuchs in the palace of the king of Babylon' (39.7). The house of David under judgement is the 'stump' in Isaiah 11; the Holy God will judge the unfaithful house of David through exile to Babylon.

During Phase 2 of Isaiah's story, a different king is prominent – King Cyrus of Persia.[6] Although David had founded Jerusalem and his son Solomon had built the First Temple, a pagan king would take on the task of David by commissioning the rebuilding of Jerusalem and its temple by sending exiles home (44.24—45.12). Furthermore, as we will discuss in the next chapter, the Servant Israel (42.1-4) takes on the royal task of bringing about justice (see Williamson 1998: 132-6) in this phase of Isaiah's story. So, in Isaiah 40—48, hopes in a coming royal messiah are not at the forefront.

During Phase 3 of Isaiah's story, a different agent is again in view – namely, the Suffering Servant who will reconstitute God's people. As we will discuss in the next chapter, although Jesus turns out to be *both* the royal Messiah *and* the Suffering Servant, it is wise not to conflate the two too quickly.

Now for Phase 4. Some interpret the absence of Davidic hopes in Isaiah 40—66 (cf. however, 55.3; 65.25) as an indication that hope in a future Davidic King from Isaiah 9.1-7, 11.1-10, and 16.4-5 does not endure in the book's final form. It seems better, however, to recognize that within Isaiah 1—39 the fulfilment of these promises sits on an undefined temporal horizon. All we know is that the light of a royal Messiah will shine after the fall of Assyria and Babylon (9.1-7; 10.33; ch. 39). Within the vantage point of the entire book, we now expect the fulfilment of the promises of a Davidic King at some point after the work of the Suffering Servant. It is amid or prior to God's final realization of his plans for the world (Phase 4) that the promises of a Davidic King will find their realization – namely, one who will rule in unending justice and bear the names of 'Wonderful Counsellor,

---

6 For an insightful account of the place of Cyrus in Isaiah's story, see Bo Lim (2018).

Mighty God, Everlasting Father, Prince of Peace' (9.6).[7] Thus, Isaiah's story invites us to situate our hope in the coming Davidic King within Phase 4, when the Holy One comes in final judgement and final salvation to make a new world for his servants.

Isaiah's Messiah and Christian reception

Isaiah's royal messianic expectations became pillars as Christians built their house of faith on the Old Testament. In Matthew's Gospel, Isaiah 7.14 becomes the first passage quoted in the New Testament, as the verse finds its fulfilment in the Virgin Mary conceiving via the Holy Spirit and bearing Immanuel, God with us (Matt. 1.22–23).[8] In Luke 1.31 NIV, Gabriel's announcement to Mary that she will 'conceive and give birth to a son, and you are to call him . . .' calls to mind Isaiah 7.14 as well. When Jesus begins his ministry in Galilee, Matthew quotes from Isaiah 9.1–2, with its expectation that a great light would break forth in the region of Galilee (Matt. 4.12–16). Although the opening of Isaiah 9 is quoted, it is surprising that the names of the king ('Wonderful Counsellor, Mighty God, Everlasting Father, Prince of Peace', 9.6) are never quoted in the New Testament. Isaiah 11 is appealed to by the apostles when they refer to Jesus as the root of David (Rom. 15.12; Rev. 5.5; 22.16). It is also possible that the Hebrew term for 'shoot' (*neṣer*) in Isaiah 11.1 informs the claim that the Messiah would be a *Nazar*ene (Matt. 2.23; see Nolland 2005: 130, who also includes the use of the verb *nṣr* in Isa. 42.6).

These passages from Isaiah also became important for the earliest apologists, but this is especially the case with Isaiah 7.14. Our focus in the rest of this chapter, then, will primarily be upon the messianic reception of Isaiah 7.14 in Christian tradition.

The apologists and Isaiah's Messiah

Justin Martyr's *Dialogue with Trypho* recounts a discussion between a sceptical Jew named Trypho and the Christian Justin, dating from around ad 150. It is a fascinating window into how a young, Gentile church attempts to justify its claims that Jesus is the Messiah of Israel's Scriptures. Trypho questions the validity of appealing to Isaiah 7.14 as a prophecy that the Messiah would be

---

7 For more on these names, see Abernethy 2016: 126–8.

8 For a discussion on the apostolic hermeneutic that enables an association between Isaiah and Matthew's use, see Blomberg (2002) and Watts (2004).

divine and born of a virgin. For, so Trypho argues, the LXX translation 'virgin' was originally 'young woman', and the passage originally refers to the time of Ahaz, particularly to his son Hezekiah. Justin counters this by arguing that the LXX translation of 'virgin' stems from Jewish elders before Christ who understood Isaiah 7.14 to anticipate something extraordinary (Justin Martyr 2003: 131). Additionally, Hezekiah did not accomplish the expectation of carrying away Samaria and Damascus (Justin Martyr 2003: 120–1), so the promised son could not be Hezekiah. Justin goes on to reason that the 'sign' of Immanuel would not be a sign if the birth was not remarkable. He then allegorically states that Christ fulfils the expectation of the child overcoming Damascus in Jesus' birth by overcoming Herod.

Tertullian (AD 150–240) also engages with numerous objections from Jews that Isaiah 7.14 cannot refer to Jesus. The opponents argue that Jesus is not actually named 'Immanuel' and the removal of power from Damascus does not take place in Jesus' time (1885a: 160–1; see also 1885c: 330–2). Appealing to Isaiah 8, Tertullian states that from the beginning it is the sense of the name, not the name itself, that is primary in Isaiah 7.14. What is more, it does not make sense that a young child could be a military conqueror, so the passage is figurative. If this is truly a 'sign', then the miraculous birth of Jesus to a virgin fits best. Although Tertullian defends Christ to Jews, he also defends the faith to Greeks who object to God taking on flesh. He does so by appealing to the trustworthiness of the Jewish Scriptures and their expectation of Christ's incarnation. 'This ray of God, then, as it was always foretold in ancient times, descending into a certain virgin, and made flesh in her womb, is in His birth God and man united' (1885b: 34–5). For Tertullian, Isaiah 7 was a central passage that supported his contention that Israel's Scriptures expected two advents of the Messiah: one in humility (in the flesh, to suffer and die) and one in glory (his second coming).

Eusebius's *Proof of the Gospel* takes a similar tack. As he makes a case that Israel's Scriptures expected God to come in the flesh (cf. esp. Eusebius 1920: 2/49–72), Isaiah 7 fits into a sequence where Isaiah sees the glory of the divine Christ in 6.1 (cf. John 12), anticipates his rejection amid Jewish hardening (6.8–13), and then predicts the birth of God in flesh among the Jews in chapter 7. Although some interpret this child to be Hezekiah or point to the Hebrew tradition of 'young woman', he argues that this would not be a miraculous 'sign' if this were the case. The abandonment of Samaria and Damascus in Isaiah 7 prefigures the time of Rome when these areas would indeed be subdued. Yet, Eusebius also offers a figurative explanation. If Damascus represents idolatry and Samaria improper worship in the human soul, the dissolution of these powers at the coming of Immanuel in 7.14 speaks of 'the stability, the calmness and peace of every soul, who received the God that was born, Emmanuel himself' (1920: 2/59).

Thus, for the defenders of the faith in the early Church, Isaiah 7.14 predicted that God would become incarnate. There is, however, a recognizable tension in defending how such a reading of Isaiah 7.14 aligns with its historical contexts and objections by the Jews.

Pre-modern Christian commentators and Isaiah's Messiah

The pre-modern Christian commentators explain Isaiah 7.14 in ways similar to the apologists. Nearly all of them are alert to Jewish traditions that read 'virgin' as 'young woman' and the challenges of reading 7.14 christologically when the verses around it are embedded in the time of Ahaz's crisis with Israel and Aram. In the early Church, the commentaries of Jerome and Eusebius follow the apologists' lines of reasoning to support christological readings of Isaiah 7.14 as opposed to Jewish traditions. Aquinas and Calvin too read Isaiah 7.14 as predicting Christ's birth, yet their defences are unique in comparison with those of the early Church in terms of how they navigate the immediate and future contexts in the passage.

Aquinas (2017) responds to five objections from Jews.

1 Jews claim that 7.14 is a sign of liberation for Jews at that time, and Christ's incarnation has nothing to do with this. In response, Aquinas claims that Isaiah is offering an 'argument from the greater: for if God will give his son for the salvation of the whole world, much more can he save you from these enemies'. In other words, even if 7.14 speaks of a distant salvation in Christ, the implication is that those in the present time of Ahaz would draw confidence knowing that God would intervene to save Judah too.

2 Jews claim that those at Isaiah's time were to see the sign, so this cannot be Christ's incarnation 800 years later. Aquinas argues that the sign is not given to Ahaz, but instead it is given generally to the house of David, which could mean at a time in the distant future.

3 Jews claim that signs come before what is signified, so, if the sign is Christ's incarnation, then this comes 800 years after the event of deliverance that the sign was to signify. Aquinas, however, points to numerous occasions in Scripture where the signified comes first.

4 Jews claim that the Hebrew *'almâ* does not mean 'virgin' but 'young woman'. Aquinas argues that it would not be a 'sign' if it only referred to an everyday occurrence (i.e. a young woman becoming pregnant through intercourse with a man). He also notes that the term can also refer to a virgin.

5 Jews claim that the child is Hezekiah's or Isaiah's son, but Aquinas argues that Hezekiah was already 25 years old by this time, and a child born to a prophet is by no means a 'sign'.

For Aquinas, then, the 'sign' of Immanuel is seen in Christ's incarnation, yet by looking forward in faith to 'God with us', the people of Ahaz's time would call on Immanuel to deliver them in their present circumstances as well. Aquinas seems so committed to exclusively applying Isaiah 7.14 to Christ that his argumentation in many of these points is strained. As I argued above, it seems better to find an initial referent in the time of Ahaz and to recognize an even greater referent and fulfilment in Christ.

Calvin (2010: 1/244) too squares off with the Jews in his interpretation of Isaiah 7.14: 'This passage is obscure; but the blame lies partly on the Jews, who, by much cavilling, have laboured, as far as lay in their power, to pervert the true exposition.' After arguing against Jewish views that the referent is Hezekiah or Isaiah's son, he critiques the view held by some Christians that 'the Prophet spoke of some child who was born at that time, by whom, as by an obscure picture, Christ was foreshadowed'. His critique is that 'this name *Immanuel* cannot be literally applied to a mere man'. So, for Calvin, Isaiah 7.14, and verse 15, can only apply to Christ. Calvin, however, argues that Isaiah shifts back to the immediate historical context in verses 7.16–17, where 'the child' does not refer to Christ but 'to all children in general' (2010: 250) – by the time the children of Judah reach the age of discernment God would deliver Judah from the dreaded lands. Although Calvin is often an exemplary interpreter, he is unsuccessful here due to his assumption that 'Immanuel' cannot refer to a mere man, for he fails to recognize how theophoric names work. This leads him to a reading where he does not have the same child in view across all of 7.14–17. Such a reading is untenable in my opinion.

As we look back over the history of interpreting Isaiah 7.14 among the apologists and Christian commentators, it is striking how Jewish objections were never far from view. Ibn Ezra (Friedländer 1873: 42), the great Jewish medieval commentator, captures well the Jewish sentiment towards these christological interpretations: 'It is to me a matter of surprise that there are those who say the prophet here refers to Jesus, since the sign was given to

Ahaz, and Jesus was born many years afterwards.' This Jewish sentiment persists for a very good reason, because a literal reading of 7.14 in historical context and chapter context supports an eighth-century BC reading. In my opinion, Calvin too quickly dismisses the possibility that 'Immanuel' could refer to a child at Isaiah's time who prefigures a greater fulfilment in Christ's incarnation. As argued above, one can satisfy the invitation to recognize that Isaiah 7.14–17 clearly addresses an immediate situation at the time of Ahaz, yet also unequivocally affirm in the light of the canonical arrangement of Isaiah 7—11 and in view of *sensus plenior* that 7.14 finds an even grander fulfilment in the Incarnation.

Isaiah's Messiah in art, poetry and music

Commentators and apologists were not the only interpreters of Isaiah. Artists, poets, and musicians were also offering their interpretations of Isaiah's Messiah, especially Isaiah 7.14. The most prominent visual representation from Isaiah is the image of the prophet Isaiah holding a scroll with the words of Isaiah 7.14 engraved in Latin or Greek, and Mary is often near. In the Basilica of San Marco (Venice), the dome of Immanuel (twelfth century AD) features Christ at the centre, surrounded by prophets and the Virgin Mary who point to him. Next to Mary stands the prophet Isaiah holding a scroll that shows Isaiah 7.14. In the St Nicholas Apse Mosaic (AD 1296) in Monaco, Mary sits on a throne with baby Jesus on her lap, while Isaiah stands by holding a scroll with Isaiah 7.14 visible in Latin. In the Siena Cathedral, various scenes from the Gospels circle around Mary and Jesus. Isaiah initiates the story of the scenes, holding a scroll with 7.14 written in it (AD 1311), as he stands beside the Virgin while she receives the angel's announcement. This tradition continues up to the present day, even in my home city of Chicago, where Christ the Savior Orthodox Church features an icon of Isaiah holding a scroll with the words of Isaiah 7.14 written in English. There are countless such examples that have been surveyed by John Sawyer (1996: 65–82).

Poets have also found inspiration from Isaiah in their attempts to speak of Jesus as Messiah. As one example, Alexander Pope (1796), the great English poet from the early eighteenth century, wrote a poem called 'The Messiah' that opens as follows:

Ye nymphs of Solyma! begin the song,
To heavenly themes sublimer strains belong.
The mossy fountains, and the sylvan shades,
The dreams of Pindus, and the Aonian maids,

Delight no more – O thou, my voice inspire,
Who touched Isaiah's hallowed lips with fire!

Rapt into future times the bard begun,
A virgin shall conceive, a Virgin bear a son!
From Jesse's root behold a branch arise,
Whose sacred flower with fragrance fills the skies;
The ethereal Spirit o'er its leaves shall move,
And on its top descend the mystic Dove.

Ye heavens! from high the dewy nectar pour,
And in soft silence shed the kindly shower!
The sick and weak, the healing Plant shall aid,
From storms a shelter, and from heat a shade.
All crimes shall cease, and ancient fraud shall fail;
Returning justice lift aloft her scale.
Peace o'er the world her olive wand extend,
And white-robed Innocence from heaven descend.

These stanzas, which open the poem, are laced with allusions to Isaiah. Pope begins by calling on God to purify his own lips just as Isaiah's were in Isaiah 6. As Pope depicts the prophetic hopes in a Messiah, he starts with the promise of the virgin birth from 7.14 ('A virgin shall conceive, a Virgin bear a son!') and meshes this with the image of Jesse's root and the Spirit empowering the Messiah from 11.1–5 ('From Jesse's root behold a branch arise . . . The ethereal Spirit o'er its leaves shall move'). What is more, although many pre-modern commentaries pay scant attention to the role of the Messiah in bringing justice within society, Pope develops themes of justice from 9.6–7 and 11.3–5 ('The sick and weak, the healing Plant shall aid . . . All crimes shall cease . . . Returning justice lift aloft her scale'), and then follows the logic of Isaiah 9 and 11 where justice is bound together with peace (9.7; 11.6–9). Pope's poem demonstrates that he was not only a good reader of these passages individually, but was also attuned to this constellation of royal messianic texts from Isaiah (7.14; 9.6–7; 11.1–10; cf. 32.1–2) and read them together.

The best-known engagement with Isaiah's messianic texts in Western society is found in Handel's *Messiah*. In June 1741, Charles Jennens sent lyrics for an opera to George Handel in London. Over the course of 24 days, Handel turned these words into a musical opera that came to be called *Messiah*. The lyrics are scriptural quotations, many of which come from Isaiah. He remarkably intersects the promises that God would return to comfort Zion (e.g. Isa. 40.1–2) with the promise of the virgin birth (7.14) and the names of the royal King (9.6), and then moves on to Isaiah's Suffering Servant (53.3–5). During the time of Handel and Jennens,[9] deism reigned; the sentiment was that God was not a personal God who works miracles. The idea of predictive prophecy, then, had no home in deism. *Messiah* boldly drew on predictive prophecy, affirmed God's ability to work miracles, and celebrated the personal nature of God. It is now a fixture in Western society during the season of Advent.

Conclusion

On the surface, applying messianic texts from Isaiah to Jesus seems straightforward and natural as one looks to the New Testament, the decor of churches, and the lyrics of Pope and Handel. Yet, from the time of the apologists to the current day in modern scholarship, there have always been questions about how to reconcile christological readings with what seems to be the plain, historical sense of these messianic texts when read in their literary and historical contexts in Isaiah. This is particularly the case with Isaiah 7.14. My hope is that this chapter challenges us to strive for readings that honour God's design to both address a historical situation and bear witness to Christ.

---

9   On the context of Handel, Jennens, and Pope amid deism, see Daniell 2003.

8

The Suffering Servant

There is perhaps no passage in Scripture more beloved and also more difficult than Isaiah 52.13—53.12 (referred to as Isaiah 53 hereafter), the famous Suffering Servant passage. Martin Luther (1972: 221) could declare: 'I delight in this text as if it were a text of the New Testament.' Yet, Brevard Childs (2001: 410) can also say: 'It is hardly necessary to remind the reader that this passage is probably the most contested chapter in the Old Testament. The problems of interpretation are many and complex.' Nearly 1,000 years before Childs, Abraham Ibn Ezra (Friedländer 1873: 239) expresses the same sentiment: 'The passage [Isaiah 53] offers great difficulties'. And about 1,100 years before Ibn Ezra, an Ethiopian eunuch was reading Isaiah 53 and the apostle Philip asked him if he understood it. The eunuch answered: 'How can I, unless someone guides me?' (Acts 8.30–31). After millennia of struggles with this text in the Church, the unrelenting conviction among Christians is that Isaiah 53 *in some way* bears witness to Jesus. Challenges emerge in the details of this passage and in trying to make sense of it within the literary flow of thought in Isaiah and in view of its historical context. In this chapter, I am under no illusion that I am offering a final word on Isaiah's Suffering Servant. I will be content if you walk away from this chapter alert to key questions people wrestle with, while retaining a sense of wonder over how Isaiah 53 bears witness to Christ and shapes the identity of the Church.

The Suffering Servant in literary and historical contexts

The 'Servant Songs' (42.1–4; 49.1–6; 50.4–9; 52.13—53.12) are a group of four passages in Isaiah 40—55 that share affinities with one another on the topic of God's Servant.

- *Song 1 Isaiah 42.1–4.* God elected his Servant and empowered him with the Spirit to bring justice gently to the nations.
- *Song 2 Isaiah 49.1–6.* The Servant recounts his calling to be Israel and restore Israel and the nations to God.

- *Song 3 Isaiah 50.4–9.* The Servant reflects on his faithful endurance in the face of suffering, trusting that God will vindicate him.
- *Song 4 Isaiah 52.13—53.12.* God will glorify the Servant, whom the members of the community now realize has suffered on behalf of their sins to set them right with God.

As noted in Chapter 3, Bernard Duhm thought these songs were later added into Isaiah 40—55, so he and his followers examined these songs in isolation from the rest of Isaiah 40—55. Yet, even if they were written later (a debated point), these songs are now strategically located within their unique literary context in various parts of Isaiah 40—55 (see Mettinger 1983). The aim, then, will be to look at how Isaiah 53 relates to the other Servant Songs within the flow of thought across Isaiah 40—55. We will do so by considering two questions: 'Who is the Suffering Servant?' and 'What does Isaiah 53 envisage?'

Who is the Suffering Servant?

The most intriguing riddle for scholars has been historical and referential in nature – trying to identify the Servant in the Servant Songs in the original historical context. Although it will become clear that I prefer a particular view, I will ultimately conclude that this line of enquiry leads us down the wrong path. Let's begin by surveying a few views that are prominent when explaining the identity of the Suffering Servant.

Christopher North (1948: 3–5) listed the four most popular theories throughout the ages that endured to his time in the 1940s. The Servant is (1) an anonymous contemporary of Second Isaiah, (2) Second Isaiah (the prophet himself), (3) collective Israel, or (4) the Messiah. In my assessment of current trends, theory 1 no longer receives much consideration. Theories 2, 3 and 4 are still dominant, yet a significant difference today from North's time is that many scholars combine these views by applying different referents to different passages. The examples that follow are illustrative rather than exhaustive. At the outset, I should clarify that these views focus on explaining the original referent in these poems, which is different from asking if and how these passages affiliate with a later referent (like Jesus and the Church) in a canonical reading.

1 The Servant as Israel. Marvin Sweeney represents a common Jewish interpretation by viewing God's Servant as Israel in all of these passages.[1]

---

1 One should note, however, that the Targum interprets these songs messianically. The LXX, by adding 'Israel' and 'Jacob' in 42.1, at least reads 42.1–4 corporately. Ibn Ezra (Friedländer 1873: 247) explains

Amid an unfolding court case that argues for Yahweh's elite sovereignty (41.1—42.13), God's Servant in 42.1-4 is the same servant already identified as 'Israel, my servant' in 41.8. This Servant will be God's means of bringing justice to the world (Sweeney 2016: 74, 78—80). Isaiah 49—54 shifts to a focus on restoring Zion's relationship with God. In Isaiah 49.1-6, God's Servant, named Israel (49.3), will declare to those abroad that they can return home to Zion. Isaiah 50.4-9 depicts how Israel, God's Servant, trusted in God even amid the nation's suffering. Ultimately, in Isaiah 53, the people of Israel understand why God hardened them (ch. 6) – their suffering amid hardness of heart resulted in a purification of sin and a repair in their breach with God. The Suffering Servant, then, is Israel who suffers in exile, and such suffering ultimately enables a return to Zion.[2] One challenge with this view, raised often throughout the centuries, is with how Israel as God's Servant can have a mission to Israel (cf. 49.3-6). This creates difficulty in explaining parts of the last three Servant Songs.

2 The Servant as a messianic figure. Jan Koole argues that all the Servant Songs are messianic.[3] In Isaiah 42.1-4, Koole acknowledges that Israel seems to be the referent, yet on the other occasions where Israel is called 'Servant' its reference to Israel is explicit. So, since 'Israel' is not mentioned in 42.1-4 and given the tremendous scope of the task in 42.1-4, the text speaks of a messiah figure (1997: 214-15). In Isaiah 49.1-6, God's Servant Messiah 'stands in' for Israel, as the true Israel, to bring Israel and the nations to God (1998: 2-7). In Isaiah 50.4-9 and 52.13—53.12, the role of suffering in the Messiah's mission is amplified and explained.

3 The Servant as Cyrus (42.1-4) and then the prophet (49.1-6; 50.4-9; ch. 53). Joseph Blenkinsopp (2002) recognizes a movement from Isaiah 40—48 to Isaiah 49—55. Within Isaiah 40—48, Cyrus is the key figure God will use (cf. 41.8; 44.26—45.13) in the re-establishment of Jacob-Israel. Since in the ancient world the Persian king was seen as the means of justice and order, it is likely that the Servant empowered to bring justice across the globe in

---

Isaiah 53 as if it were Israel, yet at the end reveals that he believes all four songs refer to the prophet.

2 Ulrich Berges (2012) also holds a corporate view. In Isa. 42.1-4, the exiles (*golah*) view themselves as God's servant, taking God's justice and Torah to the nations (2012: 337). Those returning from exile saw themselves as taking on the role of true Israel, restoring Israel back to God in 49.1-6 (2012: 344-5). In 50.4-9, a group of prophets reflect on their experiences back in Jerusalem. After these redactions, Jews among the Diaspora came to realize that although they despised Zion (those left behind), Zion's suffering was actually on behalf of the offences of the Diaspora Jews (2012: 379-81).

3 See also Chisholm 2006.

42.1–4 is Cyrus (2002: 210–11). When one reaches Isaiah 49—55, however, it is apparent that Cyrus 'has not lived up to expectations', so the prophet takes over the mantle of the Servant. The prophet suffers in the task of serving as a light to the nations and bringing people back to God (49.1–6; 50.4–9), yet the members of the community come to recognize that the prophet actually bore their sins through his silent suffering (2002: 351). One challenge with this view, raised by Childs (2001: 325), is that Cyrus's role in chapter 41 is violent, whereas the Servant of chapter 42 establishes justice gently, so identifying 42.1–4 with Cyrus seems unlikely.

4 The Servant as Israel (42.1–4) and then the prophet (49.1–6; 50.4–9; ch. 53). The most popular position among scholars today is that the Servant in Isaiah 42.1–4 is Israel and in the other songs is the prophet.[4] Within Isaiah 40—48, the focus is on God's plans for Jacob-Israel. In 41.8–9, Israel and Jacob are referred to as 'my servant' by God ('But you, Israel, my servant'), so when God says 'Here is my servant' in 42.1 it is natural to have Israel as the referent. Although Isaiah 42.1–4 presents Israel as being God's agent of gentle justice across the globe, Israel as God's Servant is revealed to be 'blind' and 'deaf' (42.18–19), and chapter 48 concludes 40—48 by depicting the continued spiritual recalcitrance of Israel. In the wake of Israel's failure as God's Servant, an individual Servant comes into view in 49.1–6. For several reasons this Servant resembles a prophet. Speaking in the first person suggests that the prophet (Second Isaiah) is speaking of God's call to be a prophet. Additionally, the mission of the Servant is prophetic; God has made his mouth like a sword (49.2) in order to bring Israel and the nations back to God. Isaiah 50.4–9 has a similar focus, as this Servant speaks (again in the first person) of God having 'given me the tongue of a teacher, that I may know how to sustain the weary with a word' (50.4). Increasingly, there is a focus on the suffering of this prophetic Servant. Isaiah 49.7 briefly mentions the Servant's suffering, as the Servant is addressed as one despised and abhorred. In 50.4–9, the prophet speaks of being beaten and spat on, and having his beard torn out. Then, in Isaiah 53, clarity comes as to how suffering can be so integral to God's plan to restore Israel and the nations to God. Second Isaiah has been beaten, perhaps killed, and the culprits have come to see that the prophet was bearing their own guilt.

---

4 For examples of this view, see Goldingay and Payne (2006), most essays in Janowski and Stuhlmacher (2004), Lessing (2011) and Wilcox and Paton-Williams (1988). H. G. M. Williamson (1998: 113–66) articulates a similar schema, yet he does not deal with Isa. 50.4–9 and chapter 53.

My own inclination is towards a view similar to the fourth view – that Israel is the original reference in 42.1–4 and that the historical experiences of a prophet could be the soil from which the other three passages spring. But in terms of an ancient referent I do not think 'Who is the Suffering Servant?' is the *best* question to be asking for a few reasons. First, even if Isaiah 42.1–4 originally described Israel, and the other songs might derive from the experiences of the historical prophet, these are now set within a literary context that opens a window for us to envisage God's future acts. In this way, these songs create a sort of eschatological, even messianic, expectation. Even if Israel failed in exile to carry out its calling, might it do so in the future? Even if the prophet's suffering became a means of bringing people to God, could not this prefigure a similar and yet greater act in the future? It seems that in the canonical form of Isaiah, the concern is not with identifying the ancient referent but with how these passages provide a lens for hoping for and discerning God's forthcoming acts of redemption. Brevard Childs (2001: 422) captures this sentiment:

> I have argued in my exegesis that the canonical shape of the book of Isaiah shows a Suffering Servant figure who was not simply viewed as a figure of the past, but assigned a central and continuing theological role in relation to the life of the redeemed community of Israel.

Second, and related, such an obsession with *who* the Suffering Servant was overlooks the literary function of these texts. David J. A. Clines (1976: 25) asks an important question:

> What if the force of the poem – to say nothing of the poetry of the poem – lies in its very unforthcomingness, its refusal to be precise and to give *information*, its stubborn concealment of the kind of data that critical scholarship yearns to gets its hands on as the building-blocks for the construction of its hypotheses?

Clines reminds us that a poem like Isaiah 53, instead of merely delivering historical information, works to envisage an alternative world and in the process to invite us as readers into a new way of viewing our present world and the future (1976: 53–4, 63). In this respect, Isaiah 53 projects a world in front of itself and invites us to consider God, his ways, and our identity in the light of that. So, perhaps the better question for us is 'What does Isaiah 53 envisage?' To this we will now turn.

What does Isaiah 53 envisage?

Isaiah 53 presents us with two complementary vantage points on the Suffering Servant: God's viewpoint and the viewpoint of the followers of the Servant. God's declarations about the Servant frame the passage (52.13–15; 53.11–12), and the body of the poem presents the words of those who have come to recognize God's work in the Servant (53.1–3; 4–6; 7–10). The outline of the passage is as follows:

1 Divine vantage point: my ghastly Servant will be exalted (52.13–15);
2 Followers' vantage point on God's Servant (53.1–10):
   (a) we initially rejected the Servant's suffering (53.1–3);
   (b) we came to understand that the Servant's affliction was on our behalf (53.4–6);
   (c) the Servant's innocent suffering was part of God's plan (53.7–10);
3 Divine vantage point: a great heritage awaits the Servant who suffered vicariously (53.11–12).

These multiple vantage points enable us to discern God's view of the Servant and to assess to what extent our experience aligns with or misaligns with the followers' experience in the body of the poem. We will walk through this poem, set aside questions about the Servant's identity, and ask instead 'What does Isaiah 53 envisage?' Although the overall 'sense' of the poem can be detected, we will be alert to the ambiguity and how the poem pushes readers beyond the known categories of their time.

1 Divine vantage point: my ghastly Servant will be exalted (52.13–15)

At the start, God speaks in the first person and declares: 'See, my servant shall prosper' (52.13a).

Although 'servant' is not a positive status today, it conveys a unique and highly esteemed status when one receives this title in association with God in the OT. After all, Abraham (Ps. 105.42), Moses (Exod. 14.31; Num. 12.7, 8; Deut. 34.5), Joshua (Josh. 24.29; Judg. 2.8), and David (e.g. 1 Sam. 19.4; 2 Sam. 3.18; 7.5, 8) are all referred to as God's servants. The idea is that a 'servant' has a significant role to undertake on God's behalf. As we have seen, God's Servant features importantly in the previous Servant Songs, and here God declares that his Servant will 'prosper'. The NRSV translates the Hebrew term *śkl* as 'prosper', but elsewhere in Isaiah the verb means 'to understand' (41.20; 44.18). I am inclined in this direction. The idea, then, could be that God's Servant will ultimately understand why God has called him into a ministry that seems so futile (e.g. 49.4).

The new-found understanding by the Servant will take place when God exalts him:

> he shall be exalted [*rûm*] and lifted up [*nāśā'*],
>   and shall be very high.
> (52.13b–c)

The language God uses of his Servant is striking. In Isaiah 6.1 ('I saw the Lord sitting on a throne, high [*rûm*] and lofty [*nāśā'*]') and 57.15 ('For thus says the high [*rûm*] and lofty [*nāśā'*] one who inhabits eternity, whose name is Holy'), the terms 'high' and 'lofty' are applied to God himself. Throughout the book God is tearing down everything else that is high and lofty, for God alone is to be exalted,[5] so it is astonishing that a figure like God's Servant will attain to an exalted status alongside God.

God recognizes that the exaltation of the Servant will be astonishing for three reasons (52.14–15). For one, the Servant is disfigured:

> so marred was his appearance,
>   beyond human semblance,
> and his form beyond that of mortals . . .
> (52.14b)

Jeremy Schipper, an expert in disability studies within the Hebrew Bible, challenges us to not merely imagine here an able-bodied person who happens to suffer. God speaks of the Servant as 'marred' in appearance, and this 'can connote an unspecified physical disability or disease' (2011: 40). Schipper ponders whether leprosy may be in view, as Duhm had posited. The social experience of this impairment – disability can never be extracted from social experience – leads people to view the Servant as not aligning with what society would expect for a human. He is perceived as an unappealing individual, and perhaps by extension as less than human; he is beyond human semblance.

Related, another reason for astonishment is that this disfigured Servant will have a role as priest among the nations. The NRSV translates 52.15a as

---

5 Isaiah 2.5–21 is a tremendous example of this. Some claim that the combination of *rûm* and *nāśā'* refers only to God in Isaiah, but this is not true. These descriptors apply to all realms of pride among humanity and to those with earthly privilege (cf. 2.12, 13, 14); God will have his day against them.

'so he shall startle many nations'. The term translated as 'startle' reflects a choice to opt for the LXX instead of the Hebrew tradition. In the Hebrew tradition the verb is *nzh*, which means 'sprinkle', and this is preserved in numerous manuscript traditions, so I am inclined to translate this phrase as: 'and he shall sprinkle many nations'.[6] Usually, in Scripture, 'sprinkling' will involve water, oil, and/or blood being spattered. Here we are not told what is sprinkled – is it blood, oil, water, or something else? Often, sprinkling is directed either upon or in front of a non-human object, such as an altar, the curtains in the holy place in the Temple, the mercy seat, or priestly garments. Yet, here humans are in view – 'he will sprinkle *many nations*'. The closest analogies to a human as the recipient of sprinkling that we have in the OT are where there is a sprinkling of oil and blood upon Aaron and his sons (Exod. 29.21; Lev. 8.30) and when there is a sprinkling of blood on to someone unclean from leprosy (Lev. 14.7).[7] In the case of Aaron and his sons, the sprinkling brings cleansing and anointing to allow them to carry out their duties in the presence of the Holy One. If this is called to mind in Isaiah 52.15, the idea is that the disfigured Servant will consecrate many nations for sacred duty in the presence of God. In the case of the leper, sprinkling with blood signifies the cleansing of the individual that allows for the leper's restoration to the Israelite camp. If this is called to mind in 52.15, the idea is that the disfigured Servant will cleanse the unclean nations so that they can become part of God's holy community (Averbeck 2012: 52). Although these are possible readings, we must keep in mind the tremendous ambiguity here. The scope of this sprinkling is unparalleled ('many nations'). It is also not clear what element (blood, water, and/or oil) the Servant actually sprinkles. This poem is pushing beyond the limits of known experience, yet it draws upon known experience in the priestly realm to point in this inconceivable direction – a disfigured Servant who sprinkles many nations.

The final astonishing feature of the Servant's exaltation is how kings will respond to him.

> kings shall shut their mouths because of him;
> for that which had not been told them they shall see,
>   and that which they had not heard they shall contemplate.
> (52.15b)

---

6 For a discussion, see Goldingay and Payne (2006: 2/294–5), who opt for the Hebrew reading too.

7 Some appeal to the covenant ceremony in Exod. 24.8, but a different verb is used there (*zrq*).

In the OT, the idiom of shutting one's mouth occurs in situations where a person has no power over the corollary. In Psalm 107.42, wickedness shuts its mouth when the upright see and delight in God's deliverance of the needy. Similarly, in Job 5.16, according to Eliphaz, God delivers the needy so the poor have hope, and as a result injustice again shuts its mouth. The kings in Isaiah 52.15b come to a point of acknowledging their powerlessness in view of the Servant's exaltation; they shut their mouths. The reason for this is that they have become unexpected witnesses to the glory of the Servant. This is unexpected because they see 'that which had not been told [spr] them' and contemplate 'that which they had not heard [šm']'. Frequently, when the verbs spr ('to tell, to recount') and šm' ('to hear') occur together, the idea is that of Israel recounting the ways of God to subsequent generations. These presumably Gentile kings have not heard the stories and promises of God, but now they are looking at and contemplating something they were not prepared for. They have seen an exalted, disfigured Servant sprinkle many nations.

Thus, God's vantage point on his Servant opens this poem in 52.13–15. God's Servant will reach a point of understanding as God exalts him with a status worthy of deity. This is astonishing because the Servant is disfigured, yet takes on a priestly role of sprinkling nations, and the kings of the nations are unexpected witnesses to the glorification of this mangled Servant.

2 Followers' vantage point on God's Servant (53.1–10)

After God's vantage point on his Servant ('*my* servant', emphasis added) in 52.13–15, a new voice arises: that of a 'we' group that speaks about God's Servant and God's work through the Servant. This 'we' group consists of the followers of the Servant. In verses 1–3, these followers recount their initial rejection of the disfigured Servant. They thought of the Servant like one would a 'young plant' or a 'root out of dry ground' (53.2) – nothing promising. What is more, in language reminiscent of God's depiction of the Servant's disfigurement (52.14), they saw nothing attractive about his appearance (53.2). Again, the Servant's disfigurement has social implications, as he is said to be 'despised and abandoned by men', 'like one who causes faces to hide from him' (53.3, my translations). This is a man of pains (mak'ōb) and acquainted with illness (ḥōlî, 53.3). Given their initial assessment of and rejection of the disfigured, despised Servant, the 'we' group appropriately opens this subunit by asking:

Who has believed what we have heard?
    And to whom has the arm of the LORD been revealed?
    (53.1)

Who would believe that God's arm (cf. 51.9; 52.10) of salvation is seen in this diseased servant? They certainly did not believe it at first.

The followers of the Servant proceed in 53.4–6 by explaining that they came to see that the affliction of the disfigured Servant was actually vicarious suffering (suffering for another). The 'he' for 'us' language infiltrates these verses, making the vicarious nature of the Servant's suffering readily apparent:

> *he* has borne *our* infirmities
>   and carried *our* diseases . . .
> *he* was wounded for *our* transgressions,
>   crushed for *our* iniquities;
> upon *him* was the punishment that made *us* whole,
>   and by *his* bruises *we* are healed . . .
> and the LORD has laid on *him*
>   the iniquity of *us all*.
> (53.4, 5, 6)

Although these followers of the Servant now see how the Servant's suffering is vicarious, there is tremendous ambiguity as to what all this means. The only other instance in the OT where someone is said to bear (*nś'*) infirmity (*ḥōlî*) is in the book of Jeremiah, where the prophet uses 'infirmity' as a metaphor for the burden of prophetic ministry that he bears (Jer. 10.19); yet, this is not the same as bearing other people's infirmities. Only here in the OT does someone 'carry' (*sbl*) a 'disease' (*mak'ōb*) or is someone 'pierced' (*ḥll*) for 'transgressions' (*peša'*) and 'crushed' (*dk'*) for 'iniquity' (*'āwôn*). Nowhere else do we read of a 'punishment [*mûsar*]' that brings wholeness (*šālôm*); nor do we hear of anyone 'laying' (*pg'*; better translated 'imposing') on another 'iniquity' (*'āwôn*). Such language may now be familiar in the Church, but the very boundaries of OT thought and linguistic convention are being pressed into a new mode of vision.

Amid the ambiguity and perplexity that would certainly arise when reading this passage in its ancient context, the vision builds upon several touch points within the world view of Ancient Israel. This allows for a 'sense' of what the passage is communicating to come through, even amid the haze of ambiguity. One of those touch points relates to *divine punishment*. 'Infirmities' (Isa. 53.4) are at times viewed as divine judgement in the OT (Deut. 28.59, 61), although this is not always the case. 'Diseases' (Isa. 53.4), better translated as 'pains', can be metaphorical for living under the judgement of God (Ps. 32.10; Jer. 30.15; Lam. 1.12, 18). The notion of divine punishment becomes explicit in the final line of Isaiah 53.4 which reads: 'we accounted him stricken, struck down by

God'. God is the one they perceived as striking him, as being 'struck down' is also a sign of judgement in the Hebrew Bible (Lev. 26.21). The idea is that the Servant has borne the punishment of disease and pain that they deserved. How this can actually take place we are not told. Yet, amid the ambiguity, the touch point of divine punishment provides an avenue of sense for ancient readers that points to God's Servant bearing the divine punishment, signified in infirmities and pains, which belongs to those who are now the followers of the Servant.

Another touch point is *priestly ritual*. The mention of 'transgressions' and 'iniquities' in verse 5 casts light on the Servant's bearing of the people's infirmities and diseases in verse 4, as does God's assessment in 53.11 ('he shall bear their iniquities'). As one attempts to make sense of this, an avenue emerges within priestly ritual. On the Day of Atonement, a priest will lay hands on a live goat and confess Israel's sins and iniquities (Lev. 16.21). He is said to 'put them [the sins] on the goat's head' (16.21 NIV) and then the goat will 'carry' (*nś'*) all of their iniquity (16.22) into a desolate land. In another passage in Leviticus, the priests are confronted for not eating the sin offering; instead, they let it burn entirely. The reason this is problematic is because God 'gave it [the sin offering] to you [the priests] to bear [*nś'*] the iniquity of the congregation, to make atonement on their behalf before the LORD' (10.17, my translation). Implied in this statement is that the priests are 'bearing' the iniquity of the people through partaking of the meat in the sanctuary. If, as the Servant 'bears' infirmity and disease, he is also bearing iniquity (cf. 53.4–5, 11), then the priestly idea of something (a goat) or someone (a priest) carrying a community's iniquity certainly resonates with the language of 53.4–6, 11.[8] The Servant is bearing the people's iniquity as a priest or goat would. The irony, however, of the Servant participating in a priestly ritual is that his deformities would have naturally ruled him out from participating in such a ritual, whether as the goat or as the priest (cf. Lev. 22.25; Mal. 1.13–14; Schipper 2011: 40).

In the final verses of the followers' vantage point on the Suffering Servant (53.7–10), they reflect upon the Servant's experience amid suffering and God's involvement. Throughout Isaiah 53, 'there is *no concrete action* that the Servant does apart from letting everything happen to him' (Clines 1976: 42). A string of passive verbs in verses 7–8 displays this:

---

8   There is a striking parallel with Lam. 5.7 ESV where the exiles say, 'Our fathers sinned, and are no more; and we bear [*sbl*] their iniquities.' This parallel gives some basis for a corporate interpretation of Isaiah 53.

He *was oppressed*, and he *was afflicted* . . .
like a lamb that is *led to the slaughter* . . .
By a perversion of justice he *was taken away* . . .
    he *was cut off* from the land of the living,
    stricken for the transgression of my people.
(53.7, 8, my emphasis)

This Servant is being acted against, and this is clearly an occasion of grave injustice ('by a perversion of justice'); verse 9 goes on to specify the innocence of the Servant, for 'he had done no violence, and there was no deceit in his mouth'. Ultimately, the Servant dies under this oppression, although some debate this. Verse 8 states that 'he was cut off from the land of the living'. Being 'cut off' (*gzr*) finds a parallel in Ezekiel 37.11, where Israel is described as being dead bones, 'cut off', in the grave. The 'land of the living' refers to being alive in the realm of earth rather than dead and in the realm of Sheol (cf. Isa. 38.11; Ezek. 26.20). So, when Jeremiah's enemies say that they want to 'cut him off [*krt*] from the land of the living' and to wipe his name out (11.19), they want to kill him. The followers profess that the Servant of God has silently been oppressed and afflicted to the point of death.

Even though the Servant dies, the followers of the Servant anticipate life continuing for the Servant:

When you make his life an offering for sin [*'āšām*],
    he shall see his offspring, and shall prolong his days . . .
(53.10b)

The NRSV translates *'āšām* as 'an offering for sin'. The key idea behind the *'āšām* is to deal with obligations, whether towards God or other people, due to guilt (Janowski 2004: 67–9). This guilt offering functions to repair a breach. So, the Philistines send back an *'āšām* with the ark they had captured, as they were guilty towards God for confiscating God's ark which belonged in Israel (1 Sam. 6.3, 4). In that case, the *'āšām* was not a sacrificial animal but instead golden tumours and golden mice given as gifts to repair the breach with Israel. An *'āšām* can also be a sacrifice in the form of a ram and further restitution (Lev. 5.14—6.7). What is unique in Isaiah 53.10 is that the human life of the Servant is the *'āšām*. Somehow, by offering his life the Servant will remedy the guilt of his followers.

After making this 'offering', the Servant's future comes into view in the second half of 53.10b. The combination of 'seeing' (*r'h*) and 'offspring' (*zera'*) only occurs here in the Hebrew Bible, but a similar idea emerges in Genesis 50.23 where we are told that 'Joseph saw Ephraim's children of the third generation'. The idea that Joseph 'saw' (*r'h*) 'children' (*bēn*) points both to Joseph's longevity and to the blessing of seeing his family line continuing across many generations. The following clause in Isaiah 53.10 continues this emphasis on longevity, as the Servant will 'prolong his days' (cf. Exod. 20.12; Prov. 28.16). Many questions naturally arise for us in an attempt to nail this verse down. How can a human offer his life as a guilt offering? Are the 'offspring' literal or figurative? How can the Servant live for any length of days when the text said he was cut off from the land of the living? Again, this depiction is venturing beyond the boundary waters of the Old Testament world view and leaves its vision hanging.

The followers of the Servant are articulating a strange message about the Suffering Servant, yet they appeal to their conviction that this is in fact God's will. Verses 6 and 10 make this explicit:

> ⁶ and the LORD has laid on him
> the iniquity of us all . . .
>
> ¹⁰ Yet it was the will of the LORD to crush him with pain . . .
> through him the will of the LORD shall prosper.
> (53.6, 10)

Again, these verses encroach on new territory. Although verse 6 reads familiarly to Christian readers, the Hebrew expression is strange. Usually, the Hebrew at the beginning of the expression would be translated as 'The LORD entreated/ encountered him', yet the occurrence of the direct object ('the iniquity of us all') complicates the typical idea. The closest parallel is in Jeremiah 15.11, which reads: 'surely I have imposed enemies on you'. This supports the reading: 'the LORD has laid on him the iniquity of us all.' Although this linguistic expression is quite novel, verse 10 strategically resonates with verse 5 ('crush'; 'pain'). There, the 'we' group, the followers of the Servant, claimed that 'he was . . . crushed for our iniquities' (53.5), and now they underscore that it was God's will to crush him (53.10).

Thus, the members of the 'we' group offer their vantage point on the Suffering Servant in 53.1–10. They invite us into their journey of conversion. They began by viewing the disfigured Suffering Servant as God-forsaken and insignificant (53.1–3). Now, however, they recognize that the suffering of the Servant was vicarious, endured on their behalf (53.4–6). They have witnessed the passive, innocent suffering of the Servant and expect him to live for a length of days (53.7–10). This they believe is all part of God's plan. They are now followers of the Servant and wonder if others will believe their report that the arm of God has been at work in a despised servant to bear their sufferings and sin. Their vantage point on the Suffering Servant is laced with ambiguity and pushes this vision beyond the parameters of thought that we find elsewhere in the Old Testament.

3 Divine vantage point: a great heritage awaits the Servant who suffered vicariously (53.11–12)

The passage concludes where it began – with God speaking in the first person about his Servant:

> [11]Out of his anguish he shall see light
> he shall find satisfaction through his knowledge.
> > The righteous one, my servant, shall make many
> > > righteous,
> > and he shall bear their iniquities.
> [12] Therefore I will allot him a portion with the great,
> > and he shall divide the spoil with the strong;
> because he poured out himself to death,
> > and was numbered with the transgressors;
> yet he bore the sin of many,
> > and made intercession for the transgressors.
> (53.11–12)

Virtually every clause in these final two verses has no equivalent in the Old Testament. What does it mean to 'see out of his anguish'? This is so ambiguous that the LXX adds the word 'light' after 'see' (53.11), as is reflected in the NRSV's translation. What 'knowledge' will bring the Servant 'satisfaction' (53.11)? How can God's Servant, God's Righteous One, make others righteous? Who are 'the great' that the Servant will have a portion with? We are again treading on unfamiliar territory, entering a dreamlike scenario where the language touches real life yet extends in incompressible directions. Several matters, however, are clear even if the particulars are opaque.

First, God is intentionally affirming and complementing the viewpoint of the 'we' group from 53.1–10. When God says 'he shall bear their iniquities' (53.11), he draws upon wording from 53.4–5. By doing so, God synthesizes the 'we' group's statements about the Servant 'bearing' infirmity and disease

(53.4) and the Servant being crushed for our 'iniquities' (53.5). The Servant's vicarious suffering is summarized by God as 'bearing their iniquities' (see 53.11). Another connection arises between verses 10 and 11. In verse 10, according to the 'we' group, the Servant's 'life' (*nepeš*) is offered, and as a result he will 'see' (*r'h*) his offspring. God affirms this by stating: 'from the anguish of his life [*nepeš*] he will see [*r'h*]' (53.11, my translation). Although the LXX adds 'light', a reader would probably draw upon verse 10 and fill in the blank with 'offspring'. This knowledge of seeing his offspring will satisfy him. A final connection, among others, between God's final word and the followers' vantage point is 'he will make intercession [*pg'*] for the transgressors' (53.12c, my translation). In this verse, God uses the verb *pg'* from verse 6, which we translated as 'YHWH imposed [*pg'*] the iniquity of us all on him' (53.6b). In verse 12, God clarifies that the divine imposition of iniquity (53.6) equates with the Servant playing the role of intercessor (53.12).

Second, it is also clear that God keeps a spotlight on the wide scope of his Servant's work. The 'we' group speaks only about how the Servant suffered vicariously for them. While this is true, God mentions the 'many' [*rabbîm*] several times: 'The righteous one, my servant, shall make *many* righteous ... he bore the sin of *many*' (53.11, 12c). Additionally, the term translated 'great' ('I will allot [the Servant] a portion with the great', 53.12a) is the same term as 'many', so *rabbîm* occurs three times in these two verses. This brings us back to God's words at the opening of the entire passage: '*many* ... were astonished at him ... he will sprinkle *many* nations' (52.14, 15, my translation). As in Isaiah 49.1–7, God's plans for the Servant extend beyond the borders of Israel. The nations too will be beneficiaries of the Servant's vicarious suffering.

Third, God reiterates that a tremendous future awaits his Suffering Servant. It is utterly ambiguous as to what it means for God to allot the Servant 'a portion with the many' (53.12a, my translation). Yet, the general sense is that a great heritage awaits the Servant among the 'many' whom he makes righteous and the 'many' whose sin he bears (53.12). If the Servant has died, is this speaking about his legacy among his followers? Is this speaking about a heritage in the afterlife? If the Servant did not actually die, is this referring to a Job-like restoration of abundance after suffering (Job 42)? Answers are not forthcoming.

Thus, the poem concludes, as it started, with God speaking about his Suffering Servant. Amid tremendous ambiguity, we can grasp that God agrees with the followers of the Servant that the Servant suffered vicariously to intercede for sin and that a great hope awaits God's Suffering Servant, yet God reminds us that the Servant's work is for 'many'.

Isaiah 53, the reader, and an open text

Having traversed the three parts of this passage (Isa. 52.13–15; 53.1–10; 53.11–12), two questions emerge that warrant further reflection: 'What's the purpose of the two voices (those of God and the 'we' group) in Isaiah 53?' and 'What do we do with all the ambiguity in this passage?'

As described above, the Suffering Servant passage opens (52.13–15) and closes (53.11–12) with God's voice. In between, the voice shifts to a 'we' group who are followers of the Servant (53.1–10). Why these two voices? Framing the passage with the divine voice gives credence to such a perplexing message – that a disfigured Servant would suffer vicariously for the sins of others to make them righteous and has a glorious future awaiting him. Questions about what this means, and how it can be, would certainly arise, but God's voice underscores that this is true and trustworthy. Why not just use the divine voice throughout, then? The 'we' group importantly invites the reader into its experience, its journey from rejecting the Servant to coming to see God's arm working through the suffering of this Servant. If readers resonate with the 'we' group, they will recognize that they should be the ones suffering (Clines 1976: 63) and that the Servant's suffering is on their behalf. The readers will come to wonder whether anyone else could possibly believe this message (53.1). Thus, the two voices are meant to authorize the perplexing message (divine voice) and to invite readers into a journey towards believing this message ('we' voice).

Now for our second question: 'What do we do with all the ambiguity in this passage?' Although a general sense of what Isaiah 53 is envisaging can be detected, ambiguity abounds, reminding us that especially for the original audience this passage pushes beyond the linguistic and conceptual modes of the time. This results in a vision that touches upon known realities yet transcends those boundaries. In some respects, the passage is like a dream. Usually our dreams have some connection with what we know of reality, yet these are bent and extended into new, perplexing directions. Isaiah 53 draws upon known realities: Israel has prophets, like Moses and Jeremiah, who suffer in God's mission; there is a priestly system with sprinkling and within which priests and goats carry iniquity; and Israel knows through exile what it means to suffer for the sins of others (cf. Lam. 5.7) and to deserve and receive divine punishment. As Isaiah 53 draws upon these and other known realities, they open new horizons towards understanding. With no referent in their midst that would make sense of these ambiguities, the vision would seem to be set on the horizon, opening up a new vision for divine activity, yet awaiting greater understanding.

G. B. Caird (1980: 57–8) illustrates the openness of this passage by picturing it as a job description advertisement:

> it describes in some detail a person whose identity is not yet known to the writer . . . He [the prophet] was undoubtedly aware that many famous men, such as Moses and Jeremiah, had sat for the composite portrait he was drawing. What he could not know was that in the end there would be only one applicant for the post.

The 'open' and ambiguous nature of Isaiah 53 seems intentional on God's part as it prepares for the Person who alone would completely fulfil this passage and bring new clarity to what had been ambiguous in the text. In Jesus Christ, a new layer of understanding comes that clarifies the intersection of vicarious suffering for the sins of others, rejection, suffering, human death, exaltation, the nations, seeing offspring, sprinkling, divine will, and more. Within the field of Old Testament studies, our inclination is to begin with understanding a passage in its original context before moving forward to Jesus, yet when there is such a lack of clarity in Isaiah 53 in the original context one should be willing to consider if this ambiguity is intentional to prepare for the fullness of time when Christ's life, suffering, death, resurrection, and Ascension would cast great light upon these ambiguities. And one is left mouth opened and jaw dropped in awe of God's kindness in providing a witness to a Suffering Servant that can only be said to derive from the inspiration of God himself.

The Suffering Servant in Isaiah's story

As has been our custom in the previous chapters, let's situate the Suffering Servant within the four phases of the story Isaiah tells.

By the time we reach the Suffering Servant, Phases 1 and 2 of Isaiah's story have passed. God has judged Israel and Judah through Assyria and Babylon, resulting in exile, as expected in Isaiah 1—39. In Phase 2, there is the expectation that God would use King Cyrus of Persia to initiate a rebuilding of God's temple in Jerusalem for Israel-Jacob (chs 40—48).

Now, in Phase 3, the Suffering Servant takes centre stage (chs 49—55). Here the central questions are: *how* can Zion's children return to the holy city of Zion, and *who* in fact are Zion's children? Immediately after summons for the exiles to 'Leave Babylon' (48.20) and to 'Leave, leave, go out from there!' (52.11, my translations), the author strategically places

Suffering Servant passages (49.1-7; 52.13—53.12; Blenkinsopp 2002: 349). The impression one is left with is that the greater return from exile (something beyond Cyrus's initiative) requires the mission of the Suffering Servant to enable it to happen. And integral to the Servant's mission is that the children who return to Zion consist of a reconstituted people. The Servant's mission would be too small if he restored only Israel to God (49.5-6). Rather, the Servant would be a light to the nations, bringing God's 'salvation . . . to the end of the earth' (49.6). The Servant would sprinkle many nations (52.15). So, a homecoming to a Zion greater than Cyrus's, where God himself will reign and rule (52.7), will require a work by the Suffering Servant by which a new community is instituted. The centrality of God's Suffering Servant in instituting this new community becomes apparent through the shift from 'servant' (singular) to 'servants' (plural) after chapter 53. The offspring of the Servant are the 'servants' of the LORD (54.17; 56.6; 65.8, 9, 13, 14, 15; 66.14; Beuken 1990). They become the community of the Servant who live faithfully as they await God's eschatological judgement and salvation (Phase 4).

As one steps into the wider story of Isaiah, a natural question is whether or not the Suffering Servant of Isaiah 40—55 is the Davidic King hoped for in Isaiah 9 and 11. As I have argued elsewhere (Abernethy 2016: 119–70), I believe it is important to keep the Suffering Servant and the Davidic King distinct in the outlook of the book of Isaiah. Their roles are decidedly different, as the Davidic King establishes justice particularly in the realm of society and the Suffering Servant plays more of a prophetic and priestly role in reconciling nations to God through suffering. Christopher North (1948: 218), who argues that the Servant Songs are messianic, states this well:

> I do not think that anything is to be gained by attempts to prove that the Servant is the Davidic Messiah of Isa. ix. and xi. Though there are undoubtedly kingly features in the Servant, there is nothing in the Songs to indicate that he was to be an anointed king . . . The Servant is a soteriological rather than a political Messianic figure.

One could refer to both the King and Servant as 'messianic', yet one would want to clarify the differences between the hopes for the messianic King and messianic Servant. Conflating the two too quickly results in a loss; even in the early Church, especially Tertullian, the early apologists argue that the Old Testament had two messiahs in view, a messiah of glory (king) and a messiah of humble suffering (servant). One can still profess that in Jesus there is a fusion of these two offices, yet in Jesus' first coming the messianic characteristics of the Suffering Servant are most prominent. Jesus' fulfilment of his royal messianic office will be more central in his second coming.

Isaiah 53 in Christian reception

Within the Christian reception of Isaiah 53, there are two prominent trends. The most prominent trend is to view Isaiah 53 as bearing witness to Jesus. Another practice has been for Christians to draw upon the Suffering Servant passage as a lens for viewing the Church and the world around them. As we will see, both trends have a basis in the New Testament.

Witness to Jesus Christ

Isaiah 53 serves as a lens for interpreting Jesus Christ in the New Testament. Michael Wilkins (2012: 112) notes that 'the New Testament authors both quote and allude to the wording or concepts of Isaiah 53 at least fifty times'. In the Gospels (Wilkins 2012: 115–32), Isaiah 53 bears witness to Jesus' being a Nazarene (*nēṣer*; 'plant' in Isa. 53.2) and the Lamb of God (John 1.29; Isa. 53.7), to his ministry of healing (Matt. 8.16–17; Isa. 53.4), reaching the Gentiles (Matt. 12.15–21; Isa. 42.1), unbelief by the Jews (John 12.38; Isa. 53.1), his pouring out his blood for many (Matt. 26.28; Isa. 53.12b), his silence en route to slaughter (Matt. 26.63; 27.12–14; Isa. 53.7), and his burial with the rich (Matt. 27.57–60; Isa. 53.9). Rikki E. Watts (1998) shows how Jesus' statement that 'the Son of Man came not to be served but to serve, and to give his life a ransom for many' (Mark 10.45) resonates with Isaiah 53 in Jesus' use of servant language, being given over to death, and acting on behalf of many. Watts (1998: 143) states:

> Mark 10.45 may be said to be an exegetical summary of the Isaianic New Exodus from the perspective of the 'Servant': the ministering 'death' of the true 'Servant' Israel, that is, Jesus, in compensation for the sins of 'the many' is the means by which Yahweh effects their redemption.

In Acts, Isaiah 53 provides the starting point for Philip to explain to the Ethiopian eunuch 'the good news about Jesus' (Acts 8.35). For Paul, as J. Ross Wagner (1998) argues, Isaiah 51—55 offers a story within which Paul takes on the role of proclaiming the message about Jesus as the Suffering Servant to the Gentiles, those who have not heard; hence, the quotation of Isaiah 52.15 in Romans 15.21. Thus, there is little doubt that Isaiah 53 was a central passage during the time of the apostles for articulating the divine purpose behind Jesus' life and journey to the cross.

The early Christian apologists and interpreters also appeal to Isaiah 53 to defend the Christian faith. Justin Martyr, in his *Dialogue with Trypho*, appeals to Isaiah 53 to explain Jewish rejection of Jesus (53.1; 2003: 50). He (2003: 64) says: 'Isaiah speaks as though in the person of the apostles, and says, *Lord, who has believed our report, and to whom is the arm of the Lord revealed?*' Additionally, he draws extensively upon Isaiah 53 to defend how a curse like the crucifixion is fitting for a messiah (2003: 140). Tertullian, in his 'Answer to the Jews' (1885a: 172) and 'The five books against Marcion' (1885c: 325–6), quotes from Isaiah 53 to make the case that the prophets anticipate two advents, one of humility and the second of honour and glory. From Eusebius to Jerome to Aquinas there is a common pattern of explaining these Servant Songs as predicting God's mission to the Gentiles, the hardening of Jews, and the death and resurrection of the Messiah, Jesus. Luther (1972: 221) continues this trend, yet Isaiah 53 also becomes a basis for supporting justification by faith, a hallmark doctrine of the Reformation. Luther states:

> But here the prophet says, 'He for us'. It is difficult for the flesh to repudiate all its resources, to turn away from self, and to be carried over to Christ. It is for us who have merited nothing not to have regard for our merits but simply to cling to the Word between heaven and earth, even though we do not feel it. Unless we have been instructed by God, we will not understand this. Therefore I delight in this text as if it were a text of the New Testament.

With Calvin, however, one finds a more nuanced interpretation of the Servant Songs. He ponders how Isaiah 42.1–4 fits within a context that speaks of the end of Babylonian captivity. He (2010: 3/284) explains that Babylonian captivity ends in the restoration of the Church under Christ's reign, so it is fitting for the prophet to 'interweave' future grace in this context. On Isaiah 49.1–6, he recognizes the challenge associated with the prophet being referred to as Israel. He (2010: 4/11) states: 'This passage must not be limited to the person of Christ, and ought not be referred to Israel alone.' Instead, Christ as head and the children of God as his body are both in view in this passage. On Isaiah 50.4–9, Calvin (2010: 4/52) falls in line with Ibn Ezra who identifies the historical prophet as the one suffering in the passage. On Isaiah 52.13—53.12, Calvin believes it speaks of Christ as the Suffering Servant, yet he also interprets the passage as a mission statement for the

Church. He states (2010: 4/106–7): 'whatever he affirms concerning himself we ought to understand as belonging also to us. Christ has been given to us, and therefore to us also belongs his ministry.' Although Christ is the primary vantage point for Calvin's reading of Isaiah 42.1–4, 49.1–6, and chapter 53, Calvin's attention to detail and historical consideration leads him to offer a more nuanced interpretation that informs our second trend in the reception of Isaiah 53 – viewing it as a lens for the Church (see 'Isaiah 53 as a lens for the Church' below).

Isaiah 53 has also had a tremendous impact in the realms of art, music, and literature in view of its witness to Jesus. John Sawyer (1996: 83–99) has catalogued this extensively, so I mention one theme within art that is particularly striking. As noted above, the deformities and abhorrence of the Suffering Servant call to mind a leprous individual, as Duhm and then Schipper argue. It is striking to me how this interpretation of Jesus in the light of Isaiah 53 manifests itself in art, where Jesus is depicted as leprous. In the Latin Vulgate, the notion of 'stricken' is translated in Isaiah 53.4 as *quasi leprosus*, which can mean 'like leprosy'. As Isaiah 53 figured prominently in the liturgy of Holy Week, the *quasi leprosus* notion in Isaiah 53 was well known across the Church. This led artists to depict the suffering Christ in such a light. In one image on an altarpiece created for a hospital ward in Isenheim, France, Matthias Grünewald (c. AD 1480–1528) portrays Jesus on the cross with diseased sores across his entire body.[9] In a host of other images from a similar time, sores and scabs are noticeable across Christ's legs and body as he stands trial before Pilate.[10] These artists drew upon Isaiah 53's vision of the Suffering Servant being deformed and *quasi leprosus* to capture Christ's appearance and social rejection amid his suffering and crucifixion. These artistic representations of Christ's suffering and death are not merely recounting what one finds in the Gospels. They allow the particular imagery from Isaiah 53 to inform their depiction of the suffering Christ, the man of sorrows.

The literary reception of Isaiah 53 is also fascinating. Some suggest that Philippians 2.5–11 is originally a hymn that models Christ's descent to death followed by glory after Isaiah 53. Bernard of Clairvaux's 'O Sacred Head, Now Wounded' (twelfth century) takes on the persona of the 'we' group of our passage. He confesses:

---

9   For a discussion of this piece and the *quasi leprosus* theme during the fifteenth to sixteenth centuries, see Marrow 1979: 52–4.

10   See esp. images 261–4 in Schiller 1972. These images from across Germany date from the fifteenth century.

What thou, my Lord, hast suffered
Was all for sinners' gain;
Mine, mine was the transgression,
But thine the deadly pain.

Philip Bliss's 'Hallelujah! What a Saviour!' (nineteenth century) begins with Isaiah 53.3:

Man of Sorrows! what a name,
For the Son of God who came,
Ruined Sinners to reclaim.
Hallelujah! What a Saviour!

In the realm of fiction, C. S. Lewis's novel *Till We Have Faces* re-mythologizes Psyche and Cupid, and in the process infuses Psyche's life and journey to sacrificial death with Isaiah 53. She touches countless people who are ill, grows weaker and weaker with each touch, and ultimately falls ill herself though many were healed through her touch (1956: 32–3). Her supportive sister Orual says: 'You healed them, and blessed them, and took their filthy disease upon yourself!' (1956: 39). This calls to mind Isaiah 53.4 ('he carried our diseases'). The people ultimately reject Psyche, considering her accursed (1956: 39). Psyche then willingly, silently, accepts the decree that she must die to break the curse of the gods upon the city-state of Glome. As Orual protests Psyche's fate, Pysche asks: 'How can I be the ransom for all Glome unless I die?' (1956: 72) In this way, Lewis casts Psyche in the guise of Isaiah's Suffering Servant, as a Christ figure.

Thus, there is a consistent, recurring affirmation among Christian interpreters, artists, hymn writers, and novelists that Isaiah 53 provides a vantage point for understanding Jesus, the suffering Christ.

Isaiah 53 as a lens for the Church

Isaiah's Suffering Servant not only bears witness to Jesus but has also provided a model for the Christian Church. We saw this in Calvin's interpretation of Isaiah 49 and 53 above. This practice has a strong precedent in the New Testament. Paul claims that his own calling is anchored in the Servant Songs by quoting from Isaiah 49.6 ('I have set you to be a light for the Gentiles, so that you may bring salvation to the ends of the earth', Acts 13.47) and Isaiah 52.15 ('Those who have never been told of him shall see, and those who have never heard of him shall understand', Rom. 15.21). In 1 Peter 2, Christ serves as an example for slaves, since Christ 'committed no sin, and no deceit was found in his mouth' (2.22; quoting Isa. 53.9).

The same pattern of drawing upon Isaiah 53 as a lens to see how the Church should live occurs in the early Church. So in the late first or early second century, Clement of Rome wrote to the believers in the church of Corinth, exhorting them to live with humility:

> For Christ is of those who are humble-minded, and not of those who exalt themselves over His flock. Our Lord Jesus Christ, the Sceptre of the majesty of God, did not come in the pomp of pride or arrogance, although He might have done so, but in a lowly condition, as the Holy Spirit had declared regarding Him.
> (*1 Clement* 16)

Clement then immediately quotes the entirety of Isaiah 53 to justify this summons to humility.

In Luther's commentary, he clearly interprets the Servant Songs christologically. Yet, this does not prevent him from drawing out moral instruction. In his exposition of Isaiah 50.4–9, he instructs Christians to expect insults and negative misinterpretations of their every action by those who resist God's word, yet, like the Servant whose face is like flint, they too can find God's word and Spirit hardening their faces to help them persevere in their calling (1972: 195).

Several more recent examples appropriate Isaiah 53 as a lens for comprehending suffering and oppression in our world today. Jon Sobrino, a Jesuit theologian in El Salvador, utilizes Isaiah's Suffering Servant to conceptualize the innocent suffering and deaths of unnamed thousands in El Salvador. He recounts Oscar Romero's transformation that led to his ministry among the poor: 'He had to learn that the church's place is among the suffering poor. The church must be immersed in the reality of the crucified peoples. The church must become a genuine Servant of Yahweh, as he would later say' (2003: 27). In a homily, while the army was murdering and driving people out of Aguilares, Romero encouraged the suffering people of that town with these words: 'You are the image of the divine victim "pierced for our offenses," of who the first reading speaks to us this morning' (2003: 29). In another sermon two years later, Romero says that Jesus so 'identified with the people that scripture scholars do not know whether the Servant of Yahweh in Isaiah is the suffering people or Christ come to redeem us' (2003: 29). Sobrino also shows how Ignacio Ellacuría, a Jesuit priest in Salvador who was assassinated nearly a decade after Romero, holds a similar outlook. He quotes Ellacuría (Sobrino 2003: 157) as saying:

> This crucified people is the historical continuation of Yahweh's servant, whom the sin of the world continues to deprive of any human decency, and from whom the powerful of this world continue to rob everything, taking everything away, even life, especially life.

Sobrino goes on to call the Church to 'read the songs of Yahweh's servant with the text in one hand and our eyes on the crucified peoples' (2003: 157). He then draws several parallels between Isaiah's Suffering Servant and these crucified peoples. Starvation, sickness, no education, and no healthcare make this people much like the 'man of sorrows, acquainted with grief' (2003: 157–8). Daily poverty has made the people ugly, having no form or beauty like the Servant. They have been despised and rejected, suffering innocently like Isaiah's Servant (2003: 158). Thus, for Sobrino, who draws upon the legacy of Romero and Ellacuría, the Servant Songs provide a lens for portraying those suffering and dying amid oppression today.

Bo Lim has brought Isaiah's Suffering Servant into the arena of race in the USA. In one article, Lim (2015) utilizes James Cone's contention that the cross and lynching tree must be understood together in US theology.[11] Lim goes a step further by bringing the Suffering Servant of Isaiah into conversation with lynching and the cross. He draws numerous parallels, such as the way perpetrators collectively act violently, the seeming anonymity and helplessness of the victim, and how these innocent victims come to be viewed as having an atoning and pacifying force. The result for Lim (2015: 120) of this triangulation of cross, lynching, and Suffering Servant is a recognition during the age of Black Lives Matter that 'receiving the gift of salvation extended through the suffering of the servant requires the ability to see not an anonymous "thug" lying dead in the street shot by police, but rather the Christ crucified'. In Lim's article 'Christ of the coronavirus', he (2020) looks at the Suffering Servant from the vantage point of racism towards Asians during the time of the coronavirus pandemic. He observes how the Suffering Servant's diseased and stricken nature aligns with leprosy, a condition that resulted in exclusion by

---

11 James Cone has little to say about Isaiah's Suffering Servant, yet he (2011: 123) states towards the end of his book: 'Blacks especially identified with the suffering of Jesus, whom they (like the early Christians) viewed as the Suffering Servant in Isaiah 53 – the one who "was despised and rejected by others," "wounded for our transgressions, crushed for our iniquities," and who, unlike Job and Jeremiah, "did not open his mouth" (Isa 53:3, 5, 7; Mt 8:17; Acts 8:32–33; 1 Pet 2:22–25).'

the community. 'Isaiah 53 exposes the injustice that can occur when those in power have the means to attribute meaning to disease; in such cases the innocent can become scapegoats.' He goes on to reflect upon violence against Asian Americans due to Covid-19 as a parallel to the violence perpetrated against the Suffering Servant. So, Lim finds affinities between the Suffering Servant and victims of racism as a means for contemporary Christians to identify with Christ's sufferings and glory.

Conclusion

As we bring this chapter to a close, let's summarize the ground we've covered. Modern scholars have often sought to identify the referent of the Servant Songs in the ancient context – is the Servant originally Israel, the Messiah, Cyrus, and/or the prophet? These passages seem intent on not revealing an original identity, so it is better to consider what the texts envisage. The vision of Isaiah 53 is one where a clear sense can be detected, yet its language and concepts push beyond the boundaries of the time. What is clear in my opinion is that God's Servant will suffer vicariously for the sins of many nations, will bear their iniquity, and will be disfigured and even die, yet God intends for this Servant to be exalted and have a great reward. Yet, how this can be or will be the case is undecipherable in its ancient context. Such ambiguity seems intentional on God's part as he knew that only in the life, death, and resurrection of Jesus Christ would a more full understanding of this passage be possible. In view of the reception of Isaiah's Suffering Servant in Christian tradition, Isaiah 53 has been an important passage for understanding Jesus and for forming the Church's own sense of mission amid suffering in the world.

9

Justice

An unassuming, grey-haired visitor with a gentle glow took the pulpit at my church in Indianapolis in the early 2000s. His text was Isaiah 1.10–17; his tenor was fire. With fervour he declared that the US Church's hands are full of blood; we need to learn to do justice and correct oppression. Some might have called the sermon cranky, but it was truly prophetic. He took on the mantle of the prophet Isaiah, taking the message that opens the book and confronting us with it. One statement towards the end of the sermon particularly unsettled me: 'The injustices here in America and around the world are so obvious that I don't even need to tell you about them.' Honestly, at that time, I was blind to present-day injustices in the USA, particularly my own culpability in injustice, yet this sermon set me on a long path, one that continues to this day, of coming to see the dire need for justice in my life, in my country, and in this world.

The preacher that day was Chester 'Chet' Wood.[1] In the 1970s, with numerous Bible degrees in tow, including a PhD in New Testament from St Andrews University in Scotland, Chet and his family set out for South East Asia to train ministers. But his training had not prepared him to address the extreme poverty and injustices that his students, and now he himself, were facing. A second conversion began, as he started rereading the Bible and reframing Christianity to include what the Bible said about justice. For four decades, Chet, his wife Delores and their children lived in the company of the poor as they taught at seminaries and made their home in South East Asia and Kenya. In the sermon and throughout his life, Chet took on a role similar to that of the prophet Isaiah. The prophets called a people who were blind to see the injustices around them, to see what God sees.

Below, the topic of justice according to Isaiah is our focus. Justice will occupy our attention in three stages: (1) key vantage points on justice in Isaiah; (2) justice in Isaiah's story; and (3) the Church's reception of justice in Isaiah.

---

1   You can read about Chet and his justice project here: <www.inpathsofrighteousness.org/about>.

Vantage points on justice in Isaiah

Entire monographs (e.g. Davies 2000; Gray 2006; Leclerc 2001) have been devoted to justice across or in select chapters of Isaiah, so it will be impossible to cover all passages relevant to our topic. Yet, if I were to choose the most important vantage points to keep in mind when trying to understand the topic of justice in Isaiah, they would be the following: social justice, the God of justice, and the agents of justice.[2] We will consider each of these in turn.

Social justice

The eighth-century BC prophets are known for confronting social injustices across society. Amos famously cries out:

> But let justice roll down like waters,
>   and righteousness like an ever-flowing stream.
> (5.24)

Micah states:

> He has told you, O mortal, what is good;
>   and what does the LORD require of you
> but to do justice, and to love kindness,
>   and to walk humbly with your God?
> (6.8)

Hosea has a similar message (4.1–2; 6.6). Each of these prophets shock their audiences, dedicated as they are to religious observances and prayer, by offering a critique in the name of God. How can they – the faithful ritualists among the people of God – really be the target of God's stinging indictments, rejection, and reprimand? These prophets are called by God to announce a sobering message, as Abraham Heschel (2001: 250) puts it, that 'deeds of injustice vitiate both sacrifice and prayer. Men may not drown the cries of the oppressed with the noise of hymns, nor buy off the Lord with increased offerings.' The prophet Isaiah joins the chorus of eighth-century prophets who confront the civic and religious establishment with the news that being on the wrong side of justice puts you on the wrong side of God, no matter how many sacrifices or prayers one offers.

---

2   Although I could start with God, it will prove useful to begin by defining social justice in Isaiah.

Injustice in Zion

Isaiah 1—39 and 56—66 routinely address the topic we refer to as 'social justice'.[3] Although 'social justice' has many political connotations today, I use it simply to refer to God's concern for justice at a social level, particularly God's concern that the socially vulnerable receive just treatment within society. Isaiah 1 strategically opens the entire book on this note. God is fed up with his people's sacrifices (1.11), does not want them to assemble in his temple (1.12), cannot bear their religious festivals (1.13–14), and is not listening to their prayers (1.15) because their hands are full of blood (1.15). As a result, God calls them to the following actions:

> Wash yourselves; make yourselves clean;
>> remove the evil of your doings
>> from before my eyes;
> cease to do evil,
>> learn to do good;
> seek justice,
>> rescue the oppressed,
> defend the orphan,
>> plead for the widow.
> (1.16–17)

As is common in Hebrew poetry, the lines progress from generalizations to specifics, and in the process the rhetorical focus of the passage becomes clear. Cleansing (1.16a) takes the form of no longer doing evil before God (1.16b). In order to do this, the people of Israel need to not only stop doing evil (1.16c) but positively learn to do good (1.17a). What does it look like to do good? It involves actively seeking justice (1.17b), particularly justice that rescues the oppressed (1.17c). To spell this out further, this passage concludes with two particular groups of vulnerable people who are easily oppressed: the orphan and the widow (1.17d). The pairing of the orphan and widow is common in the Hebrew Bible (e.g. Exod. 22.21; Ps. 68.6; Job 22.9; 24.3), with 'foreigner' at times included (e.g. Deut. 10.18; 14.29; Jer. 7.6; 22.3; Zech. 7.10 (includes 'poor' too); Mal. 3.5), so such a pair probably signifies all who are vulnerable in general.

---

3   For a relevant study on the different uses of justice between Isaiah 40—55 and Isaiah 1—39 and 56—66, see Leclerc 2001; Oswalt 1997; Rendtorff 1993.

One finds a similar message in the subsequent poem about Zion, the Whorish City (1.21–26). The first half of the poem tells the story of how God's faithful city, Zion, is now a whore, for

> she . . . was full of justice [mišpāṭ],
> righteousness [ṣedeq] lodged in her –
>   but now murderers!
> (1.21)

As Moshe Weinfeld (1995: 8; cf. 25–44) has shown, the combination of mišpāṭ ('justice') and ṣedeq/ṣedāqâ ('righteousness') evident here is a common way for those in the Hebrew Bible to refer 'primarily to acts on behalf of the poor and less fortunate classes of the people'. At one time, apparently, acting on behalf of the vulnerable to ensure equity was characteristic of Zion, but this was no longer the case. Zion's leaders are more interested in accumulating wealth than ensuring justice for all; if the price is right, they turn a blind eye towards injustice:

> Everyone loves a bribe
>   and runs after gifts.
> They do not defend the orphan,
>   and the widow's cause does not come before them.
> (1.23)

The second half of the poem portrays God's plan to purge the city through his wrath and restore judges (šōpēṭ) who will ensure justice – Zion will again be a 'city of righteousness [ṣedeq]', a 'faithful city' (1.26). Thus, from the start of the book, as in 1.16–17 so also in 1.21–26, the most vulnerable in society have God's attention: the orphan and widow.

It is not mere happenstance that the opening chapter of Isaiah confronts its readers and hearers on two occasions with God's demand that the vulnerable in society experience justice. This introduces a theme that recurs throughout the book. For instance, in the 'Song of the Vineyard' (5.1–7), God reveals the identity of his putrid vineyard:

> For the vineyard of the LORD of hosts
>   is the house of Israel,
> and the people of Judah
>   are his pleasant planting;

he expected justice [*mišpāṭ*],
  but saw bloodshed [*mišpāḥ*];
righteousness [*ṣᵉdāqâ*],
  but heard a cry [*ṣᵉʿāqâ*]!
(5.7)

The 'justice' (*mišpāṭ*) and 'righteousness' (*ṣᵉdāqâ*) pair again appears, calling to mind God's expectations that social justice would prevail across his nation. Yet, in a clever play on words, God sees *mišpāḥ* ('bloodshed') instead of *mišpāṭ* ('justice') and hears *ṣᵉʿāqâ* ('a cry') rather than *ṣᵉdāqâ* ('righteousness').

'Keep justice'

Isaiah 56 opens the final section of the book with a call to social justice:

Keep justice [*mišpāṭ*], and do righteousness [*ṣᵉdāqâ*],
  for soon my salvation will come,
    and my righteousness [*ṣᵉdāqâ*] be revealed.
(56.1 ESV)

This opening verse weds together the call for social justice from First Isaiah with Second Isaiah's emphasis on God's saving justice.[4] With God soon coming to set the world right (56.1b), God's servants are commanded to promote social justice – indicated by the word pair of 'justice' and 'righteousness' – in the meantime. Isaiah 58 unpacks further God's concern for social justice, which many scholars envisage as being set in a post-exilic era. As in Isaiah 1, the targets of Isaiah 58 assume that their religious fasting and Sabbath-keeping places them in good standing with God. They are behaving

as if they were a nation that practised righteousness [*ṣᵉdāqâ*]
  and did not forsake the ordinance [*mišpāṭ*] of God.
(58.2)

This combination of *ṣedāqâ* and *mišpāṭ* ironically surfaces in the very next line: 'they ask of me righteous judgements [*mišpeṭê-ṣedeq*]' (58.2). John Goldingay (2014: 165) captures the irony here well: 'they look for Yhwh to behave toward

---

4   Rolf Rendtorff (1993: 181–9) argues that Isa. 56.1 weds together First Isaiah and Second Isaiah in this verse.

them with *mišpāṭ ûṣᵉdāqâ* but do not embody these characteristics in their own life.' As the rest of the chapter reveals, the people are oppressing and beating their workers, turning their back on those in need, and seeking only their own gain. They keep religious fast-days, but what God seeks is true fasting. Is this not:

> to loose the bonds of injustice,
>   to undo the thongs of the yoke,
> to let the oppressed go free,
>   and to break every yoke?
> Is it not to share your bread with the hungry,
>   and bring the homeless poor into your house;
> when you see the naked, to cover them,
>   and not to hide yourself from your own kin?
> (58.6–7)

If one deprives oneself of food for religious fasting, one should also be willing to give food to those in need.

Covenantal or natural law

It is apparent, then, that social justice is significant in Isaiah, particularly in chapters 1—39 and 56—66. The question arises, however, as to where Isaiah derives this ethic from. For some (e.g. Calvin), the laws of Sinai provide the impetus for Isaiah to champion God's desire for justice among God's covenant people. Certainly, there are numerous laws in the Pentateuch that call for the protection of the orphan and widow (Exod. 22.21; Deut. 10.18; 24.17), and the pair of justice and righteousness emerges on a few occasions (Lev. 19.15; Deut. 16.18; cf. Gen. 18.19), yet Isaiah never directly quotes these laws, and social justice was a common element across the Ancient Near East (Williamson 2012: 22–43). As a result, scholars such as John Barton (2003) and Hugh Williamson (2012) argue that the ethic of Isaiah is grounded in wisdom deriving from 'natural law' in the sense 'that certain moral norms are felt to be *natural*, in tune with the way things are, or likely to be held by everyone in virtue of some innate moral sense' (Barton 2003: 32–3). God, however, is not removed from the equation of Barton's and Williamson's 'natural law' because the prophet's sense of what is fitting relates closely to one's proper place before God as Creator and King (see Barton 2003: 138–44; Williamson 2012: 65–72). Whether covenantal or natural law forms the basis for Isaiah's call for justice, what is most significant is Isaiah's burning conviction that justice derives from God's own commitment to justice and the urgency for humans to align with that.

The God of justice

The most important vantage point on justice in Isaiah is to see God as the God of justice. Several passages will offer us a window into this.

'He shall judge between the nations'

God's involvement with justice is apparent in the second part of the book's dual introduction (ch. 1; 2.1–5). In Isaiah 1, God chastised his unjust people and called them to live justly (1.2–20), and then declared that he would transform unjust Zion into a city of righteousness after judgement (1.21–31). Immediately after this, the scene shifts to Zion in its glory with all nations streaming to it (2.2). The purpose of their pilgrimage to Zion becomes clear in verses 3–4:

> Many peoples shall come and say,
> 'Come, let us go up to the mountain of the LORD,
>   to the house of the God of Jacob;
> that he may teach us his ways
>   and that we may walk in his paths.'
> For out of Zion shall go forth instruction,
>   and the word of the LORD from Jerusalem.
> He shall judge between the nations,
>   and shall arbitrate for many peoples;
> they shall beat their swords into ploughshares,
>   and their spears into pruning-hooks;
> nation shall not lift up sword against nation,
>   neither shall they learn war any more.
> (2.3–4)

The nations' desire is to receive instruction from God – a stark and ironic contrast with Israel in Isaiah 1, where God's people are spoken of as if they were Sodom and Gomorrah. In 2.4, justice comes to the fore. It begins with what God will do: 'he shall judge [*šāpaṭ*] . . . and shall arbitrate [*yākaḥ*]'. In Isaiah's outlook, the task of 'judging' and 'arbitrating' is essentially a royal task. This is why this combination of verbs occurs twice to describe the task of the future King from Jesse's stump (11.3–4). Certainly, the scene of all nations streaming to Zion already calls to mind God's kingship. As Jensen

(1973: 90) puts it: 'Yahweh's sovereignty as king extends not simply over Judah, of course, but over all nations; when the nations come streaming to His throne in Jerusalem they are acknowledging Him as their rightful sovereign.' What they seek from God, at an international scale, is justice. In this scene, the sort of justice they desire is God's just decisions on the various disputes arising between nations. With an all-wise God ruling over the world and offering his judgements, the results are awe-inspiring. The nations will disarm and focus on cultivating their lands rather than training for war (2.4). Thus, from the start of the book, the destiny of world peace rests upon the hope that God will rule as a just king over the entire world.

'Exalted by justice'

Another strong declaration of God's commitment to justice occurs in Isaiah 5.16:

> But the LORD of hosts is exalted by justice,
>   and the Holy God shows himself holy by righteousness.

There is a level of ambiguity here that Walter Moberly's (2001) article title on this verse captures well: 'Whose justice? Which righteousness?' Is God exalted in the light of his own acts of justice, or when his people act justly? What sort of justice and righteousness are in view – juridical, punitive, or salvific? As for the second question, the sort of justice and righteousness in view is the social justice noted above, as this is how the word pair 'justice' and 'righteousness' usually functions; this is also apparent in the parable of the Vineyard in 5.7, part of the immediate context. So, returning to our first question, 'Whose "social justice" is in view?', an instinctive inference is to focus on human justice, where God's people act justly towards others. Yet, as Moberly (2001: 62) observes, 'justice' and 'righteousness' that come about in the human sphere through the Davidic King are attributed to 'the zeal of the LORD of hosts' (9.7). So, God is not disconnected from human action. A likely interpretation of 5.16, then, is that social justice can bring God glory because he is the one accomplishing this through human agency. Thus, God's own glory is tied up with justice and righteousness within the social spheres, for God is a God of justice.

'I will bring near my righteousness'

God's justice is also on display in Isaiah 40—55, yet justice has a unique flavour here in comparison with the social justice variety that dominates Isaiah 1—39.

The familiar justice–righteousness word pair, with its concern for justice for the vulnerable in a given society, does not occur in Isaiah 40—55; instead, here justice and righteousness are set within a global arena where nations await God's just decisions that will set the entire world right. Our observations here will be limited to two.

First, the arena of justice is global and international in Isaiah 40—55. The nations are summoned to draw near for 'judgement' (41.1). God's Servant will bring 'justice to the nations' (42.1, 4). God's justice will go out 'for a light to the peoples' (51.4). God will bring his 'deliverance' (righteousness) near to the peoples and coastlands who wait for him (51.5). Within this global arena, the revelation of God's justice towards nations will make it clear how incomparable he is.

Second, within this global scene, justice pertains more to a right ordering of the world (i.e. salvation) through God's just decisions than to localized social justice. For example, consider 51.4–5:

> [4] Listen to me, my people,
>   and give heed to me, my nation;
> for a teaching will go out from me,
>   and my justice for a light to the peoples.
> [5] I will bring near my deliverance swiftly,
>   my salvation has gone out
>   and my arms will rule the peoples;
> the coastlands wait for me,
>   and for my arm they hope.

In verse 4, 'teaching' (*tôrâ*) parallels 'justice' (*mišpāṭ*). As in 2.3–4 (Leclerc 2001: 121), where *tôrâ* relates to God's judging, the nations in 51.4 will receive instruction (*tôrâ*), namely a decree (*mišpāṭ*), pertaining to their international circumstances. In verse 5, the instruction and justice from verse 4 develop in a salvific direction through the parallel of 'deliverance' (*ṣedeq*) and 'salvation' (cf. 45.8; 46.12–13; 51.6, 8). The sense across verses 4–5 is that God's just decisions will set the nations 'right' (translated by the NRSV as 'deliverance'), will save them. The verb translated as 'rule' in verse 5 is the verb 'to judge' (*šāpaṭ*; cf. 2.3), so the line would better read: 'my arms will judge the peoples'. The grand hope of the nations, then, is that God will serve as the international Judge whose just decisions will set the nations in order, and hence they would experience God's salvation. Thus, in

Isaiah 40—55, justice fundamentally relates to the desire of Israel and the nations for God to issue forth his just decisions across the world so that all will be set right.

'I love justice'

In my opinion, it is hard to find a more moving portrayal of God's commitment to justice than we find in Isaiah 56—66. In Isaiah 59, God is displeased with what he sees because 'there was no justice' (59.15b). The problems God sees are stockpiled at the start of chapter 59. Hands, fingers, lips, and tongues contribute to evil, as individuals murder and lie (59.3). Cases brought to court are a sham (59.4). People are quick to run towards evil, and their minds are fixed on iniquity (59.7). As a result, a social reality of justice and righteousness is far from them (59.9, 14; Leclerc 2001: 148). As the LORD sees this, he is 'displeased', or, more literally, 'this was evil in his eyes' (59.15), for justice is absent among his people. As a result, God moves to action; he takes the matter of justice into his own 'arm':

> The LORD saw it, and it displeased him
>   that there was no justice.
> He saw that there was no man,
>   and wondered that there was no one to intercede;
> then his own arm brought him salvation,
>   and his righteousness upheld him.
> He put on righteousness as a breastplate,
>   and a helmet of salvation on his head;
> he put on garments of vengeance for clothing,
>   and wrapped himself in zeal as a cloak.
> According to their deeds, so will he repay,
>   wrath to his adversaries, repayment to his enemies;
>   to the coastlands he will render repayment.
> So they shall fear the name of the LORD from the west,
>   and his glory from the rising of the sun;
> for he will come like a rushing stream,
>   which the wind of the LORD drives.
> 'And a Redeemer will come to Zion,
>   to those in Jacob who turn from transgression,' declares
>   the LORD.
> (59.15b–20 ESV)

Arrayed as a warrior and clothed in righteousness and salvation, the Divine Warrior comes in judgement against all that is unjust and sets the world aright in salvation (see Abernethy 2016: 88–94). It is fitting, then, that God says a few chapters later: 'I the Lord love justice' (61.8).

By way of summary, justice in the book of Isaiah must be seen from the vantage point of God. The book opens with the grand hope that all nations will live at peace as God offers his judgements on the cases of the nations (2.2–4). God's very glory is wrapped up in whether or not there is social justice among his people (5.16). Furthermore, God's justice extends beyond the internal, social dimensions of Israel; his just decrees are the ultimate hope of the nations, as his justice will result in the entire world being set aright (51.4–5). Finally, moved by the absence of justice in the world, God takes it upon himself to right his world (59.15–20). The following quote from Abraham Heschel (2001: 272, 275), although primarily related to Amos, is relevant for Isaiah as well: 'Righteousness is a vast and mighty stream because God is its unfailing source . . . to defy it is to block God's almighty surge.'

Agents of justice

Amid God's zeal and love for justice, the question naturally arises as to whether he uses intermediaries to carry out his plans for justice. Although God's use of agents may not exhaust his enactment of justice in the world, such individuals certainly play a key role in Isaiah's vision. Four agents invite our attention: the Davidic King, the Servant, the servants, and the Messenger.[5]

The Davidic King

Within Isaiah 1—39, there are three, possibly four, passages that speak of a future Davidic King. In all of these passages, the chief task of the king will be to ensure social justice. In Isaiah 9, the Davidic King will 'establish and uphold [his throne] with justice [$mišpāṭ$] and righteousness [$ṣᵉdāqâ$]' (9.7). In Isaiah 11, the shoot from Jesse's stump will be endowed with a spirit of wisdom (11.2–3a) that will enable him to guarantee justice for the vulnerable:

---

5 The most significant study on this topic is H. G. M. Williamson's 1998 monograph, *Variations on a Theme.*

He shall not judge by what his eyes see,
  or decide by what his ears hear;
but with righteousness [ṣedeq] he shall judge [šāpaṭ] the
    poor,
  and decide with equity for the meek of the earth;
he shall strike the earth with the rod of his mouth,
  and with the breath of his lips he shall kill the wicked.
Righteousness [ṣedeq] shall be the belt around his waist,
  and faithfulness the belt around his loins.
(11.3b–5)

In Isaiah 16, amid a scene where the exiles of Moab are fleeing oppression, hope emerges in the form of a throne in David's tent where a 'ruler who seeks justice [mišpāṭ] and is swift to do what is right [ṣedeq]' will sit on the throne in faithfulness (16.5). In the final text, which is more proverbial in nature than futuristic, Isaiah 32.1 again attaches the task of social justice to royalty:

See, a king will reign in righteousness [ṣedeq],
  and princes will rule with justice [mišpāṭ].

Within the first half of Isaiah, the chief agent who will serve as a vehicle for promoting social justice is the messianic Davidic King.

The Servant

In Isaiah 40—55, the scene shifts from the internal affairs in Israel to the world stage amid exile. As a result, as discussed above, the concept of justice shifts towards an emphasis on how God's sovereign rule over the world will result in his just decrees issuing forth to set everything right among the nations. In Isaiah 42.1–4, the Servant, whom we argued in Chapter 8 is Israel in this passage, is to play a vital role in bringing God's justice (i.e. just decrees) to the nations. 'Justice' (mišpāṭ) is repeated three times in this passage:

I have put my spirit upon him;
  he will bring forth *justice* to the nations . . .
he will faithfully bring forth *justice*.
He will not grow faint or be crushed
  until he has established *justice* in the earth;
  and the coastlands wait for his teaching.
(42.1, 3b–4, my emphasis)

Since Israel is blind, its people are not ready to be God's Servant, so a new Servant takes over who embodies the essence of Israel (and is named as such) and will reconcile Israel and the nations to God (49.1–7). Ironically, however, this Suffering Servant would experience injustice ('By a perversion of justice he was taken away', 53.8), yet through this suffering would create a community of servants who would bring God's justice to the world (56.1).

The servants and the Messenger

In Isaiah 56—66, two chief agents of justice are the servants and the Messenger. In Isaiah 56.1-8, the final section of the book opens by redefining God's people. Whether one is a foreigner or a eunuch, faithfulness to God's covenant expectations warrants the status of being one of God's servants (56.6). By starting the section with an exhortation to 'keep justice, and do righteousness' (56.1 ESV), a commitment to social justice is a chief indicator of covenant faithfulness for God's servants. These 'servants' are the offspring of the Servant; they are those made righteous by the righteous Servant: 'the righteous one [ṣaddîq] . . . shall make many righteous [ṣādaq]' (53.11). In 54.17 NKJV, God declares that

> This is the heritage of the servants of the LORD,
> And their righteousness [ṣᵉdāqâ] is from Me.

Beuken (1990: 68) captures well this shift from the Servant as the righteous one to the servants as righteous: 'God guarantees that the Servant will excel in "righteousness" and will transfer it to those who belong to him, so that "righteousness" will also become the essence of their life (53.11; 54.17).' Thus, it is the offspring of the Servant, God's servants, who are empowered and called to promote justice and righteousness in their spheres as they await the coming of God's ultimate display of righteousness and salvation (56.1).

The second chief agent of Isaiah 56—66 is the Anointed Messenger in Isaiah 61. Although this Messenger has affinities with the Davidic King and the Servant, this is a ministry of proclamation:[6]

> [1] The Spirit of the Lord GOD is upon me,
>   because the LORD has anointed me
> to bring good news to the poor;

---

6 For a survey of debates about the identity of this Messenger, particularly in the light of the Davidic King and Suffering Servant, see Abernethy 2016: 160–7.

> he has sent me to bind up the broken-hearted,
> to proclaim liberty to the captives,
>   and the opening of the prison to those who are bound;
>   ² to proclaim the year of the LORD's favour,
>   and the day of vengeance of our God;
>   to comfort all who mourn;
>   ³ to grant to those who mourn in Zion –
>   to give them a beautiful headdress instead of ashes,
>   the oil of gladness instead of mourning,
>   the garment of praise instead of a faint spirit;
>   that they may be called oaks of righteousness,
>   the planting of the LORD, that he may be glorified.
>   (61.1–3 ESV)

This well-known passage, quoted by Jesus in Luke 4, begins by recounting God's empowerment for the task. Backed by the Spirit and the anointing of God, seven infinitives spell out the purpose (61.1–2) and results (61.3) of the Messenger's mission: 'to bring good news . . . to bind up . . . ²to proclaim . . . to comfort . . . ³to grant . . . to give'. Through proclaiming the good news that God's reign is ushering in a new era of liberty, the poor, the broken-hearted, the captives, the imprisoned, and those mourning will find healing, be free, and break forth in praise.

Thus, amid God's love for and quest to promote justice, several chief agents arise across the book whom he empowers by the Spirit for the task. The Davidic King leads the way in promoting social justice within society. The Servant Israel is unable to carry out its mission of bringing God's just decrees to the nations, but the Suffering Servant is a Righteous One who will experience injustice yet through suffering will create a new community of righteous servants. The Anointed Messenger will proclaim the good news of the in-breaking of God's rule that sets captives free.

Justice in the story of Isaiah

Having considered three essential vantage points on justice in Isaiah (social justice, the God of justice, and agents of justice), it is now time to ask how justice fits into the four phases of Isaiah's story (see Chapter 4).

In Phase 1, injustice is a significant reason why the Holy One will judge Israel through Assyria and Babylon. The book opens by speaking of those in the audience as rebellious children, more stupid than barn animals, wounded people, as bad as the leaders of Sodom and Gomorrah, and behaving like whores. The reason is that their 'hands are full of blood' (1.15) and their court systems are so corrupt that the widow and orphan cannot receive a fair hearing (1.23; cf. 1.17; 5.23). They plunder the goods of and crush the poor (3.14–15). They are like a vineyard that produces putrid grapes, for God expected social justice from them, but instead their land is full of outcry (5.7). The rich acquire field after field and house after house, leaving nothing for the poor (5.8). Their laws favour the rich, and the poor cannot get a fair trial (10.1–2). As a result of such injustice, God will turn his hand against whorish Zion in purifying wrath (1.24); its people will experience judgement through exile (10.4). Yet, this is not the end of God's story, as these chapters anticipate a time when Zion will be righteous (1.26), when God will offer justice to the nations (2.2–4), and when a Davidic King will promote social justice (9.7; 11.1–5; 16.5; 32.1).

In Phase 2, God raises up King Cyrus of Persia for righteous purposes. In Isaiah 41, a court case is unfolding where God makes a case for his superiority before the nations. In verse 2, God speaks of rousing up someone from the east (Cyrus) whom God will enable to conquer the nations. The term 'righteousness' (*ṣedeq*) occurs in this clause, which is very difficult to understand in Hebrew. Some translate it with a focus on victory:

> Who stirred up one from the east,
>   whom victory [*ṣedeq*] meets at every step?
> (41.2 ESV; cf. NRSV)

Others emphasize righteousness:

> Who has stirred up one from the east,
>   calling him in righteousness to his service?
> (41.2 NIV; cf. NKJV)

I prefer the latter because one finds a similar statement about Cyrus in 45.13:

> I have aroused him in righteousness [*ṣedeq*],
>   and I will make all his paths straight;
> he shall build my city
>   and set my exiles free.

156

In both 45.13 and 41.2, we find the same verb, 'to arouse', and the same noun, 'righteousness' (ṣedeq), so the sense is similar. In 45.13, however, God's purpose for Cyrus as it relates to Jerusalem is more explicit. King Cyrus is to be a vehicle of righteousness in the sense that he will set aright God's ruined city and allow exiles to return home.

In Phase 3, the Suffering Servant continues the story of justice and righteousness. With God's Servant Israel blind and unable to fulfil its purpose of bringing justice to the nations (42.1–4, 18–20), the Suffering Servant emerges as 'the righteous one' (53.11). Through his own experiences of injustice (53.8) at the hands of the people, this Righteous One will have offspring, a new community of servants, who will be set right and truly be Zion's inhabitants. These servants will find that 'their righteousness' is from God (54.17 NKJV).

Phase 4 of Isaiah's story sits as a looming storm and beautiful sunrise on the horizon. The Holy One will come in final judgement and final salvation to make a new world for his servants. Somewhere, either within Phase 4 or between Phases 3 and 4, hopes for an age of justice and righteousness will find their realization. Zion will again be the Righteous City (1.26). All the world will stream to God for his peace-imparting justice (2.3–4). A Davidic King will promote social justice (9.7; 11.3–5; 16.5). All nations will receive God's just instruction (51.4–5). God will take matters into his own arm to establish justice (59.15b–20). The Messenger will proclaim the good news of liberation as God's reign breaks upon the world (61.1–3). Yet, in the meantime, as God's servants await the ultimate realization of these promises, their calling is clear:

> Keep justice [mišpāṭ], and do righteousness [ṣᵉdāqâ],
> for soon my salvation will come,
>   and my righteousness [ṣᵉdāqâ] be revealed.
> (56.1 ESV)

As for readers today, where do you fit with the story of justice in Isaiah? For those who believe Jesus is the Suffering Servant, it is in Isaiah 56.1 that we find our place in the story. The Suffering Servant, the Righteous One, experienced grave injustices to include us among God's righteous servants. And the call to 'Keep justice, and do righteousness' meets us as we await God's final realization of his promises. If we obey these commands, we find ourselves called to take up the mantle of God's Servant – Israel and the Suffering Servant – and be willing to promote justice in the world even amid difficulty. If we ignore our call to pursue social justice and become encrusted in our 'modes' of religious duty, then we align with the audiences in Isaiah 1 and 58 who need to hear the prophetic rebukes.

The Church's reception of justice in Isaiah

As we turn to how the Church has received Isaiah's message about justice, an acknowledgement is essential from the start. Christians, in every age, have failed in their own ways to be the conduit of justice that God seeks from his servants. Whether through wilful disobedience, indifference, or shameful ignorance, those in the Church have been found wanting time and time again in this area. The stinging messages of Isaiah 1, 5, and 58 remain a necessary rebuke of and caution for the Church. With that being said, the focus below is more positively on how justice in Isaiah has been interpreted and utilized by the Church.

Injustices Jesus faced

The early Church interpreted the topic of justice in Isaiah in view of the life of Christ. According to Eusebius, Isaiah 1 speaks of the religious leaders during the time of Christ. He (2013: 5) states:

> We are talking about those who were rulers of the nation during the times of the Savior, who dared to act against the Lord. They thought that God was placated with burnt offerings and drink offerings and other bodily acts of worship according to the law.

The reason that their hands are said to be 'full of blood' (1.15) is because they murder Christ, 'in keeping with the slaughter of countless prophets'. Similarly, Jerome (2015: 84) appeals to Jesus' parable of the Wicked Tenants (Matt. 21.38), in which tenant farmers kill the owner's heir, to explain how their 'hands are full of blood'. Along similar lines, in the case of Isaiah 5.7, Jerome (2015: 134) understands the 'outcry' God hears as the outcry of Jesus' blood during his Passion. Thus, one strand of Christian reception of justice in Isaiah was to interpret the injustices confronted by Isaiah in the light of the injustices Jesus faced.

The Church and social justice

Another way justice in Isaiah has been viewed relates to God's desire for his church to live justly in the world. Jerome interprets Isaiah 56.1 as a call to live justly in the present because God's ultimate justice is coming. He reasons that since the Saviour himself is justice (1 Cor. 1.30) and since the Church needs to train its senses for discerning good and evil (Heb. 5.14), the people of God should 'keep judgment at all times' (2015: 707). Such judgement should lead us to not be partial to rich or poor (Lev. 19.15) or great or small (Deut. 1.17). And since justice signifies 'all points of morality', 'one who does a single justice is shown to have fulfilled all the virtues, which follow each other in succession and cleave to each other' (Jerome 2015: 707). Aquinas (2017), similarly, interprets the command to 'do justice' as a call to 'do every virtue', for justice conforms to all the other virtues.

During the Reformation, Martin Luther understood exhortations towards social justice as a means by which God condemns the sinner under the law. On Isaiah 1.15 ('your hands are full of blood'), Luther (1969: 18) says:

> Consider how many monsters there are in the world, and how much ungodliness. We do everything except what love demands; we give much for monstrous and godless religions but nothing for the need of the poor. Clean before men, but unclean, cruel, and murderers before God.

In response to the call to 'defend the fatherless' (see 1.17), Luther (1969: 19) declares: 'Would that we only realized that this is our duty! For it is evil for us to think smugly that we are living a good life.' When Isaiah describes how everyone loves a bribe (1.23), Luther (1969: 22) again appeals to the condemnation of the law: 'The law of nature is the law of God, and the prophets teach that one person owes love to the other. Therefore no one will be excused.' He (1972: 260) uses a similar tactic in his interpretation of Isaiah 56.1: 'Keep justice. These are words of the Law. The prophet demands that the people make themselves fit and capable for grace . . . This is a brief statement of the Lawgiver who condemns the guilty and the innocent.' Thus, for Luther, Isaiah's message about social justice is a means of condemnation for those in the Church to see their need for Christ.

John Calvin too uses Isaiah's message of justice as an opportunity to confront sin, yet he also interprets Isaiah's calls for justice more positively. In the case of Isaiah 1, Calvin explains that the clause 'your hands are full of blood' is a figure of speech about how the more powerful 'deceive and take advantage' of the underprivileged. Calvin (2010: 1/62) presses this point home by admonishing fellow ministers to follow Isaiah's tactics as they confront those in their own spheres:

This circumstance ought to be carefully observed; for on the same grounds must we now deal with wicked men, who oppress the poor and feeble by fraud and violence, or some kind of injustice, and yet cloak their wickedness by plausible disguise.

Amid such failure to carry out justice, Calvin encourages the oppressed with the comforting word that God himself cares for the widow and orphan (Exod. 22.22–24; Deut. 10.18–19). Calvin (2010: 1/170) operates similarly in his reading of Isaiah 5.7. After a brief explanation of the verse, he transitions: 'Let us now understand that the same things are addressed to us.' He reasons that because the Gentile Church has been grafted into the Jewish olive tree (Rom. 11.24), so the Church must assess whether it is bringing forth fruits of injustice similar to those of Ancient Israel. For Calvin, however, Isaiah's message about justice is not only negative, but also serves as a call for the Church to live justly. In his comments on 56.1 ('keep justice'; 'do righteousness'), Calvin (2010: 4/175) argues that this exhortation

includes all the duties which men owe to each other, and which consist not only in abstaining from doing wrong, but also in rendering assistance to our neighbours. And this is the sum of the second table of the Law, in keeping which we give proof of our piety, if we have any.

Calvin, then, seems to align with the tenor of the prophetic words. On occasions when the prophet confronts the audience about injustice (1.15–17; 5.7), this is an opportunity to expose sin. When the prophet commands the people to 'keep justice' in 56.1, this is a reminder to love our neighbour as ourselves, the second table of the law.

Civil rights and Isaiah

The book of Isaiah has been a beacon of hope for a greater day of justice for black America. The examples of Harriet Beecher Stowe and Martin Luther King, Jr, will illustrate this.

Prior to the US Civil War (1852), Harriet Beecher Stowe, an abolitionist, published her classic novel *Uncle Tom's Cabin* to expose the evils of slavery. In the novel, she recounts the story of a slave, Tom, for whom the Bible is precious. As Tom draws upon Scripture, there is a brief interlude by the narrator that beautifully captures Stowe's view of the Bible (Stowe 1877: 173):

These words of an ancient volume, got up principally by ignorant and unlearned men, have, through all time, kept up, somehow, a strange sort of power over the minds of poor, simple fellows, like Tom. They stir up the soul from its depths, and rouse, as with trumpet call, courage, energy, and enthusiasm, where before was only the blackness of despair.

In the same spirit, the Preface (1877: viii) that sets the course for the entire book concludes with three verses, based on the Authorized (King James) Version:

He shall not fail nor be discouraged
Till He have set judgment in the earth. [Isa. 42.4]

He shall deliver the needy when he crieth,
The poor, and him that hath no helper. [Ps. 72.12]

He shall redeem their soul from deceit and violence,
And precious shall their blood be in His sight. [Ps. 116.15]

Before wading into the sorrowful story of slavery, Stowe presents Isaiah 42.4, Psalm 72.12, and Psalm 116.15 as a vista of hope, showing that a greater day will come, perhaps even as a result of writing this book. Isaiah's vision of the Servant who will not relent in his quest to bring justice across the earth leads the way in this list.

The illustrious civil rights reformer, Martin Luther King, Jr, drew routinely upon three texts from Isaiah's vision of justice. Isaiah 2.4 was an important verse for King as his leadership in the non-violent protest movement took form. On 3 December 1956, one year after the bus boycott in Montgomery, Alabama, King took the pulpit of Holt Street Baptist Church before an overflowing crowd. The title of his message was: 'Facing the challenge of a new age'. King (2000b: 452) marvels about how God had turned Montgomery, which was once 'the Cradle of the Confederacy' into 'the cradle of freedom and justice'. He is struck by the power of non-violent resistance. After situating the plight of blacks historically within the view of this moment in time, King (2000b: 461) calls for the audience to join in ushering in a new age by gaining political power through the ballot, through legislation, through investing finances, through developing excellence in upcoming leaders, and through being willing to 'stand up and protest against injustice wherever we find it'. At the culmination of his message, he (2000b: 462) declares (emphasis added):

If we will join together in doing all of these things we will be able to speed up the coming of the new world – a new world in which men will live together as brothers; a world in which *men will beat their swords into ploughshares and their spears into pruning-hooks.*

This imagery from Isaiah 2.4 works so beautifully for King because it envisages a time of non-violence when the justice of God will prevail and peace will abound. Over the next year, King would appeal to Isaiah 2.4 in a very similar manner in at least three other speeches.[7]

The best-known passage of Isaiah used by Martin Luther King, Jr, is Isaiah 40.4–5. On 28 August 1963, King stood before the Lincoln Memorial in Washington, DC, in front of a quarter of a million people and delivered his now-famous 'I have a dream' speech. A comparison between the manuscript for his speech and the speech he delivered reveals that he improvised at the most famous moments in his presentation. A wonderful production of King's address makes plain where he improvised (<freedomsring.stanford.edu>). As he comes to the pinnacle of this improvised dream, he quotes Isaiah 40.4–5:

I have a dream that one day every valley shall be exalted, every hill and mountain shall be made low, the rough places will be made plain, and the crooked places will be made straight, and the glory of the LORD shall be revealed, and all flesh shall see it together. This is our hope.

This quotation from Isaiah 40.4–5 occurs on a number of occasions in King's other speeches too. For example, in 'The birth of a new nation' (7 April 1957), upon returning from a trip to Ghana, he offers hope to those in Montgomery when he says (2000a: 166):

I can hear Isaiah again, because it has profound meaning to me, that somehow 'every valley shall be exalted, every hill and mountain shall be made low, the rough places will be made plain, and the crooked places will be made straight, and the glory of the LORD shall be revealed, and all flesh shall see it together'. That's the beauty of this thing: all flesh shall see it together. Not some from the heights of Park Street and others from the dungeons of slum areas. Not some from the pinnacles of the British Empire

---

7   These appeals occur in his speeches 'Desegregation and the future' (15 December 1956), 'A realistic look at the question of progress in the area of race relations' (10 April 1957), and 'Some things we must do' (5 December 1957). The talks can be accessed online at Stanford University's King Institute.

and some from the dark deserts of Africa. Not some from inordinate, superfluous wealth and others from abject, deadening poverty. Not some white and not some black, not some yellow and not some brown, but all flesh shall see it together. They shall see it from Montgomery. They shall see it from New York. They shall see it from Ghana. They shall see it from China.

For King, Isaiah's portrait of God as one who can revolutionize the world, exalting valleys, lowering hills, straightening the crooked, and smoothing what is rough, provides grounds for hope that God can birth a new nation, an America where there is freedom and justice for all.

A final passage important in King's vision of justice is Isaiah 61.1–3. On 5 June 1966, King delivered a sermon entitled 'Guidelines for a constructive church'. It is recorded and available online and well worth listening to. During a time when guidelines were being set forth across the USA for integrating schools, he turns to the Church and asks about what its guidelines should be. King (1998) states:[8]

> Somewhere behind the dim mist of eternity, God set forth his guidelines. And through his prophets, and above all through his son Jesus Christ, he said that, 'There are some things that my church must do. There are some guidelines that my church must follow.' And if we in the church don't want the funds of grace cut off from the divine treasury, we've got to follow the guidelines. (*That's right*) The guidelines are clearly set forth for us in some words uttered by our Lord and Master as he went in the temple one day, and he went back to Isaiah and quoted from him. And he said, 'The Spirit of the Lord is upon me, because he hath anointed me (*Yes, sir*) to preach the gospel to the poor, (*Yes, sir*) he hath sent me to heal the broken-hearted, to preach deliverance to the captives, and recovering of sight to the blind, (*Yes*) to set at liberty them that are bruised, to preach the acceptable year of the Lord.' These are the guidelines.

In the rest of his sermon, King unpacks three guidelines from Isaiah 61. The Church should 'seek to heal the broken-hearted', 'preach deliverance to them that are captive', and 'preach the acceptable year of the Lord'. At a powerful moment in the sermon, King declares:

---

8   The italicized words in parentheses are responses from King's audience, not King's words.

Some people are suffering. (*Make it plain*) Some people are hungry this morning. (*Yes*) [*clap*] Some people are still living with segregation and discrimination this morning. (*Yes, sir*) I'm going to preach about it. (*Preach it; I'm with you*) I'm going to fight for them. I'll die for them if necessary, because I got my guidelines clear. (*Yes*) And the God that I serve and the God that called me to preach (*Yes; Amen*) told me that every now and then I'll have to go to jail for them. (*Make it plain*) Every now and then I'll have to agonize and suffer for the freedom of his children. (*Yes*) I even may have to die for it. But if that's necessary, I'd rather follow the guidelines of God (*Yes*) than to follow the guidelines of men. (*Yes*) The church is called to set free (*Yes*) those that are captive, (*Yes, sir*) to set free those that are victims of the slavery of segregation and discrimination, those who are caught up in the slavery of fear and prejudice. (*Make it plain*)

King's suggestion that he would be willing to die for those suffering as he embodied the calling of Isaiah 61 became reality two years later.

Conclusion

Within every part of the book of Isaiah, justice comes into view. During a time of social injustice within Israel and disorder between nations, the book of Isaiah confronts injustice, implores God's servants to practise social justice (1.16–17; 56.1; ch. 58), and offers hope that God will make justice a reality through his Davidic King, Suffering Servant, and Anointed Messenger. In the reception of Isaiah's message of justice by the Church, we are invited to consider Jesus' experiences of injustice, our own guilt in injustice, our call to seek justice right now, and the hope Isaiah offers to weary pilgrims who long for a just world.

10
In the end, worship

We are now at the end of our journey together. We've traversed the paths trod by interpreters past and present (Chapters 2 and 3), scanned the entire range of the (hi)story Isaiah tells (Chapter 4), and trekked along the paths of the Holy One, Zion, the Davidic Messiah, the Suffering Servant, and justice (Chapters 5–9). As you continue this journey, remember this is not a journey you are taking alone. Many have come before you to clear out paths for successful travel and many will come after you, for this mountain will endure and continue to invite pilgrim souls to explore its beauty. Yet, before I leave you, you need to know where this journey ends. The summit of Mount Isaiah is Worship.

Praise infiltrates Isaiah unlike any other prophetic book. Joseph Blenkinsopp (2018: 37–85) catalogues at least 25 hymns or passages with hymnic influence across all sections of Isaiah. What is particularly striking is how nearly all of the major sections (1—12; 13—27; 28—35; 40—55; 56—66) of Isaiah culminate in praise. In Isaiah 1—12, there is the expectation that the Holy One would judge Israel and Judah through Assyria, and then renew Zion (2.2-4; 4.2-6) and raise up a Davidic Messiah (9.6-7; 11.1-9), yet the entire collection ends with the expectation of praise:

> You will say in that day:
> I will give thanks to you, O LORD,
>   for though you were angry with me,
> your anger turned away,
>   and you comforted me . . .

> Sing praises to the LORD, for he has done gloriously;
>   let this be known in all the earth.
> Shout aloud and sing for joy, O royal Zion,
>   for great in your midst is the Holy One of Israel.
> (12.1, 5–6)

Isaiah 13—27 also crescendoes in praise. In this section, Isaiah's messages of divine judgement and salvation extend beyond Israel and Judah to the nations in the Oracles Against the Nations (13—23) and to a cosmic and eschatological scale in the so-called 'Mini-Apocalypse' (24—27). The destiny of these visions finds its telos in a regathering of God's people at Zion in worship:[1]

> And on that day a great trumpet will be blown, and those who were lost in the land of Assyria and those who were driven out to the land of Egypt will come and worship the LORD on the holy mountain at Jerusalem. (27.13)

Isaiah 28—35 returns to the historic realities of the eighth century BC through a series of woes against Israel and Judah, yet interspersed are signals of hope that culminate in Isaiah 35:

> And the ransomed of the LORD shall return,
>   and come to Zion with singing;
> everlasting joy shall be upon their heads;
>   they shall obtain joy and gladness,
>   and sorrow and sighing shall flee away.
> (35.10; cf. 51.11)

The journey of the weary exiles will culminate with a fresh season of joy and worship in Zion. As a shameless plug, my wife, Katie, wrote a song based on Isaiah 35 after the passing of her brother. Jodee Lewis performs it beautifully under the title 'The Redeemed of the Lord'.[2] It captures this wondrous hope of returning to Zion with joy because of God's return as King.

In Isaiah 40—55, the anticipated return from Babylon (40—48) gives way to a more grandiose salvation. Upon God's return as King to Zion, the watchmen announce this news and call for joy to spread:

> Listen! Your sentinels lift up their voices,
>   together they sing for joy;
> for in plain sight they see

---

1 As far as I am aware, Willem Beuken (2009) is one of the few who observes how worship plays an important role in the structure of Isaiah in the light of 27.13; 52.7-10; and 66.15-24.

2 Katie Abernethy, 'The Redeemed of the Lord' (2018), track 9 on Jodee Lewis, *Buzzard's Bluff*. Digital download: <https://jodeelewis.bandcamp.com/track/the-redeemed-of-the-lord>.

the return of the Lord to Zion.
Break forth together into singing,
  you ruins of Jerusalem;
for the Lord has comforted his people,
  he has redeemed Jerusalem.
(52.8–9)

In chapter 54, barren Zion is called to 'Sing . . . burst into song' (54.1). Isaiah 40—55 concludes with a vision of God's servants rejoicing amid a creation that is coming to life to join in the praise:

For you shall go out in joy,
  and be led back in peace;
the mountains and the hills before you
  shall burst into song,
  and all the trees of the field shall clap their hands.
Instead of the thorn shall come up the cypress;
  instead of the brier shall come up the myrtle;
and it shall be to the Lord for a memorial,
  for an everlasting sign that shall not be cut off.
(55.12–13)

The final section of the book (chs 56—66) presents worship as the endgame. It opens with the subversive announcement that faithful foreigners will have a special place in God's house where they will joyfully gather to worship God in prayer and sacrifice (56.7–8). The entire book ends similarly with a vision where Gentiles come to God's glory in Zion, are chosen to serve as priests and Levites, and worship God:

From new moon to new moon,
  and from sabbath to sabbath,
all flesh shall come to worship before me,
says the Lord.
(66.23)

In contrast to the start of the book where God rejected the Israelites' worship on the Sabbath and at the new moon (1.11–14), the final positive note in the book is the expectation that all flesh will worship God. Yet, this destiny of worship for God's servants is contrasted even in the end with a warning –

there will be those who miss out on this destiny and experience God's fiery wrath instead (66.24).

As you set out on your journey up Mount Isaiah, remember that God's mission of judgement and salvation across era after era, his use of Cyrus and a Suffering Servant, and the hopes of Zion's restoration and a Davidic Messiah culminate in an era when all people will worship before the saving, holy King.

Bibliography

Abernethy, A. T., 2014. *Eating in Isaiah: Approaching the role of food and drink in Isaiah's message and structure*. BIntS 131; Leiden: Brill.

——, 2016. *The Book of Isaiah and God's Kingdom: A thematic-theological approach*. NSBT 40; Downers Grove, IL: IVP Academic.

—— and Goswell, G., 2020. *God's Messiah in the Old Testament: Expectations of a coming king*. Grand Rapids, MI: Baker.

Allis, O. T., 1951. *The Unity of Isaiah: A study in prophecy*. Philadelphia, PA: Presbyterian & Reformed.

Aquinas, T., 2017. *Expositio super Isaiam ad Litteram*. Trans. J. Madden; Aquinas Institute; <https://aquinas.cc/la/en/~Isaiah>.

Augustine of Hippo, 1887. *City of God*, in P. Schaff (ed.), *Nicene and Post-Nicene Fathers. First Series: Vol. 2*. Edinburgh: T&T Clark/Grand Rapids, MI: Eerdmans: 1–511.

Averbeck, R. E., 2012. 'Christian interpretations of Isaiah 53', in D. L. Bock and M. Glaser (eds), *The Gospel According to Isaiah 53: Encountering the Suffering Servant in Jewish and Christian theology*. Grand Rapids, MI: Kregel: 33–60.

Baer, D. A., 2006. '"It's all about us!" Nationalistic exegesis in the Greek Isaiah (chapters 1–12)', in C. M. McGinnis and P. K. Tull (eds), *'As Those Who Are Taught': The interpretation of Isaiah from the LXX to the SBL*. SBL Symposium Series 27; Atlanta, GA: SBL: 29–47.

Barstad, H. M., 1989. *A Way in the Wilderness. The 'second exodus' in the message of Second Isaiah*. JSSM 12; Manchester: University of Manchester Press.

Barton, J., 2003. *Understanding Old Testament Ethics: Approaches and explorations*. Louisville, KY: Westminster John Knox.

Berges, U., 2002. 'Der neue Himmel und die neue Erde im Jesajabuch: Eine Auslegung zu Jesaja 65:17 und 66:22', in F. Postma (ed.), *The New Things: Eschatology in Old Testament prophecy. Festschrift for Henk Leene*. Maastricht: Uitgeverij Shaker: 9–15.

——, 2012. *The Book of Isaiah: Its composition and final form*. Trans. M. C. Lind; Sheffield: Phoenix.

Beuken, W. A. M., 1990. 'The main theme of Trito-Isaiah: "the servants of YHWH"', *JSOT* 47: 67–87.

——, 2002. '"Lebanon with its majesty shall fall. A shoot shall come forth from the stump of Jesse" (Isa 10:34–11:1): interfacing the story of Assyria and the image of Israel's future in Isaiah 10–11', in F. Postma (ed.), *The New Things: Eschatology in Old Testament prophecy. Festschrift for Henk Leene*. Maastricht: Shaker: 17–33.

——, 2004. 'The manifestation of Yahweh and the commission of Isaiah: Isaiah 6 read against the background of Isaiah 1', *Calvin Theological Journal* 39: 72–87.

——, 2009. 'YHWH's sovereign rule and his adoration on Mount Zion: a comparison of poetic visions in Isaiah 24–27, 52, 66', in A. J. Everson and H. C. P. Kim (eds), *The Desert will Bloom: Poetic visions in Isaiah*. 4th edn; SBLAIL 4; Atlanta, GA: SBL: 91–108.

Blenkinsopp, J., 2000. *Isaiah 1–39: A new translation with introduction and commentary*. AB 19; New York, NY: Doubleday.

——, 2002. *Isaiah 40–55: A new translation with introduction and commentary*. AB 19A; New York, NY: Doubleday.

——, 2018. *The Beauty of Holiness: Re-reading Isaiah in the light of the Psalms*. London: T&T Clark.

Blomberg, C., 2002. 'Interpreting Old Testament prophetic literature in Matthew: double fulfillment', *TJ* 23: 17–33.

Brendsell, D., 2014. *'Isaiah Saw His Glory': The use of Isaiah 52–53 in John 12*. BZNW 208; Berlin: de Gruyter.

Brooke, G. J., 2006. 'On Isaiah at Qumran', in C. M. McGinnis and P. K. Tull (eds), *'As Those Who Are Taught': The interpretation of Isaiah from the LXX to the SBL*. SBL Symposium Series 27; Atlanta, GA: SBL: 69–85.

Brownlee, W. H., 1964. *The Meaning of the Qumran Scrolls for the Bible with Special Attention to the Book of Isaiah*. New York, NY: Oxford University Press.

Brueggemann, W., 1998. *Isaiah 1–39*. Westminster Bible Companion; Louisville, KY: Westminster John Knox.

——, 2001. *The Prophetic Imagination*. 2nd edn; Minneapolis, MN: Fortress.

Bunyan, J., 2003. *The Pilgrim's Progress*. New York: Oxford University Press.

Caird, G. B., 1980. *The Language and Imagery of the Bible*. Philadelphia, PA: Westminster.

Calvin, J., 2010 (original 1559). *Commentary on the Book of the Prophet Isaiah*. 4 vols; trans. W. Pringle; Bellingham, WA: Logos Bible Software.

Carr, D. M., 1996. 'Reading Isaiah from beginning (Isaiah 1) to end (Isaiah 65–66): multiple modern possibilities', in R. F. Melugin and M. A. Sweeney (eds), *New Visions of Isaiah*. JSOTSup 214; Sheffield: Sheffield Academic: 188–218.

Carter, C. A., 2018. *Interpreting Scripture with the Great Tradition: Recovering the genius of premodern exegesis.* Grand Rapids, MI: Baker Academic.

Chapman, S. B., 2018. 'Theological interpretation as a traditional craft', in A. T. Abernethy (ed.), *Interpreting the Old Testament Theologically: Essays in honor of Willem A. VanGemeren.* Grand Rapids, MI: Zondervan: 109–20.

Childs, B. S., 1979. *Introduction to the Old Testament as Scripture.* London: SCM.

——, 2001. *Isaiah.* OTL; Louisville, KY: Westminster John Knox.

——, 2004. *The Struggle to Understand Isaiah as Christian Scripture.* Grand Rapids, MI: Eerdmans.

Chisholm, R. B., Jr, 2006. 'The christological fulfillment of Isaiah's Servant Songs', *BSac* 163: 387–404.

Clements, R., 1990. 'The Immanuel prophecy of Isa. 7:10–17 and its messianic interpretation', in E. Blum et al. (eds), *Die Hebräische Bibel und ihre zweifache Nachgeschichte: Festschrift für Rolf Rendtorff zum 65. Geburtstag.* Neukirchen-Vluyn: Neukirchener: 225–40.

Clifford, R. J., 1972. *The Cosmic Mountain in Canaan and the Old Testament.* Cambridge, MA: Harvard University Press.

Clines, D. J. A., 1976. *I, He, We, and They: A literary approach to Isaiah 53.* JSOTSup 1; Sheffield: JSOT.

Cogan, M., 2003a. 'Cyrus Cylinder (2.124)', in *COS* 2: 314–16.

——, 2003b. 'Sennacherib's siege of Jerusalem (2.119B)', in *COS* 2: 302–3.

Cone, J., 2011. *The Cross and the Lynching Tree.* Maryknoll, NY: Orbis.

Conrad, E. W., 1991. *Reading Isaiah.* OBT; Minneapolis: Augsburg.

Couey, J. B., 2015. *Reading the Poetry of First Isaiah: The Most Perfect Model of the Prophetic Poetry.* Oxford: Oxford University Press.

Coxe, A. C., 1885. *Ante-Nicene Fathers.* Vol. 3. Edinburgh: T&T Clark/Grand Rapids, MI: Eerdmans.

Cyril of Alexandria, 2008. *Commentary on Isaiah.* 3 vols; trans. R. C. Hill; Brookline, MA: Holy Cross Orthodox.

Daniell, D., 2003. *The Bible in English: Its history and influence.* New Haven, CT: Yale University Press.

Darr, K. P., 1987. 'Like warrior, like woman: destruction and deliverance in Isaiah 42:10–17', *CBQ* 49: 560–71.

——, 1994. *Isaiah's Vision and the Family of God.* Literary Currents in Biblical Interpretation; Louisville, KY: Westminster John Knox.

Davidson, A. B., 1904. *Old Testament Prophecy.* Ed. J. A. Paterson; Edinburgh: T&T Clark.

Davies, A., 2000. *Double Standards in Isaiah: Re-evaluating prophetic ethics and divine justice.* BIntS 46. Leiden: Brill.

Davis, E., 2009. *Scripture, Culture, and Agriculture: An agrarian reading of the Bible.* New York, NY: Cambridge University Press.

Dekker, J., 2007. *Zion's Rock-Solid Foundations: An exegetical study of the Zion text in Isaiah 28:16.* Oudtestamentische Studiën, Old Testament Studies 54; Leiden: Brill.

Delitzsch, F., 1890. *Biblical Commentary on the Prophecies of Isaiah.* 4th edn; Edinburgh: T&T Clark.

Dines, J., 2004. *The Septuagint.* Understanding the Bible and Its World; London: T&T Clark.

Dionysius, 1897. *Dionysius the Areopagite, Works.* Vol. 2. Trans. J. Parker; London: J. Parker & Co.

Driver, S. R., 1904. *Isaiah: His life and times and the writings which bear his name.* 2nd edn; London: Francis Griffiths.

Duhm, B., 1922 (original 1892). *Das Buch Jesaia.* 4th edn; Göttinger Handcommentar zum Alten Testament; Göttingen: Vandenhoeck & Ruprecht.

Dumbrell, W. J., 1985. 'The purpose of the book of Isaiah', *Tyndale Bulletin* 36: 111–28.

Ellinger, K., 1928. *Die Einheit des Tritojesaja (Jesaja 56–66).* BZAW 9; Stuttgart: W. Kohlhammer.

Eusebius of Caesarea, 1920. *The Proof of the Gospel, Being the Demonstratio Evangelica of Eusebius of Caesarea.* 2 vols; trans. W. J. Ferrar. New York, NY: Macmillan.

——, 2013. *Commentary on Isaiah.* Ed. J. C. Elowsky; trans. J. J. Armstrong; Ancient Christian Texts; Downers Grove, IL: IVP Academic.

Evans, C. A., 1988. 'On the unity and parallel structure of Isaiah', *VT* 38: 129–47.

Ewald, G. H. A. von, 1875–81. *Commentary on the Prophets of the Old Testament.* 5 vols; trans. J. F. Smith. London: Williams & Norgate.

Fischer, I., 2012. 'Isaiah: The book of female metaphors', in L. Schottroff and M.-T. Wacker (eds), *Feminist Biblical Interpretation: A compendium of critical commentary on the books of the Bible and related literature.* Trans. T. Steiner; Grand Rapids, MI: Eerdmans: 303–18.

Fischer, J., 1937. *Das Buch Isaias: Übersetzt und Erklät. 1. Teil: Kapitel 1–39.* Bonn: Peter Hanstein.

——, 1939. *Das Buch Isaias: Übersetzt und Erklät. 2. Teil: Kapitel 40–66.* Bonn: Peter Hanstein.

Flint, P. W., 1997. 'The Isaiah scrolls from the Judean desert', in C. C. Broyles and C. A. Evans (eds), *Writing and Reading the Scroll of Isaiah: Studies of an interpretive tradition.* VTSup 70.2; Leiden: Brill: 481–9.

Friedländer, M. (ed. and trans.), 1873. *The Commentary of Ibn Ezra on Isaiah. Vol. 1: Translation of the Commentary.* London: Society of Hebrew Literature.

Gadamer, H.-G., 1989. *Truth and Method.* 2nd edn; New York, NY: Continuum.

Goldingay, J., 2014. *Isaiah 56–66: A critical and exegetical commentary.* ICC; London: T&T Clark.

—— and Payne, D., 2006. *Isaiah 40–55,* 2 vols; ICC; New York, NY: T&T Clark.

Goswell, G., 2013. 'Royal names: naming and wordplay in Isaiah 7', *WTJ* 75: 97–105.

——, 2014. 'Isaiah 16: a forgotten chapter in the history of messianism', *SJOT* 28: 91–103.

——, 2015. 'The shape of messianism in Isaiah 9', *WTJ* 77: 101–10.

Gray, G. B., 1912. *A Critical and Exegetical Commentary on the Book of Isaiah, I–XXXIX.* ICC; Edinburgh: T&T Clark.

Gray, M., 2006. *Rhetoric and Social Justice in Isaiah.* LHBOTS 432; London: T&T Clark.

Hayes, J. H. and Irvine, S. A., 1987. *Isaiah, the Eighth-Century Prophet: His times and his preaching.* Nashville, TN: Abingdon.

Heffelfinger, K. M., 2011. *I Am Large, I Contain Multitudes: Lyric cohesion and conflict in Second Isaiah.* BIntS 105; Leiden: Brill.

Heim, F. A. and Hoffmann, W., 1839. *Die großen Propheten Jesaja, Jeremia, Hesekiel, Daniel erbaulich ausgelegt aus den Schriften der Reformatoren.* Winnenden.

Heschel, A. J., 2001. *The Prophets.* Perennial Classics; New York, NY: HarperOne.

Heskett, R., 2007. *Messianism within the Scriptural Scrolls of Isaiah.* LHBOTS 456; London: T&T Clark.

Hibbard, J. T. and Kim, H. C. P. (eds), 2013. *Formation and Intertextuality in Isaiah 24–27.* SBLAIL 17; Atlanta, GA: SBL.

Horgan, M. P., 1979. *Pesharim: Qumran interpretations of biblical books.* CBQMS 8; Washington, DC: Catholic Biblical Association of America.

Ironside, H. A., 1952. *Expository Notes on the Prophet Isaiah.* Ironside Commentary Series 9; Neptune, NJ: Loizeaux.

Jang, S.-H., 2012. 'Hearing the word of God in Isaiah 1 and 65–66: a synchronic approach', in R. B. Carden and J. Kelso (eds), *The One Who Reads May Run: Essays in honour of Edgar W. Conrad.* LHBOTS 553; New York, NY: T&T Clark: 41–58.

Janowski, B., 2004. 'He bore our sins: Isaiah 53 and the drama of taking another's place', in B. Janowski and P. Stuhlmacher (eds), *The Suffering*

Servant: Isaiah 53 in Jewish and Christian sources. Trans. D. P. Bailey; Grand Rapids, MI: Eerdmans: 48–74.

—— and Stuhlmacher, P. (eds), 2004. *The Suffering Servant: Isaiah 53 in Jewish and Christian sources.* Trans. D. P. Bailey; Grand Rapids, MI: Eerdmans.

Janzen, J. G., 1986. 'Rivers in the desert of Abraham and Sarah and Zion (Isaiah 51:1–3)', *Hebrew Annual Review* 10: 139–55.

Jensen, J., 1973. *The Use of tôrâ by Isaiah: His debate with the wisdom tradition.* CBQMS 3, Washington, DC: Catholic Biblical Association of America.

Jerome, 2015. *Commentary on Isaiah: Including St. Jerome's translation of Origen's Homilies 1–9 on Isaiah.* Trans. T. P. Scheck; Ancient Christian Writers 68; New York, NY: Newman.

Jones, A., 2010. 'A Thanksgiving sermon, preached Jan 1, 1808, in St. Thomas's or the African Episcopal Church, Philadelphia on account of the abolition of the African Slave Trade, on that day, by the Congress of the United States (1808)', in M. Simmons and F. A. Thomas (eds), *Preaching with Sacred Fire: An anthology of African American sermons, 1750 to the present.* New York, NY: W. W. Norton: 68–76.

Justin Martyr, 2003. Dialogue with Trypho. Ed. M. Slusser; rev. T. P. Halton; trans. T. B. Falls; Selections from the Fathers of the Church 3; Washington, DC: Catholic University of America Press.

Katanacho, Y., 2005. 'Christ is the owner of Haaretz', *Christian Scholar's Review* 34: 425–41.

——, 2013. *The Land of Christ: A Palestinian cry.* Eugene, OR: Pickwick.

Kim, B., 2018. *'Lengthen Your Tent-Cords': The metaphorical world of Israel's household in the book of Isaiah.* Siphrut 23; University Park, PA: Eisenbrauns.

Kim, H. C. P., 2003. *Ambiguity, Tension, and Multiplicity in Deutero-Isaiah.* Studies in Biblical Literature 52; New York, NY: Peter Lang.

King, M. L., Jr, 1998. 'Guidelines for a constructive church', in C. Carson (ed.), *A Knock at Midnight: Inspiration from the great sermons of Martin Luther King, Jr.* New York, NY: IPM/Warner: 101–16.

——, 2000a. 'The birth of a new nation', in C. Carson, S. Carson, A. Clay, V. Shadron and K. Taylor (eds), *The Papers of Martin Luther King, Jr. Vol. 4: Symbol of the Movement, January 1957–December 1958.* Berkeley, CA: University of California Press: 155–67.

——, 2000b. 'Facing the challenge of a new age', in C. Carson, S. Carson, A. Clay, V. Shadron and K. Taylor (eds), *The Papers of Martin Luther King, Jr. Vol. 4: Symbol of the Movement, January 1957–December 1958.* Berkeley, CA: University of California Press: 451–63.

King, P., 1992. 'Jerusalem', *ABD* 3: 747–66.

Kissane, E., 1941. *The Book of Isaiah. Vol. 1: I–XXXIX*. Dublin: Richview.

——, 1943. *The Book of Isaiah. Vol. 2: XL–LXVI*. Dublin: Richview.

Knight, D., 2011. *Law, Power, and Justice in Ancient Israel*. Library of Ancient Israel; Louisville, KY: Westminster John Knox.

Knight, J., 1995. *The Ascension of Isaiah*. Guides to Apocrypha and Pseudepigrapha 2; Sheffield: Sheffield Academic.

Koole, J. L., 1997–8. *Isaiah III*. 2 vols; trans. A. Runia; HCOT; Kampen: Pharos.

Kuenen, A., 1877. *The Prophets and Prophecy in Israel: An historical and critical inquiry*. Trans. A. Milroy; London: Longmans, Green & Co.

Laato, A., 1998. *About Zion I Will Not Be Silent: The book of Isaiah as an ideological unity*. Coniectanea biblica, Old Testament 44; Stockholm: Almqvist & Wiksell.

Landy, F., 2001. *Beauty and the Enigma: And other essays on the Hebrew Bible*. JSOTSup 312; Sheffield: Sheffield Academic.

——, 2002. 'Prophetic intercourse', in A. G. Hunter and P. R. Davies (eds), *Sense and Sensitivity: Essays on reading the Bible in memory of Robert Carroll*. LHBOTS 348; London: Bloomsbury T&T Clark: 261–79.

Leathes, S., 1891. *The Law in the Prophets*. London: Eyre & Spottiswoode.

Leclerc, T. L., 2001. *Yahweh Is Exalted in Justice: Solidarity and conflict in Isaiah*. Minneapolis, MN: Fortress.

Lee, N. C., 2015. *Hannevi'ah and Hannah: Hearing women biblical prophets in a woman's lyrical tradition*. Eugene, OR: Cascade.

Lessing, R., 2011. 'Isaiah's servants in chapters 40–55: clearing up the confusion', *Concordia Journal* 37: 130–4.

Levenson, J. D., 1984. 'The Temple and the world', *Journal of Religion* 64: 275–98.

——, 1985. *Sinai and Zion: An entry into the Jewish Bible*. New Voices in Biblical Studies; New York, NY: HarperCollins.

Lewis, C. S., 1956. *Till We Have Faces: A myth retold*. Grand Rapids, MI: Eerdmans.

Liebreich, L. J., 1954. 'The position of chapter six in the book of Isaiah', *HUCA* 25: 37–40.

——, 1956a. 'The compilation of the book of Isaiah', *JQR* 46: 259–77.

——, 1956b. 'The compilation of the book of Isaiah', *JQR* 47: 114–38.

Lim, B. H., 2015. 'The lynching of the Suffering Servant of Isaiah: death at the hands of persons unknown', *Ex Auditu* 31: 108–20.

——, 2018. 'A theological interpretation of the Cyrus passages in Isaiah', in A. T. Abernethy (ed.), *Interpreting the Old Testament Theologically: Essays in honor of Willem A. VanGemeren*. Grand Rapids, MI: Zondervan: 176–89.

——, 2020. 'Christ of the coronavirus: a meditation on Isaiah 53 for Good Friday', *Inheritance*. 9 April 2020. <www.inheritancemag.com/stories/christ-of-the-coronavirus>.

Lowth, R., 1868 (original 1778). *Isaiah: A new translation; with a preliminary dissertation and notes, critical, philological, and explanatory*. London: William Tegg.

Luther, M., 1969. *Lectures on Isaiah: Chapters 1–39*. Ed. H. C. Oswald; trans. H. J. A. Bouman; Luther's Works 16; St Louis, MO: Concordia.

——, 1972. *Lectures on Isaiah: Chapters 40–66*. Ed. H. C. Oswald; trans. H. J. A. Bouman; Luther's Works 17; St Louis, MO: Concordia.

McDonald, J., 1814. *Isaiah's Message to the American Nation: A new translation of Isaiah chapter XVIII with notes critical and explanatory, a remarkable prophecy, respecting the restoration of the Jews, aided by the American Nation, with an universal summons to the Battle of Armageddon, and a description of that solemn scene*. Albany, NY: E. & E. Hosford.

Marrow, J. H., 1979. *Passion Iconography in Northern European Art of the Late Middle Ages and Early Renaissance: A study of the transformation of sacred metaphor into descriptive narrative*. Kortrijk: Van Ghemmert.

Marti, D. K., 1900. *Das Buch Jesaja*. Tübingen: Mohr Siebeck.

Mettinger, T. N. D., 1983. *A Farewell to the Servant Songs: A critical examination of an exegetical axiom*. Lund: CWK Gleerup.

Moberly, R. W. L., 2001. 'Whose justice? Which righteousness? The interpretation of Isaiah v 16', *VT* 51: 55–68.

Motyer, J. A., 1993. *The Prophecy of Isaiah: An introduction and commentary*. Downers Grove, IL: IVP.

Moyise, S. and Menken, M. J. J. (eds), 2005. 'Introduction', in *Isaiah in the New Testament: The New Testament and the Scriptures of Israel*. New York, NY: T&T Clark: 1–5.

Muilenburg, J., 1956. 'The book of Isaiah: chapters 40–66', in G. A. Buttrick et al. (eds), *Interpreter's Bible*. 12 vols; Nashville, TN: Abingdon: 5: 381–773.

Nolland, J., 2005. *The Gospel of Matthew*. NIGTC. Grand Rapids, MI: Eerdmans.

North, C. R., 1948. *The Suffering Servant in Deutero-Isaiah: A historical and critical study*. London: Oxford University Press.

Ollenburger, B. C., 1987. *Zion, the City of the Great King: A theological symbol of the Jerusalem cult*. Sheffield: JSOT.

Orelli, C. von, 1904. *Der Prophet Jesaja*. München: Beck.

Osborne, W. R., 2018. *Trees and Kings: A comparative analysis of tree imagery in Israel's prophetic tradition and the Ancient Near East.* BBRSup 18; University Park, PA: Eisenbrauns.

Oswalt, J. N., 1986. *The Book of Isaiah: Chapters 1–39.* NICOT; Grand Rapids, MI: Eerdmans.

——, 1998. *The Book of Isaiah: Chapters 40–66.* NICOT; Grand Rapids, MI: Eerdmans.

Otto, R., 1958. *The Idea of the Holy.* Trans. J. W. Harvey; New York, NY: Oxford University Press.

Pao, D. W., 2000. *Acts and the Isaianic New Exodus.* WUNT 130; Tübingen: Mohr Siebeck.

Philips, K. L., 2015. 'Studies in Abraham Ibn Ezra's exegesis of the Latter Prophets with particular reference to his commentary on Isaiah 40–66.' PhD diss.; University of Cambridge.

Pope, A., 1796. 'Messiah: A Sacred Eclogue', in *A Select Collection of Poems.* New-London, CT: Springer's: 123–6.

Porter, S. E. and Pearson, B. W. R., 1997. 'Isaiah through Greek eyes', in C. C. Broyles and C. A. Evans (eds), *Writing and Reading the Scroll of Isaiah: Studies of an interpretive tradition.* VTSup 70; Leiden: Brill: 2: 531–46.

Reimer, D. J., 2012. 'On triplets in a trio of prophets', in I. Provan and M. J. Boda (eds), *Let Us Go Up to Zion: Essays in honour of H. G. M. Williamson on the occasion of his sixty-fifth birthday.* VTSup 153; Leiden: Brill: 203–17.

Rendtorff, R., 1984. 'Zur Komposition des Buches Jesaja', VT 34: 295–320.

——, 1993. *Overtures to an Old Testament Theology.* Trans. M. Kohl; OBT; Minneapolis, MN: Fortress.

Ricoeur, P., 1981. *Hermeneutics and the Human Sciences.* Trans. and ed. J. B. Thompson; Cambridge: Cambridge University Press.

Roberts, J. J., 2015: *First Isaiah.* Hermeneia; Minneapolis, MN: Fortress.

Sanders, F. K. and Kent, C. F., 1899. *The Messages of the Later Prophets: Arranged in the order of time, analyzed and freely rendered in paraphrase.* 2 vols; London: James Clarke.

Sawyer, J. F. A., 1996. *The Fifth Gospel: Isaiah in the history of Christianity.* New York, NY: Cambridge University Press.

——, 2018. *Isaiah through the Centuries.* Wiley Blackwell Bible Commentaries; Chichester: Wiley Blackwell.

Schibler, D., 1995. 'Messianism and messianic prophecy in Isaiah 1–12 and 28–33', in P. E. Satterthwaite, R. S. Hess and G. J. Wenham (eds), *The Lord's Anointed: Interpretation of Old Testament messianic texts.* Grand Rapids, MI: Baker: 87–104.

Schiller, G., 1972. *Iconography of Christian Art. Vol. 2: The Passion of Jesus Christ.* Trans. J. Seligman; London: Lund Humphries.

Schipper, J., 2011. *Disability and Isaiah's Suffering Servant.* New York, NY: Oxford University Press.

Schultz, R. L., 1999. *The Search for Quotation: Verbal parallels in the Prophets.* JSOTSup 180; Sheffield: Sheffield Academic.

Seiler, G. F., 1792. *Das größere biblische Erbauungsbuch Altes Testament. Teil 7: Die Propheten Jesaias und Jeremias.* 8 vols; Erlangen.

Seitz, C. R., 1988. 'Isaiah 1–66: making sense of the whole', in C. R. Seitz (ed.), *Preaching and Reading the Book of Isaiah.* Philadelphia, PA: Fortress: 105–26.

——, 1991. *Zion's Final Destiny: The development of the book of Isaiah. A reassessment of Isaiah 36–39.* Minneapolis, MN: Fortress.

——, 1993. *Isaiah 1–39.* Interpretation; Louisville, KY: John Knox.

——, 2007. *Prophecy and Hermeneutics: Toward a new introduction to the Prophets.* Studies in Theological Interpretation; Grand Rapids, MI: Baker Academic.

Shalev, E., 2013. *American Zion: The Old Testament as a political text from the Revolution to the Civil War.* New Haven, CT: Yale University Press.

Skehan, P. W. and Di Lella, A. A., 1987. *The Wisdom of Ben Sira: A new translation with notes, introduction and commentary.* AB 39; New York, NY: Doubleday.

Smith, E., 1825. *View of the Hebrews: Or, The Tribes of Israel in America.* 2nd edn; Poultney, VT: Smith & Shute.

Smith, G., 2009. *Isaiah 40–66: An exegetical and theological exposition of Holy Scripture.* NAC 15B; Nashville, TN: B&H Academic.

Sobrino, J., 2003. *Witnesses to the Kingdom: The martyrs of El Salvador and the crucified peoples.* Maryknoll, NY: Orbis.

Sommer, B. D., 1997. *A Prophet Reads Scripture: Allusion in Isaiah 40–66.* Stanford, CA: Stanford University Press.

Spinks, B., 1991. *The Sanctus in the Eucharistic Prayer.* Cambridge: Cambridge University Press.

Spinoza, B., 2007. *Theological-Political Treatise.* Trans. M. Silverthorne and J. Israel; ed. J. Israel. Cambridge: Cambridge University Press.

Stead, M. R., 2009. *The Intertextuality of Zechariah 1–8.* LHBOTS 506; New York, NY: T&T Clark.

Steck, O. H., 2000. *The Prophetic Books and Their Theological Witness.* Trans. J. D. Nogalski; St Louis, MO: Chalice.

Stowe, H. B., 1877. *Uncle Tom's Cabin: Or, Life Among the Lowly.* Boston, MA: James R. Osgood & Co.

Stromberg, J., 2011. *Isaiah after Exile: The author of Third Isaiah as reader and redactor of the book*. OTM; Oxford: Oxford University Press.

Stulman, L. and Kim, H. C. P., 2010. *You Are My People: An introduction to prophetic literature*. Nashville, TN: Abingdon.

Sweeney, M. A., 2014. 'Eschatology in the book of Isaiah', in R. J. Bautch and J. T. Hibbard (eds), *The Book of Isaiah: Enduring questions answered anew. Essays honoring Joseph Blenkinsopp and his contribution to the study of Isaiah*. Grand Rapids, MI: Eerdmans: 179–95.

——, 2016. *Isaiah 40–66*. FOTL; Grand Rapids, MI: Eerdmans.

Telfer, C. K., 2016. *Wrestling with Isaiah: The exegetical methodology of Campegius Vitringa (1659–1722)*. Reformed Historical Theology 38; Göttingen: Vandenhoeck & Ruprecht Academic.

Tertullian, 1885a. 'An answer to the Jews', in A. Roberts, J. Donaldson and A. C. Coxe (eds), *Latin Christianity: Its founder, Tertullian*. Vol. 3. Trans. S. Thelwall; Ante-Nicene Fathers; Buffalo, NY: Christian Literature Company.

——, 1885b. 'The apology', in A. Roberts, J. Donaldson and A. C. Coxe (eds), *Latin Christianity: Its Founder, Tertullian*. Vol. 3. Trans. S. Thelwall; Ante-Nicene Fathers; Buffalo, NY: Christian Literature Company.

——, 1885c. 'The five books against Marcion', in A. Roberts, J. Donaldson and A. C. Coxe (eds), *Latin Christianity: Its founder, Tertullian*. Vol. 3. Trans. Peter Holmes; Ante-Nicene Fathers; Buffalo, NY: Christian Literature Company.

Tiemeyer, L.-S., 2010. *For the Comfort of Zion: The geographical and theological location of Isaiah 40–55*. VTSup 139; Leiden: Brill.

Torrey, C. C., 1928. *The Second Isaiah: A new interpretation*. Edinburgh: T&T Clark.

Tov, E., 1997. 'The text of Isaiah at Qumran', in C. C. Broyles and C. A. Evans (eds), *Writing and Reading the Scroll of Isaiah: Studies of an interpretive tradition*. VTSup 70; Leiden: Brill: 2: 491–511.

Tull, P. K., 2009. 'Persistent vegetative states: people as plants and plants as people in Isaiah', in A. J. Everson and H. C. P. Kim (eds), *The Desert Will Bloom: Poetic visions in Isaiah*. SBLAIL 4; Atlanta, GA: SBL: 17–34.

——, 2010. *Isaiah 1–39*. Smyth & Helwys Bible Commentary; Macon, GA: Smyth & Helwys.

Ussishkin, D., 2013. 'Sennacherib's campaign to Judah: the events at Lachish and Jerusalem', in A. T. Abernethy, M. G. Brett, T. Bulkeley and T. Meadowcroft (eds), *Isaiah and Imperial Context*. Eugene, OR: Pickwick: 1–34.

van der Kooij, A., 2006. 'Interpretation of the book of Isaiah in the Septuagint and in other ancient versions', in C. M. McGinnis and P. K. Tull (eds), *'As*

Those Who Are Taught': The interpretation of Isaiah from the LXX to the SBL. SBL Symposium Series 27; Atlanta, GA: SBL: 49–68.

Vermeylen, J., 1977–8. *Du prophète Isaïe à l'apocalyptique: Isaïe, I–XXXV, miroir d'un demi-millénaire d'expérience religieuse en Israël.* 2 vols; Paris: Gabalda.

——, 1989. 'L'Unité du livre d'Isaïe', in J. Vermeylen (ed.), The Book of Isaiah – Le Livre d'Isaïe: Les oracles et leurs relectures. Unité et complexité de l'ouvrage. BETL 81; Leuven: Peeters: 11–53.

Wagner, J. R., 1998. 'The heralds of Isaiah and the mission of Paul: an investigation of Paul's use of Isaiah 51–55 in Romans', in W. H. Bellinger, Jr, and W. R. Farmer (eds), *Jesus and the Suffering Servant: Isaiah 53 and Christian origins.* Harrisburg, PA: Trinity: 193–222.

——, 2002. *Heralds of the Good News: Isaiah and Paul 'in concert' in the letter to the Romans.* NTSup 101; Leiden: Brill.

——, 2013. *Reading the Sealed Book: Old Greek Isaiah and the problem of Septuagint hermeneutics.* FAT 88; Tübingen: Mohr Siebeck.

Walton, J. H., 1987. 'Isa 7:14: what's in a name?', *JETS* 30: 289–306.

Watts, R. E., 1997. *Isaiah's New Exodus and Mark.* WUNT 88; Tübingen: Mohr Siebeck.

——, 1998. 'Jesus' death, Isaiah 53, and Mark 10:45: a crux revisited', in W. H. Bellinger, Jr, and W. R. Farmer (eds), *Jesus and the Suffering Servant: Isaiah 53 and Christian origins.* Harrisburg, PA: Trinity: 125–51.

——, 2004. 'Immanuel: virgin birth proof text or programmatic warning of things to come (Isa 7:14 in Matt 1:23)?', in C. A. Evans (ed.), *From Prophecy to Testament: The function of the Old Testament in the New.* Peabody, MA: Hendrickson, 92–113.

Webb, B. G., 1990. 'Zion in transformation: a literary approach to Isaiah', in D. J. A. Clines, S. E. Fowl and S. E. Porter (eds), *The Bible in Three Dimensions.* JSOTSup 87; Sheffield: JSOT, 1990: 65–84.

Wegner, P. D., 1992. *An Examination of Kingship and Messianic Expectation in Isaiah 1–35.* Lewiston, NY: Mellen.

——, 2011. 'How Many Virgin Births Are in the Bible? (Isaiah 7:14): A Prophetic Pattern Approach', *JETS* 54: 467–84.

Weinfeld, M., 1995. *Social Justice in Ancient Israel and in the Ancient Near East.* Minneapolis, MN: Fortress.

Wenham, G. J., 1972. '*Bĕtûlāh*: "a girl of marriageable age"', *VT* 22: 326–47.

Wilcox, P. and Paton-Williams, D., 1988. 'The Servant Songs in Deutero-Isaiah', *JSOT* 42: 79–102.

Wildberger, H., 1991. *A Continental Commentary: Isaiah 1–12.* Minneapolis, MN: Fortress.

Wilkins, M. J., 2012. 'Isaiah 53 and the message of salvation in the four Gospels', in D. L. Bock and M. Glaser (eds), *The Gospel According to Isaiah 53: Encountering the Suffering Servant in Jewish and Christian theology*. Grand Rapids, MI: Kregel: 109–32.

Willey, P. T., 1997. *Remember the Former Things: The recollection of previous texts in Second Isaiah*. SBLDS 161; Atlanta, GA: Scholars.

Williamson, H. G. M., 1985. *Ezra, Nehemiah*. WBC 16; Dallas, TX: Word.

——, 1994. *The Book Called Isaiah: Deutero-Isaiah's role in composition and redaction*. Oxford: Clarendon.

——, 1998. *Variations on a Theme: King, Messiah and Servant in the book of Isaiah*. Didsbury Lectures 1997; Carlisle: Paternoster.

——, 2001. 'Isaiah and the Holy One of Israel', in A. Rapoport-Albert and G. Greenberg (eds), *Biblical Hebrew, Biblical Texts: Essays in memory of Michael P. Weitzman*. JSOTSup 333; Sheffield: Sheffield Academic: 22–38.

——, 2008. *Holy, Holy, Holy: The story of a liturgical formula*. Julius-Wellhausen-Vorlesung 1; Berlin: de Gruyter.

——, 2012. *He Has Shown You What Is Good: Old Testament justice*. Cambridge: Lutterworth.

——, 2018. *Isaiah 6–12: A critical and exegetical commentary*. ICC; London: Bloomsbury.

Willis, J. T., 1978. 'The meaning of Isaiah 7:14 and its application in Matthew 1:23', *Restoration Quarterly* 21: 1–18.

Wise, M., Abegg, M., Jr, and Cook, E. 1996. *A New Translation: The Dead Sea Scrolls*. New York, NY: HarperOne.

Young, E. J., 1958. *Who Wrote Isaiah?* Grand Rapids, MI: Eerdmans.

Younger, K. L., Jr, 2003a. 'Summary Inscription 4 (2,117C)', in *COS* 2: 287.

——, 2003b. 'Summary Inscription 13 (2.117G)', in *COS* 2: 292.

——, 2003c. 'Nimrud Prisms D (2.118D)', in *COS* 2: 295.

Copyright acknowledgements

Index of biblical references

Index of authors

Index of authors

Ricoeur, P. ix
Roberts, J. J. 107
Romero, O. 139–40

Sanders, F. and C. Kent 27
Sawyer, J. 5–6, 114, 137
Schibler, D. 101, 103
Schiller, G. 137
Schipper, J. 123, 127, 137
Schultz, R. 33
Seiler, G. 25–6
Seitz, C. 2, 32, 38, 42, 86
Shalev, E. 98
Skehan, P. W. and A. A. Di Lella 10–11
Smith, E. 97–8
Smith, G. 27, 47, 50
Smith, W. R. 27
Sobrino, J. 139–40
Sommer, B. 33
Spinks, B. 72
Spinoza, B. 7, 25
Stead, M. R. 9
Steck, O. H. 42
Stowe, H. B. 160–1
Stromberg, J. 30–1
Stulman, L. and H. C. P. Kim 33–4
Sweeney, M. A. 36, 79, 118–19

Telfer, C. 23
Tiemeyer, L.-S. 35
Torrey, C. 29, 36
Tov, E. 11
Tull, P. K. 33, 102

Ussishkin, D. 45

Vermeylen, J. 30, 36
Vitringa, C. 20, 23

Wagner, J. R. 13, 14, 135
Walton, J. 106
Watts, I. 95
Watts, R. 13, 110, 135
Webb, B. 33, 85
Wegner, P. D. 101, 106
Weinfeld, M. 145
Wenham, G. J. 106
Westermann, C. 31
Wilcox, P. and D. Paton-Williams 120
Wildberger, H. 31, 106
Wilkins, M. 135
Willey, P. Tull 33
Williamson, H. G. M. 9, 30–1, 35, 60, 63,
 64, 80, 101, 103, 105–9, 120, 147, 152
Willis, J. T. 106
Wise, M., M. Abegg and E. Cook 12
Wood, C. 142

Young, E. J. 28
Younger, K. L. 44–5

ANCIENT AUTHORS

Augustine of Hippo 4, 94, 97
Clement of Rome 71–2, 139
Cyril of Alexandria 16, 69, 93
Dionysius 69, 72
Eusebius of Caesarea 15–17, 23, 47–8, 68,
 93, 95–7, 111–12, 136, 158
Ibn Ezra, A. 19–20, 23, 26, 113–14,
 117–19, 136
Jerome 3–4, 16–18, 23, 47, 48, 59, 69, 93,
 95, 96–7, 112, 136, 158–9
Jesus ben Sira 10–11, 26
Josephus 11, 26, 96
Justin Martyr 14–16, 23, 110–11, 136
Tertullian 15–16, 111, 134, 136
Theodoret 16

Index of subjects

Ahaz 42–3, 80, 87; death of 43; sign to 106–14

allegorical interpretation 16–19, 21, 23, 92, 111; *see also* christological interpretation

angels, angelic beings 58–9, 68, 71–3; revelation through 19, 69

Aram: fall of 38, 43; war against Ahaz 43, 44–5, 80, 106–8

art, reception 72–3, 114–16, 137–8, 160–4; *see also* Isaiah, book of

Assyria: era of 37, 44–6; judgement by 38, 42–3, 45–6, 54–5, 65, 86–8, 102–3, 107–9, 133, 155, 165; judgement of 43, 46, 56, 65, 102–3, 109; salvation from 10, 45–6, 81–2, 85–6; *see also* nations

Augustine, interpretation of Isaiah 4, 94, 97

authorship 28–9; 'First Isaiah' 30, 36, 146; 'Second Isaiah' 30, 33, 35–6, 64, 118, 120, 146; 'Third Isaiah' 30–1, 64; Josephus 26; in pre-modern interpretation 26–37; in rabbinical interpretation 19; in Reformation interpretation 26; *see also* Isaiah, book of

Babylon: and dating of Isaiah 19–20, 26, 35; era of 28, 37, 86, 103; exile in 9, 19–20, 38, 81, 85; judgement by 42–4, 46, 54–5, 65, 86–8, 91–2, 102–3, 109, 133, 155; judgement of 44, 46–7, 56, 63, 65, 109; King Hammurabi 105; oracles against 26; return from 49,

65–6, 133, 136, 166–7; *see also* exile, to Babylon

barrenness 89–90; imagery of 51–2, 66, 82–3, 89–90, 167; *see also* Zion, Lady Zion

blindness: in interpretation 8, 41, 142; recovering sight 163; spiritual metaphor 49, 89, 120, 154, 157; towards injustice 40, 41, 82, 142, 145, 157; *see also* eyes

Calvin, John 21–3; interpretation of Isaiah: on Isaiah 7.14 113–14; on justice 159–60; on law 147; on the 'righteous one' 47; on 'seeing God' 70; on Servant Songs 136–8; on the 'shepherd' 48; on Zion 93–4; 96–7; *see also* reception history of Isaiah

canon 121; canonical approach 31–2, 34–5, 38–9, 108

christological interpretation 36, 68–71; of Isaiah 7.14 112–14, 116; of Isaiah's Messiah 110–16, 155; and justice 158–63; of Luther 20–1, 38; *sensus plenior* 106–8, 114; of the Servant Songs 133, 135–41; of Zion 92–3, 96–8

Church: in Isaiah 20–3; symbolized by the Suffering Servant 118, 135–41; symbolized by Zion 93–9; use of Isaiah 5–7, 56, 68, 72–3, 112, 134, 158–64; *see also* reception history of Isaiah

comfort: for the afflicted 41, 160; for exiles 22; for Zion/Jerusalem 10, 85, 89, 91, 115, 155, 165–7

creation 72; new 54, 56–7, 83–5, 92, 167

Index of subjects

2022. 01. ૨   ૨૧.૬૦